New Business Opportunities in Latin America

Trade and Investment
After the Mexican Meltdown

Louis E.V. Nevaer

QUORUM BOOKS
Westport, Connecticut • London

Library of Congress Cataloging-in-Publication Data

Nevaer, Louis E. V.
New business opportunities in Latin America : trade and investment
after the Mexican meltdown / Louis E.V. Nevaer.
p. cm.
Includes bibliographical references and index.
ISBN 1–56720–023–0 (alk. paper)
1. Latin America—Commerce—United States. 2. United States—
Commerce—Latin America. 3. Free trade—Latin America. 4. Latin
America—Economic integration. I. Title.
HF3230.5.Z7U55 1996
382'.098073—dc20 95–38752

British Library Cataloguing in Publication Data is available.

Library of Congress Catalog Card Number: 95–38752
ISBN: 1–56720–023–0

First published in 1996

Quorum Books, 88 Post Road West, Westport, CT 06881
An imprint of Greenwood Publishing Group, Inc.

Printed in the United States of America

The paper used in this book complies with the
Permanent Paper Standard issued by the National
Information Standards Organization (Z39.48-1984).

10 9 8 7 6 5 4 3 2 1

For

Teodoro Varela
1921–1995

and

Charles S. Tabor IV
1956–1995

and
Rosa Raquel Romero de Barajas

CONTENTS

Appendices

PREFACE

In December 1994 the leaders of the New World, with the exception of Cuba, gathered in Miami, Florida, for the Summit of the Americas. This historic meeting culminated in the announcement that the nations of the Western Hemisphere would form a free trade zone, no later than the year 2005, which would bring down barriers across and usher in an age of free trade among all the Americas. These optimistic words were made possible by the developments that engulfed the world only a few years prior to this meeting. The collapse of the Soviet Union and Eastern Europe, as much from the bankruptcy of their ideologies as from the bankruptcy of their treasuries, ended in a most definite manner the competition between two competing dreams.

Nikita Khrushchev's pronouncement that communism would "bury" the West echoed with irony, a voice carried across the corridors of a mausoleum. In a single generation from the time of Khrushchev's visit to the United States, American ideology had prevailed. For the nations of the Western Hemisphere, exhausted by the burden of being rendered pawns, a renewed vigor took hold. Cuba, once a slave to the will of the United States, had willingly become a slave to the will of the Soviet Union, and now was set adrift, bankrupt and hopeless, lost in its own madness. More than anything else, it is the insanity of Cuba that has galvanized other Latin American countries to avoid the same mistakes, the same failures. That Latin Americans, too, are more demanding, of themselves and of their leaders, serves as a catalyst for reform. After all, satellites have been circling the earth beaming images of American democracy and the material benefits of a market system into the homes of the Latin Americans, giving shape to their visions and aspirations for two decades now. And people the world over want what they see on television.

Latin America, as the next century approaches, looks not to the mother countries, Spain and Portugal, but to the power of American culture. It is the seductive consequence of what America stands for and represents that finds a believing audience throughout the New World. At a time in the history of the United States when Americans have lost faith and grown jaded and disillusioned in their own country, it is remarkable how believing in the American Dream immigrants from Latin America remain. Whether they are from Buenos Aires or Guatemala City, Latin Americans who come to the United States are prepared to scrub floors on their hands and knees because they have faith in America, in what is possible here, and what they can achieve with their lives if given the chance. Horatio Alger is alive and well, and learning English at night school at a community college near you.

The Summit of the Americas, therefore, is a defining moment in Latin American history, for it represents the conclusive turning away from Europe and stands as a bold affirmation of identity: the people of the Americas are Americans. For much of this century, to their regret, Latin Americans traveled to Europe—Madrid, London, Paris, Rome—and brought back the most peculiar ideas imaginable. The emotional and historic traumas that torment the Europeans from so many centuries of hate and warfare did little to improve the lives of Latin Americans. A society's success can be measured by the number of options it offers its members. By this standard, Latin America has not been successful. It is evident through television and movies, in the marginal role Latin Americans play in the world's contemporary scene, by the cumbersome efforts required to make Latin contributions noticeable. Through the movement of people back and forth across borders and through the international availability of U.S. television, aspirations have changed. Latin Americans now want to travel to New York and Miami, Los Angeles and Chicago. They have seen the future, and it is the United States that captivates their imagination and defines their ambitions. The Summit of the Americas, then, is an articulation that what Latin Americans now wish to import is the American Dream.

The American Dream is corporate America's dream as well.

INTRODUCTION

In Latin America there are no miracles, only mirages.

In few other places do appearances deceive as successfully as they do here. The landscape, which is filled with such vast wealth, both natural and human, is also one of tragedy. It is a peculiar place, however, in that, unlike other places in the world where similar disorder and despair exist, Latin America is remarkably free of warfare. Apart from lingering civil unrest in some Central American countries; a so-called insurrection in southern Mexico, more pathetic than menacing; and a waning rebel movement in Peru, the mainland of the Americas is free of armed conflict. No other land mass on the planet, including Western Europe, can make such a claim. Another claim that renders this hemisphere singular is its vast resources. These are both in raw materials, which the West has always coveted, as well as a diverse heritage of many cultures. Latin America is a multicultural place, one that proudly boasts legacies from all the corners of the world, as well as numerous indigenous peoples whose achievements equal those of any other civilization in beauty and refinement.

The images of Latin America reflect this diversity. Print and television media advertisements for airlines and hotels, for instance, deliver a staccato of vivid images: the pyramids of the Maya, the nightlife of Rio, the colonial churches of Colombia, macaws in flight over a rain forest canopy. For the corporate officer who is unfamiliar with Latin American culture and whose command of Spanish (or Portuguese) is rudimentary, the task of understanding this continent can be daunting. The fact of the matter, however, remains that the peoples with whom the United States and Canada share the hemisphere are becoming integrated into what we think of when we think of "America." This process of acculturation is not some future event; it has already happened. If it is not immediately visible, perhaps this is because in being so diverse, Latin America has entered American life under cover of darkness across an unsecured border; the U.S. Census expects that in the year 2000 there will be more "Hispanics" in the United States than African Americans, and more people speak Spanish at home than speak any other foreign language.

Corporate America is well aware of this. Consider the changes that have occurred over the last decade. For instance, think about the increased frequency with which U.S. airliners have bilingual presentations of safety procedures prior to take-off. On most major carriers' afternoon flights bound for Miami, which arrive in time to make connections to Latin American destinations, this is the standard. Another example is found in the blossoming of Spanish-language billboards throughout urban centers. The question of language is pivotal; while divisive as a political issue, from a business point of view it is immaterial: *a seller speaks in the language of the buyer.* This is a truism in market economies, where there is competition among several producers of goods and services. Only in economies where there is a single seller, or a regulated one, does the buyer have to acquiesce to the conditions established by the seller. But in America, the increasing number of Hispanics[1]—and their economic clout—has required corporate America to reach out to this population in Spanish.

Language is indeed a barrier. It also disguises the precise nature of the presence of Hispanics in American life. Consider the difference between Hispanics and African Americans. That the latter share a common cultural and historical background in America, for the most part, facilitates creating a unity. A book like *Roots* speaks to the African-American experience. There is nothing similar for Hispanics. Americans of Cuban ancestry share a far different historical and cultural experience in America from Americans of Mexican ancestry. It is therefore a difficult matter to attempt to speak to the entire Hispanic audience. In the summer of 1995, for instance, two films were simultaneously released. One, *My Family,* spoke to the Mexican-American experience, and the other, *The Perez Family,* dealt with the Cuban presence in the United States. Neither film appealed to the entire Hispanic population.[2] Both quickly passed from memory, as inconsequential things often do.

This kind of market segmentation is exactly what we find in Latin America. The nations of the region, now embarked on a program of hemispheric integration through free trade zones and economic blocs, are as anxious about what this all means as are Hispanics within the United States. The soothing rhetoric of politicians aside, there is apprehension, often born of mistrust and ignorance, among Latin Americans. There is comfort in all of this for corporate officers, for instead of being confronted by an entire hemisphere, it is important to recognize that the diversity and differences require different strategies. In the same way that apart from the broadest of themes—Spanish, Catholicism, Native American legacies—there are few other ideas from which to flesh out a portrait of Latin America.

The differences, however, inherently reveal different levels of success. The Summit of the Americas confirmed in no uncertain terms the commitment to move to freer markets, economic integration, and the interdependence born of market-driven forces. "We now have a flight plan that will keep us busy for years to come," Mexican Foreign Minister José Angel Gurría announced in Miami, with sweet naïveté. Within days, the panorama had changed dramatically. The thirty-four leaders who gathered at the Summit of the Americas barely had time to unpack their luggage when Mexico crashed landed. Panic spread across the continent that the Mexican fiasco would derail free trade throughout the hemisphere. Latin America, which consists of 450 million people, was stunned at the dramatic developments in Mexico, and the impact throughout the region. Nations like Argentina and Brazil were engulfed by uncertainty as they struggled to restore investor confidence. Others, like Costa Rica and Honduras, saw their belief in market reform come into question as the pieces of Mexican economic liberalization were sorted out by officials from the International Monetary Fund (IMF), the World Bank, and the U.S. Treasury Department.

Despite this setback, 1995 saw the continent move forward, embracing market-driven reforms and embarking on trade negotiations. The aspirations of Latin America remain intact. This is fortuitous, for it offers corporate America the singular opportunity to participate in the development of these nations' economies. There are many needs and desires throughout Latin America. There are many opportunities. This book examines the nations of Latin America and provides a fundamental understanding of how the region works. From one end to the other, there are intricate opportunities the likes of which the United States has not seen since the conclusion of World War II, when Europe and Japan lay in shambles. The economic integration of the region is a drama that will unfold, not without some surprises, as Mexico demonstrated, over the next fifty years. That is a considerable amount of time in which to see sound business plans, properly implemented with perseverance and hard work, come to fruition. This is what America is all about, and what Latin America is about to become.

NOTES

1. The term *Hispanic* is an abitrary one. In the United States there are individuals who consider themselves "Latin," "Hispanic," "Latino," "Cuban-American,"

"Mexican American," "Chicano," "Puerto Rican," another designation, or simply, "American." The only characteristic they hold in common is that Spanish or Portuguese (or, to a lesser degree, another Iberian language, such as Catalan or Basque) is the primary language at home. This confusing array of terms is instructive of the diversity of this segment of the American population. For purposes of clarity the umbrella term *Hispanic* is used in this book.

2. Curiously, the term "Asian American" is a political, not economic one. The nations of Asia are immensely diverse, and to lump together an American of Thai ancestry with one of Korean lineage is incorrect. Such blanket labels, in some ways, are offensive, for what the term "Asian American" really means is an American with slanted eyes, which is, in and of itself, racist.

PART I

The Emergence of Free Trade in Latin America

1

ON AMERICAN BUSINESSMEN IN LATIN AMERICA

There are tremendous opportunities in Latin America as the new century dawns. The nations of the New World have embarked on an ambitious program to implement a hemispherewide free trade zone. This enthusiastic embrace of the market system is a historic repudiation of communal, socialist, statist, and communist philosophies and ideologies that have kept Latin America impoverished far too long. The irony of it all is that Latin America consists of rich lands inhabited by poor people. The United States has an enviable role to play in helping the processes of democracy and economic liberalization. The United States, far from displaying "imperialist" designs, as has been the case in the past, is positioned to be a partner in the development of sustainable market economies, with middle-class citizens and functioning democratic institutions, from Alaska to Argentina.

This development is compelling. But Latin America is not the United States, or Canada. There are differences that can create stumbling blocks. The liberalization of the hemisphere, however, continues. American businessmen, who in increasing numbers are doing business in Latin America, can be overwhelmed by the diversity of the region, both geographical and cultural. Questions concerning personal issues—including language difficulties, health concerns, cultural practices, race and gender relations, and so on—abound throughout corporate America. There are also concerns about the kinds of insurance coverage one should have, how to comply with the requirements of the U.S. Foreign Corrupt Practices Act, and the most appropriate banking and financial arrangements in specific countries. There are far too many differences throughout the hemisphere to offer advice that is applicable everywhere all the time. Apart from general observations that are platitudes—urban centers the world over are dangerous at night—it is impossible to be more specific other than to make the observation that cultural differences pose the greatest confusion. In both social and business settings, manners, habits, and practices tend to differ, and Latin Americans may appear peculiar to the American businessperson, just as an American businessman or woman will at times perplex his or her host in Latin America.

It is therefore vital that American executives make use of two invaluable resources: an experienced travel agent and the U.S. State Department. A good travel agent can keep an executive informed as to the mundane but important things, including seasons and weather conditions, travel documents required, and accommodations and services available. The State Department issues travel advisories that, at times, border on the alarmist. Nevertheless, these bulletins advise Americans as to the changing political, health, and economic developments around the hemisphere. A breakout of cholera here, the imposition of curfews there, the imposition of exchange controls in another place are part of the unfolding drama in the lives of Latin Americans. The same is true in the United States: Miami and Los Angeles have imposed curfews in recent years, breakouts of diseases are reported in isolated places from time to time, the Treasury Department requires that sums of cash or equivalents be reported if they exceed $10,000 US when entering the United States, and heightened security measures are imposed at times at the nation's airports, such as during the Persian Gulf War. State Department travel advisories are useful, and they can be accessed by calling (202) 647-5225.

At the same time, there are certain characteristics about life in Latin America that converge in unexpected ways to give rise to a unique business culture. These nuances can puzzle American businesspeople, and oftentimes require time to figure out. While some offend American sensibilities, such as the virtual absence of businesswomen in Latin America, for the most part they are value neutral, meaning no moral judgments are made. They are treated as cultural peculiarities of a regional business culture. Understanding these norms will help an American executive understand better the mindset of his Latin American colleague, associate, or client, thereby moving things along. Several of these peculiarities of Latin American business culture will now be discussed.

AMERICAN OPTIMISM VERSUS LATIN AMERICAN PESSIMISM

The United States is built on an ideal, and in so being is an optimistic society. American optimism, which at times borders on naïveté, stands in stark contrast to the worldview of Latin America. Americans believe tomorrow will be better than today, whereas Latin Americans are more cynical, and contemptuous of such a view. For a variety of reasons, both historical and cultural, Latin Americans possess a pessimism that Americans find disturbing. Indeed, American executives find tremendous frustration in understanding how skeptical and reserved Latin Americans are about what is possible and what is desirable. American optimism stumbles when it encounters the enduring belief in the presence of evil. To understand the reasons for this it is necessary to think in terms of a single life. When we are young, we think the world will go on forever because we believe that we ourselves will go on forever. It is as we age that the limits imposed by mortality become apparent and are often denied. In contrast, the lives of Latin Americans are impoverished by the tragedy around them—no matter how wealthy one is, it is impossible to escape bearing witness to the misery of others. Their lives are tempered by the limitations of the physical, whether it is in the nature of the climates, which so often result in medical afflictions that shorten life spans, or the poverty of societies, which deny the inalienable rights Americans take for granted. The terror of poverty fosters pessimism, for one is reminded of its horror every day, everywhere. An acquaintance in Mexico City, proud of his Porsche Carrera Turbo, wanted to show off its power, but where in Mexico is there a highway built well enough so as to not damage such a vehicle? What good is having an elite vehicle if all the roads are filled with potholes or strewn with gravel? The power of optimism encounters the limitations imposed by pessimism at every turn. It is in this context that Latin Americans are tempered in their ambitions and goals. This pessimism historically has been attributed to the chastising nature of Catholicism and the stoicism, often called fatalism, of the Native American philosophies. Of equal influence, of course, is reality, a reality that delineates limitations, injustices, and failures. Where Americans are ready to say, *Why not?* Latin Americans find refuge in lamenting, *If only*.

THE QUESTION OF PEASANTS

In English, the word "peasant" carries negative connotations. It is a derogatory term, seldom used. In Spanish, "peasant" is "campesino." The word, however, is more generous in its meaning, more accurately translated as "country folk," with the positive affirmations of honesty, hard work, generosity, and kindness that this term evokes. These virtues recall a pastoral life and the values of our agrarian past of a by-gone era. Of course the connotations of "simple" folk is included, but it is done so in a generous way. Humility is a virtue we praise, but it is usually not found in powerful business or political leaders we admire. In Latin America there is nothing wrong with the term "peasant," although it implies a lack of

sophistication, or perhaps corruption, often associated with urban dwellers, which is to say city slickers. The only negative associations with "campesino" reside in the fact that rural dwellers are now almost exclusively
"Indian" peoples, who suffer discrimination. The frustrations are many.
Not unlike the United States where Native American societies languish,
in Latin America, as is the case the world over, native peoples do not
participate fully in the lives of their nations. In *The Great Deep,* this is how
James Hamilton-Paterson sums up the situation: "The world is dotted with
groups of demoralized tribespeople, drunk in shacks and shanties at the
margins of the societies that have disinherited them. Exasperated and not
always unsympathetic officials complain about the inertia and fecklessness
of Aborigines or [Native Americans], how pathetically they connive in
their own degradation."[1]

The failure to assimilate into the modern nation-state frustrates officials
around the world. It also creates images and stereotypes that others try to
overcome. In *The Exile,* David Rieff reports Gloria Sanchez, an outspoken
Cuban Miamian, as making the following point: "Anglos [non-Cuban
white Americans] hate us . . . because we are not like Mexicans or Puerto
Ricans. We won't get down on our knees. We accept some of America but
not everything. We weren't just peasants."[2] The implication seems to be
that Mexicans in America are "merely" peasants. The antagonisms among
Hispanics in the United States are due, to a great extent, to perceptions
of the American population at large to Spanish-speaking Americans. In
the West, where there are more Americans of Mexican ancestry, the issues
are different from those in the Southeast, where there are more Americans of Cuban ancestry, for instance. Californians have a different view of
what Hispanics are all about than Floridians, who are more familiar with
Cuban Americans, and New Yorkers encounter more Puerto Ricans and
have their perceptions influenced. The heterogeneous nature of Latin
America makes it impossible to make generalizations that accurately characterize the peoples of Spanish America. Joan Didion, writing in *Miami*
about Cubans, expresses the cultural discomfort the Black Legend has
engendered in the English-speaking world:

This question of language was curious. The sound of spoken Spanish was common
in Miami, but it was also common in Los Angeles, and Houston, and even in the
cities of the northeast. What was unusual about Spanish in Miami was not that it
was so often spoken, but that it was so often heard: in, say Los Angeles, Spanish
remained a language only barely registered by the Anglo population, part of the
ambient noise, the language spoken by the people who worked in the car wash
and came to trim the trees and cleared the tables in restaurants. In Miami Spanish
was spoken by the people who ate in the restaurants, the people who owned the
cars and the trees, which made, on the socioauditory scale, a considerable difference.[3]

It is evident that Americans have different expectations of Latin Americans. It is almost as if in the sophisticated metropolises of Latin America—Mexico City, Caracas, Buenos Aires, and so on—no one spoke Spanish. One suspects that Americans believe that only humble country folk are to be found throughout Latin America. It is undeniable that unskilled Mexican labor is everywhere throughout California, but there are multitudes of highly skilled professionals living very successful lives throughout south Florida. The prejudices Joan Didion expresses, ironically, have become the self-limiting parameters Americans of Mexican ancestry impose upon themselves. As Richard Rodriguez states: "Success is a terrible dilemma for Mexican Americans, like being denied some soul-sustaining sacrament. Without the myth of victimization—who are we? We are no longer Mexicans. We are professional Mexicans. We hire Mexicans."[4]

What is imperative for corporate officers to understand is that there are no negative connotations to the term "campesino," and in most cases it speaks longingly of a simpler time when life was uninterrupted by fax machines and digital pagers, and has no derogatory intent.

THE WAGES OF IGNORANCE

A corollary to the conceptualization of "peasant" as "country folk" is the curious importance ignorance plays in preserving the status quo of many Latin American countries. In authoritarian countries, which includes some Latin American countries, the state has a vested interest in denying people education in order to manipulate them. As Richard Rodriguez observes in *Days of Obligation,* "Information in an authoritarian society is power. In Mexico, power accumulates as information is withheld." The easiest way to withhold information is to deny education. In Latin America there are countries filled with illiterate multitudes the way the Southern Cone (Cono Sur) countries are not. By keeping people ignorant they can be kept dependent—dependent on a paternalistic state that takes care of its citizens the way an indulgent parent takes care of a child. The irony in all of this is obvious: An uneducated person is not a skilled worker. The dilemma for countries like Mexico remains one of educating people enough so that they can work in factories—economic development—but not enough to think and act for themselves—political empowerment. To achieve these goals, by contemporary standards, is immoral. Slavery in everything but name offends our sensibilities. It also makes little economic sense. A nation of ignorant workers makes for a small consumer market. That a few might very well enjoy the privileges inherent in exploiting the many is clear, but the tragedy is monumental on a human scale. The most difficult aspect about being an American in Latin America is to witness the exploitation of humans on such a scale. It is heartbreaking to see the Mexicans work so hard, struggling with such a determination to maintain their dignity as they confront humiliation after humiliation. In the summer of 1995, as the Mexican economy began to experience the full impact of the Zedillo administration's austerity program, a French colleague and I sat at an outdoor cafe in Mexico City's Zona Rosa. We remarked how passively the Mexicans accepted their fate. In the United States people would be rioting against the government if measures anywhere near as severe as these were imposed. My colleague concurred, saying the French would revolt rather than endure such Draconian measures. The people of Latin America, for some reason, are prepared to let their rights be violated without putting up much resistance. The observations of the Emperor Maximilian sounded as true today as they did when first made:

For a time the Emperor had thought the Indians would be his officials. But slowly he was forced to realize what could happen if Mexico was ruled by men who had never had responsibility and did not understand it. There was what he and the Empress called "a nothingness" about the masses of the Mexicans, which found them passive in the face of bandit raids against their villages and made difficult the procurement of men willing to do anything for the Empire or for anything else. The French said it was because Mexico was a half-breed and mongrel country, lazy, debased, unambitious; but the Emperor and Empress were unable to reach beyond that and say the problem was the result of the people's subjugation by the Spanish and the Church.[5]

Foreigners feel a subconscious anger at Latin Americans. A Dutchman who lives in Havana is frustrated at how the Cuban people quiver and refuse to rise up. "I keep telling them it's their country—they have a right to riot," he explains, "but they don't listen to me." The need of authoritarians to exploit ignorance affects the ability to conduct business. Consider in-bond factories in the Mexican state of Yucatan. It is not unheard of for people in this part of the country to be unable to sign their own names. On pay day, they receive their wages in cash, and have to affix their fingerprints on the payroll to indicate they received their pay. It is not a little discomforting for an American businessman to conduct business in this way. It is, however, how Mexico's ruling party remains in power. Before becoming president, Ernesto Zedillo served as Secretary of Education and under his tenure, for the first time in this century, literacy rates among "Indians" declined. This was no accident. It was a national policy designed to counteract the ascendance of National Action, the opposition party known as PAN, which was making tremendous gains as Mexico's population became more educated and the economy developed. Electoral fraud is easier to carry out when intimidation is the order of things. The systematic exploitation of the most impoverished members of Mexican society remains the foremost strategy in the ruling party's efforts to hold onto power. For some countries again, the challenge has been twofold: How do you educate people so that they can be workers in a modern factory, but not enough to think for themselves? How do you educate people so foreign investors will have confidence in the nation's work force, but not enough for them to demand political participation through free elections? For countries like Mexico, it has been increasingly difficult to balance these opposing needs of the authoritarian leaders; developed economies require workers who are educated and can think for themselves, whereas authoritarian regimes do not. It is difficult at times to remain indifferent to the way these societies exploit their own citizens: To endeavor to deny another human being an education borders on evil. Thus the dual curses of ignorance and passivity in the face of injustice is perhaps the most intriguing puzzle of Latin America.

BUSINESS VERSUS PERSONAL RELATIONSHIPS

More than in the United States, throughout Latin America business relationships become personal ones. One does business with friends and people one trusts. This is in sharp contrast with the United States, where one's life is more neatly compartmentalized between public and private. For American executives, there is the question of ethical considerations as personal relationships evolve. It is not uncommon to be invited to a Latin American colleague's home and meet his family. This is not unknown in the United States or Europe, either. It is almost nonexistent among say, the Japanese, who find it unacceptable to welcome business associates into their homes. But in Latin America, where the rigors of society melt away under the glare of pragmatism, other circumstances arise. Consider, for instance, the complications in a business relationship that has become a close personal one. In both Mexico City and Buenos Aires I have become good friends with business associates whose families I have met. But in both cases, when we are entertaining or being entertained on business, my Latin American colleagues are accompanied by women who are not their wives. Thus, American businessmen become unwilling accomplices in duplicity, which becomes more discomforting when, in the case of one Latin American associate, he has several women friends. Social situations become cumbersome—I know he is cheating on his wife, but I am often confused as to which mistress is being used to cheat on another mistress. That he has children by women other than his wife only further complicates matters. This is all in sharp contrast with American norms; I have, for instance, never attended the birthday party of an American colleague's mistress, or the wedding of an American colleague's illegitimate daughter. Latin American societies, for all their stereotypes of being repressive bastions of oppressive Catholicism, are in fact very fluid in their mores, and approximate the social tolerances of the

Mediterranean countries of Italy, France, and Spain. In the United States, remembering a colleague's wife's name is sufficient; in Latin America keeping all the names straight is somewhat more challenging.

RELIGIOUS CONDUCT

Few other themes are as immaterial as religion in the business life of Latin Americans. Pragmatism prevails, although ritualized mysticism constitutes an integral—and riveting—part of the cultures of the region. American executives should find comfort in and tolerance of vestiges of an irrational past, spectacle that amuses and intrigues but is of no consequence. Historical aberrations, such as the Inquisition apart, Latin Americans are not any more zealous than any other human society on earth. Its Christianity is more tolerant and forgiving, as the social mores concerning fidelity reveal, than other forms of Christianity. This has its roots in philosophical differences. Catholics do not pretend to know the mind of God, whereas Christian Fundamentalists are convinced that they do. In a real, practical sense it renders religion absent from the business life of Latin America, however much the spectacle of mysticism abounds. It is not uncommon, for instance, to have new offices or businesses blessed by a Catholic priest. However peculiar it might appear to an American, it is as harmless as it is charming. Few Latin Americans are immune from indulging in these practices. A Mexican businessman I know, a consummate sophisticate if ever there was one, had a Catholic priest bless—and sprinkle with holy water—all the cubicles when his new offices were opened. In an in-bond factory on the outskirts of Buenos Aires, the factory workers had portraits of a saint on the wall in the lunch room. Religious relics suffuse these societies, but in a harmless way. The legalistic excesses of Americans—class action lawsuits barring religious icons from public spaces—are absent in Latin America. One day a few years ago in Brazil I was surprised when I noticed dried blood on the doorstep to a franchise that had opened earlier that week, when I remembered that a shaman had held a ceremony the previous evening. After a couple of phone calls my suspicions—animal blood was used in a ceremony to keep evil spirits away—were confirmed. For most Americans this is all outside the realm of normal business practices. At the same time, in the United States, for some inexplicable reason, the noun "Catholic" is almost exclusively preceded by the adjective "devout." In Latin America such creatures are few and far between: if the nature of a human is to sin, then Latin Americans do an admirable job of following human nature. In Latin America, therefore, religion is a cultural manifestation of no greater significance or discriminatory bias than showing up at the office in the United States with take-out sushi or ravioli to eat quietly at one's desk. In societies where faith and power are tenuous, there is little competition between these ideas. To be sure there is tremendous faith—the Pope fills stadiums in Latin America the way the Super Bowl does in the United States—but religion remains a spectator sport, satisfying a primitive voyeuristic need. The exact nature of their religious convictions, often displayed against a background of faith, not unlike their political beliefs, is as incomprehensible as it is pervasive. As such, mindful respect and tolerance of the inconsequential is the prudent course of action; let a priest sprinkle holy water to his heart's content, provided one makes sure his or her personal computer is adequately protected from the downpour.

HEIGHTENED ELEMENT OF RISK

On a personal level, there are many rewards for American executives in Latin America. There is the satisfaction of contributing to the economies of nations purposefully working to raise their standards of living. When American express package delivery companies, such as FedEx, UPS, and DHL, enter a new market, they are being innovative and offering a new service that did not exist before. In the United States one can compete, but in Latin America one can compete—while being a pioneer. On a human level, there is pride in bringing this kind of innovation, which is often denied in developed countries where much has grown mundane. There is also the very real rush of adrenaline when engaged in activities that are fraught with danger. Flying aboard a Russian-made Cuban military jet from Havana to the island of Curacao in the company of agents of the Cuban government armed with diplomatic passports and brief cases with several million dollars is not a routine business activity in corporate America. The sense of lawlessness and danger is seductive, even if it isn't for the faint of heart. The excitement is as real as the adrenaline rush, reportedly; and there is an undeniable element of fun, invariably. The United States is so developed that there are few realms, apart from the underworld, where the wild, wild West of the past century endures. In Cuba, the arbitrary reality of business life—at any moment one or one's associates may fall out of favor with Fidel Castro and face arrest or expulsion—creates excitement; a few days prior to arriving in Havana in 1995, executions by firing squads in an eastern province had taken place. Not unlike sex, for which humans are hard-wired to run risks, doing business in some Latin American markets continues to prove irresistible to some American businessmen, legalities back home notwithstanding. It isn't only Cuba that offers an "Indiana Jones" business climate, to a discomforting degree. Consider another example. Once, upon arriving in Guatemala City with clients, shortly after checking into our hotel, the front desk rang up. "I suggest you fill the bathtub with water," I was informed. "And if you would be kind enough, please inform the others in your party." When asked why, the gentleman volunteered that a coup was underway. This sort of thing happens regularly enough, he explained, and "the military only legitimizes its take-over by claiming it has the people's support. To do this they shut off the water and cut the power until people from all over town converge in rallies. Then they turn the water and lights back on." It also helps to have the presence of mind to dash out and purchase aspirin; shopping becomes more difficult once martial law is declared and curfews are in effect. It turned out it took three days before the massive rallies in support of the new dictator could be arranged. Filling the bathtub with water was a strategic move to ensure we could, at a minimum, flush the toilets while we languished in the hotel when the curfew was in place, and hesitatingly ventured forth during daylight hours while the military secured the city. Calls to our travel agent proved futile; it would be impossible to return to the airport before curfew went into effect. Business meetings, needless to say, had to be rescheduled, as the entire country had been rescheduled. There are few instances in which the business environment within the United States offers similar escapades. There is, of course, tremendous excitement for those executives who thrive on adrenaline rushes in this kind of turmoil, but it is also a reminder that the State Department provides travel advisories that offer timely advice on prevailing conditions.

THE CHARACTER OF OFFICIALS

An enduring problem with doing business in Latin America is the ethical issues about the men and women with whom one must conduct business. There is no Latin American country where officials and business leaders at some point are not less than admirable individuals. This is true in the United States, as well. The difference is how pervasively the reprehensible public figures cross the stages of nationals' lives of Latin American countries. That a good number of leaders, whether Panama's General Manuel Noriega or Cuba's Fidel Castro, have come to power through the use of force has a great deal to do with how they conduct themselves. Another consideration, too, is the fact that impoverished societies seldom afford all their members access to social refinement. Manners are as scarce as education in Latin America. This is all compounded by the insecurities of Latin Americans, particularly those from those countries with large "Indian" populations. Indeed, the secure act differently from the insecure. The inferiority complexes of the countries with large "Indian" and mixed-race populations have given rise to a culture of consumerism obsessed with superficial status symbols. The confidence of the Cono Sur countries, in contrast, leaves the people here less prone to fall prey to coarse displays of wealth. Latin Americans from the "Indian" countries aspire to civility, not sophistication. Latin Americans from the Cono Sur countries, on the other hand, discern the shades of cosmopolitanism. It is enough for a

Mexican to know the fundamentals of dinner wines, but an Argentine is expected to be able to distinguish among dessert liqueurs. Consider the following anecdote.

At the Pacific Stock Exchange in San Francisco, the San Francisco Chamber of Commerce is hosting a dinner for Carlos Hank González, Mexico's Secretary of Tourism. In a country renowned for corruption, González is considered perhaps the most corrupt Mexican of all. This is impressive, worthy of a Presidential Lifetime Achievement Award. Nonetheless, here we are among the business leaders of San Francisco, assorted city and state officials, undeniably distinguished citizens, a small contingent of groupies from the Friends of Mexico, the fawning press, all of us assembled to hear this exemplary gentleman speak. And speak, he does. "Mexico is so rich and fertile," he says, "few places in the world are as blessed." On he continues, weaving fantastic tales of resorts and beaches, highrise hotels and lowrise exclusive retreats. It is all there: emerald rain forests, pristine mountain waterfalls, more sunny days on sunny beaches than any other place on earth, sophisticated cities of unspeakable refinement, secluded colonial towns, exquisite ancient pyramids to trample over. Mexico has it all. It's all there in Mexico.

"They say pandas do not breed outside China," he says, a snide reference to those reluctant pandas at the National Zoo in Washington, D.C. who refuse to procreate. "But in Mexico, our pandas make baby pandas!" The audience laughs. I laugh. He is so vulgar I am entranced. He is so pompous I am fascinated. I am in awe of the charm he oozes as he schmoozes ever so effortlessly, captivated by the polished manner of this ruthless thief. No matter that he is corrupt, I think. No matter that he represents everything that is wrong with Mexico, I convince myself. I am enchanted. Nothing he has done is beyond redemption. Nothing he has done he has been able to prevent himself from doing, I lie to myself. I look around. Everyone is mesmerized. Only Richard Rodriguez, seated two chairs to my right, is not impressed by this fraud. If Adolf Hitler were Mexican, he would be a hit at a San Francisco Chamber of Commerce dinner at the Pacific Stock Exchange.

The only awkward moment comes after dessert, during the question and answer portion of the show when, as the Secretary of Tourism makes the case for American investment in Mexican resorts, one woman stands, an American of Mexican ancestry, ostensibly to make the point that *all* investments, no matter how apparently secure, entail some sort of risk.

It is the late 1980s and Mexico, a deadbeat debtor nation, remains a risk. The Secretary of Tourism pretends acoustics and language are a problem and answers an entirely different point. The investment banker to my left mutters almost inaudibly under his breath, "Stupid bitch." He turns to me, shaking his noble Wasp head slightly. I smile. His bank is financing yet another self-contained resort development in overdeveloped Cancun.

I don't know who I like more: the questioner, the Secretary of Tourism, or Richard Rodriguez, who rolls his eyes. As this affair ends I find myself speaking with the Secretary of Tourism for a moment. I shake his hand and I mock him for a second. He pretends not to understand, his graceful smile never leaves his face for a moment. I am enchanted by a pro of unchallenged skill.

Among Argentines, in contrast, cosmopolitanism forbids such vulgarity. This is not to be confused with civility, as Americans understand civility, however. This is Argentina after all. This is a country that, less than a generation ago, had a government that was kidnapping its own citizens, drugging them unconscious, and throwing living people off low-flying airplanes into shark-infested waters as a way of dealing with political opponents. To be civilized does not preclude being immoral or criminal. To be sophisticated does not mean one cannot be corrupt, or evil. That one's aspirations for civility are realized does not preclude betraying decency. Latin Americans of the Cono Sur countries, like the European ancestors that nurtured them, are masters of betrayal. This is all important to understand from day one. American executives cannot help but encounter individuals such as Hank González, for men like him populate public offices throughout Latin America. There is no subtle way to disguise the unpleasant truth: Unsavory characters hold positions of power in Latin America with greater frequency than they do in the United States. American businesspeople who do business in Latin America will hear horror stories. And those who do business in Latin America long enough will *live* horror stories.

CORRUPTION, EVERYONE?

The Foreign Corrupt Practices Act governs how Americans are to conduct themselves abroad. It is illegal for American executives to pay bribes or engage in any other activity that can be construed as "corruption." At the same time, in a competitive world, it cannot be denied that a competitive advantage can be readily had by oiling the wheels of bureaucracies or winning favor by making a payment of some kind. To make matters worse, there is the eternal perception of Latin American societies as being hopelessly corrupt. The truth of the matter is that corruption is not as widespread as stereotypes would have us believe. To be sure, there are poor ethics—to be generous is classifying the problem—among those of authority throughout Latin America. Corruption at the highest levels of government is customary, but the same can be said of all societies. Is there a more astounding example of systematic institutional corruption as that which led to the savings and loan scandal, which cost American taxpayers a still-unknown sum? Indeed, in many cases Latin Americans, out of frustration at their inability to achieve sustainable economic growth and enduring democracies, are inclined to believe the worst of their governments, exaggerating corruption. In so doing, there is an easy scapegoat for any failure: Things that go wrong do so because of corruption somewhere along the line and not because of poor management or bad luck. In Mexico, for instance, this predisposition to be damning of the country is so prevalent and perverse it is called "malinchismo." A malinchista is one who criticizes Mexico, or desires what is foreign—meaning American—in an act of deprecating what is Mexican. But every Mexican is a malinchista, as both consumer patterns and frustration with the lethargic and oppressive political system demonstrate. In fact, Mexicans, who resent having to repress their regional and ethnic identities by being forced to adopt a "national" identity that is mostly fictitious, are the first to label anything the result of corruption. To hear Mexicans speak, there is not one honest human being in the whole country. That may be true of public officials, such as police officers and petty bureaucrats who are wont to abuse their authority to a remarkable degree. But the truth is different. Mexicans, like all other Latin Americans, are no more corrupt or immoral than any other people in the world. "I hope you have not been leading a double life, pretending to be wicked and being really good all the time. That would be hypocrisy," Oscar Wilde wrote in *The Importance of Being Earnest*. It has been my experience that the people of Latin America are as kind and gentle, generous and charming as the people of small towns and large cities throughout the United States. Latin Americans, if truth be told, pretend to be evil, more out of frustration than out of conviction.

DOUBLE STANDARDS

While corruption is not as widespread as is often believed, arrogance is a different matter. Latin Americans from the larger countries—Mexico, Brazil, and Argentina—are inclined to hold amusing ideas of themselves. Within a week of the implementation of the North American Free Trade Agreement (NAFTA), for example, Mexicans believed they had "arrived" and it was intriguing to see their arrogance. They demanded in indirect and effusive ways to be treated as "First World" citizens. This was never articulated, but in body language, allusions, and inferences, this was the expectation. There is nothing of substance with these demands. That is, of course, because being "First World" is more than a trade agreement. The Mexicans want to be treated as First World citizens without having to measure up to First World standards. "The only thing First World about Mexico," an American executive said in November 1994, "are the prices. But ask for a telephone that works, or properly starched shirts, or electricity that doesn't come and go, and then we're back at the Third World." The double standard is transparent: Third World economies demanding First World consideration. It is problematic, and outright annoying, that the basic infrastructure and civil comforts are not reliable. Quality fluctuates more than some exchange rates during a severe devaluation, and reliability is an aspect of the will of God.

PERCEPTIONS OF AMERICANS

As discussions develop between American executives and their counterparts, and if language does not pose that great a barrier, it is only a matter of time before Latin Americans' curiosity and fascination with the United States becomes apparent. The United States proves intriguing precisely because of the export of American culture through films, television programs, magazines, books, news reports, and so on. For many Latin Americans this is how perceptions are formed and expectations created. This appeal is without a doubt a competitive advantage for American executives. At the same time, it is crucial to understand how incorrect perceptions take shape. Latin Americans, while in awe of the spectacular achievements of the United States in economic, political and cultural terms, stand aghast at the violence and chaos that seems to permeate American lives. The images from Hollywood—violent films, television programs that portray empty lives and bankrupt morals, magazines that examine the most sordid details of the lives of celebrities and public figures, sensationalist voyeurism into domestic violence and public failures—are beamed into Latin America from satellites around the clock. News reports from the United States offer little in reassurance. In the 1990s I have had to defend American foreign policy when it has been indefensible, and explain the legal technicalities that resulted in a mistrial of the Menendez brothers who confessed killing their parents. There is concern about the darker side of the American character, whether it is in the form of police brutality, shooting tourists, cannibal-murders, or cross-burning white supremacists. Latin Americans are bombarded with images of violence and racism, of dysfunctional families and irresponsible citizens. They are, in short, bombarded by American television, which is enough to give anyone pause to wonder. When arriving at any capital in Latin America, after checking into your room, turn on the television and surf the channels. You are bound to see American television shows, either with subtitles, with voice-overs, or in English. Then imagine what these people must think if this is what they have on which to base their opinions about America and Americans. It is a humbling experience. A prudent strategy is to be honest in admitting that the United States is not perfect and problems do exist, but that these images portray sensationalism more than fact. Latin Americans, whose lives are encumbered by distortions in their own countries, will understand. A danger of great consequence is that curiosity is not reciprocal; Latin Americans are much more intrigued by the United States than Americans are by Latin America. It is not unusual to have Americans be quizzed about the United States. The result is often that Americans find Latin Americans somewhat boorish or boring; people who ask endless questions about mundane things while one is indifferent to his or her host are indeed boring. It is, however, a question of diplomacy to spare Latin American feelings, never letting them let on how tedious they are by asking questions about the United States. After all, one can always forgive those one finds boring, but never those who find one boring. Therefore, be generous in explaining anything about America, but do not take this opportunity to dwell on problems. Recognize, however, that there are limits to what one can explain. A Peruvian government official was disappointed with my response to his question to know what Michael Jackson was all about, so he could explain it to his teenage daughter. I shrugged my shoulders and said that some things are inexplicable. But as an American in a foreign land, it is imperative to bear in mind that the most important impression of the United States is how one is perceived. It is bad form to be critical of the one's own country, whether one is Latin American or not. It is also important that, if the relationship has developed to a point of friendship, humor can assuage fears and reassure. For instance, when asked by a Colombian gentleman if it was true that half of all marriages in the United States ended in divorce, a potential polemic came to a happy end when I replied that *that* was the good news—the bad news is that the other half end in the death of a spouse. After mischievous smiles are exchanged, the subject should be changed.

NOTES

1. James Hamilton-Paterson, *The Great Deep: The Sea and its Thresholds* (New York: Random House, 1992), p. 272.

2. David Rieff, *The Exile: Cuba in the Heart of Miami* (New York: Simon & Schuster, 1993), p. 139.

3. Joan Didion, *Miami* (New York: Simon & Schuster, 1987), p. 63.

4. Richard Rodriguez, *Days of Obligation: An Argument with My Mexican Father* (New York: Viking Penguin, 1992), p. 70.

5. Gene Smith, *Maximilian and Carlota: A Tale of Romance and Tragedy* (New York: William Morrow, 1973), p. 130.

2

THE FACE OF LATIN AMERICA IN PERSPECTIVE

Latin America is too heterogeneous to speak of as one entity. The peoples and societies of Latin America are as varied as in other areas of the world, such as Europe. Romance languages, Spanish colonialism, Catholicism, Native American peoples are the bones on which rest the individual cultures, societies, and lives of the people who live throughout the hemisphere. These broad historical events and cultural characteristics punctuate the evolution of Latin America, of course, but these are limited, and limiting, when attempting to understand the nuances and differences among peoples as diverse and a landscape as sweeping. But if sense is to be made of Latin America, and of the emerging business opportunities as the nations of the hemisphere embrace market-driven economies, it is necessary to categorize these nations. Only then can the business opportunities and markets be assessed and appropriate strategies implemented. There is no question that there are tremendous opportunities in Latin America. How to approach these markets, however, is another matter.

From Mexico to Argentina, the nations of the regions have embarked on free trade as a development model. The Mexican Meltdown of December 1994—ten days short of the first anniversary of the North American Free Trade Agreement—has raised questions about how to implement free trade. This is fortunate, for it forces a more tempered and disciplined approach to regional integration. The reckless manner in which the Mexicans embarked on a free trade agreement offers lessens for other Latin American nations. As the Mexican bubble burst, repercussions shook the financial capitals of the Americas, sending finance ministers scurrying for cover, negotiating credit lines at international lending bodies, implementing austerity programs, defending their currencies, traveling to the financial centers of the industrialized nations to reassure international investors, and appearing on television programs explaining to their fellow citizens why each nation was not like Mexico. Calm had been restored by the summer of 1995 and negotiations for establishing a hemispherewide free trade zone, as outlined at the Summit of the Americas, continued, perhaps in a more cautious manner.

Heterogeneous or not, however, from a business point of view, it is necessary to categorize the nations of Latin America in order to have a more disciplined set of strategic plans and objectives. Latin American countries fall into three categories. These are Core, Periphery, and Caribbean Basin nations.

Core Countries: Core countries are those that rest upon the Sierra and the Andes mountain ranges. These are mountainous nations that were blessed with highly advanced Native American societies when the Europeans first arrived. They are *mestizo* cultures, meaning their people are the descents of both Native American and European ancestors and civilizations. The countries included in this category are Bolivia, Colombia, Ecuador, Guatemala, Mexico, and Peru.

Periphery Countries: Periphery countries are those that surround the core countries. They are marked by the absence of large Native American populations and their people are almost exclusively of European descent. Paraguay is an exception; the intermingling of races has been so extensive there that its people are singular. For the most part, however, these are "transplanted" Europeans, meaning that they are European societies that have evolved on American soil. The periphery countries are Argentina, Brazil, Chile, Paraguay and Uruguay.

Caribbean Basin: The Caribbean Basin includes the island nations of the Caribbean sea, the nations of Central America, with the exception of Guatemala, and those that straddle the northern shoulder of the South American continent. The mainland nations included are Costa Rica, El Salvador, Honduras, Jamaica, Nicaragua, Panama, and Venezuela. Belize, French Guiana, Guyana, and Suriname fall in this category but are only briefly mentioned in the survey presented.

AUTHORITARIANS VERSUS DICTATORS

The distinctions between core countries and periphery ones, at first, seems insignificant. From an American perspective, all that matters is the unending stream of bad news that spills forth from Latin America. It's a coup in one place, an upheaval in the other, as relentless as a plague of locusts. The boom-and-bust cycles, too, are as familiar as they are frustrating. Mexico booms, then it crashes. Peru rises like a phoenix from the ashes of despair. So it goes, like a game of musical chairs where reversals of fortune are in order every time the music stops. But there are patterns in all of this. There are clear distinctions between the two main groups of Latin American countries. Core countries are characterized by authoritarian regimes, while periphery countries alternate between democracies and dictatorships. The reasons for these distinctions are historical, cultural, and economic.

In *Dictatorships and Double Standards* Jeane Kirkpatrick advances a theory of government that shaped American foreign policy during the Reagan administration. In this infamous book, Kirkpatrick argues that there are clear distinctions between right-wing and left-wing dictatorships. "Although there is no instance of a revolutionary 'socialist' or Communist society being democratized," Kirkpatrick writes, "right-wing autocracies do sometimes evolve into democracies—given time, propitious economic, social, and political circumstances, talented leaders, and a strong indigenous demand for representative government."

Thus, she can lump together Nicaragua's Anastasio Somoza and Iran's Shah in one breath, labeling them as "traditional rulers of semitraditional societies." From the classifications offered, it is argued the United States can morally support right-wing dictators, but must oppose left-wing dictators. It becomes unclear, however, if it makes much difference to the people who live under a dictatorship where on the political spectrum their oppressors lie. Oppression is oppression, regardless of how it is delivered. Writing of Czarist Russia in the nineteenth century, the Marquis de Custine, a Frenchman who journeyed throughout the Russian empire, wrote, "To tremble is not to disdain; we never despise that which excites our fear." If some kinds of dictatorships endure it is because they are feared, not because of their politics. Indeed, the Kirkpatrick theory places so many conditions for the eventual evolution of democracies of right-wing authoritarian governments as to be meaningless. The requirements of "time" and "a strong indigenous demand" for democracy could very well mean enough time for people to be fed up and revolt against a system that is bankrupt—which is precisely what happened throughout the left-wing autocracies in Eastern Europe and the former Soviet Union. This is not different from the rebellion against the right-wing dictatorship in Argentina, but rather than this being the result of "talented leaders," it was their incompetence during the war with England over the Falkland or Malvinas (the name one uses depends on one's political persuasion) Islands. It was the economic and ideological bankruptcy of Marxism and the right-wing generals' breathtaking stupidity that toppled these dictatorships, not imagined differences among "authoritarian" governments.

The collapse of the Soviet Union and the melting of Marxism from the face of Europe disproved the Kirkpatrick thesis in no uncertain terms. Nevertheless, the false theory remains a central part of American thinking

in the formulation of foreign policy toward Latin America. This surprises
in its irrationality. There is, of course, nothing wrong with arguing a theory that later is disproved. There is, however, something sad about not
changing one's ideas to reflect empirical data. That Jeane Kirkpatrick
steadfastly insists on an incorrect theory to bolster her career is not an
unfamiliar practice among the men and women who served in the Reagan
administration. There are misgivings about the level of intellectual honesty required to remain so stubborn, unless one assumes that the same
cognitive dissonance that afflicted the more paranoid members of the
Reagan administration who indulged arms-for-hostages fantasies also afflicted the UN ambassador. The argument presented, however, is both
irrational and unreasonable, which underscores the irrelevance of the
Kirkpatrick thesis regarding Latin America. To a great extent, Jeane Kirkpatrick's diatribes detract from the business of understanding Latin America precisely because they clutter intelligent discourse. For our purposes,
it is imperative that American businessmen understand the fundamental
differences in the political economies of core versus periphery countries.
It is important to understand these distinctions because it is important to
understand the minds of the men who run the systems of Latin American
societies, how they see the world, and their place in it.

Core nations are authoritarian, meaning they are characterized by significant numbers of "Indian" peoples. The majority of their citizens are
mestizos and there is widespread illiteracy. These societies were patterned
on patrimonial models in which the state dispenses patronage as a means
of exerting institutional control. Poor people are dependent on the government for their livelihood, and in turn they support the government.
In the same way that in the American South the plantation owner had
patron-client relationships with those within his domain, so too in Latin
America have hacienda owners exercised similar control over the lives of
their charges. In contemporary society, this patron-client relationship
based on raw dependence has been transferred to the state through ruling
oligarchies or authoritarian systems. Periphery countries, on the other
hand, have been traditionally encumbered by dictators. These countries,
the children of European people and ideas, have fundamental democratic
institutions that are taken over by the military. Power, through one-man,
or one-general, rule, is attained through brutal force. In periphery countries, where the population is well educated and Westernized, military
rule, not unlike power plays in Europe, are born of ideological conflicts,
carried out by zealots. Whether it is to fight communism or "Jews," the
dictators of the periphery countries profess to be fighting to save Western
civilization, while enriching themselves as an added bonus. In core countries, such pretenses are almost unheard of, except when testifying before
U.S. congressional committees. The authoritarians of core countries are
in power for economic purposes, belittling the inability of their compa-

triots to be capable of self-government in mocking, patronizing terms. The dictators of periphery countries, on the other hand, lament the "necessity" for the military to intervene, but intervene it must to save the nation from civilians it deems irresponsible or dangerous.

Periphery dictators are on divine missions, often invoking faith. Their unquestioning moral right, and the murderous logic in which it often ends, have devastated the lives of millions in Argentina, Brazil, Chile, Paraguay, and Uruguay. That extremes of this nature exist with dark consequences across the continent suggests the decadence in thought that is possible when ideas develop in a vacuum. An individual who lives alone with very little contact is at risk for being peculiar, speaking to himself, voicing strange ideas, becoming a little batty. For societies, the same is true. Whether it is Americans in the nineteenth century driven by religious fervor to build Utopias across the vast stretches of the Midwest, or evolving transplanted European societies in the Southern Cone, the murderous extremes of logic degenerate into perversions of morality. None of the Utopian schemes in America succeeded, and in Latin America, European psychosis plagues the periphery countries in a frightening political zealousness.

Core country authoritarian regimes are neurotic, obsessed with their parentage, haunted by irrational notions of "bastardy." The people from core countries feel their blood is tainted by the savagery of the "Indian." These are fears that haunt them, and manifest themselves in annoying interruptions in social and business life. Periphery dictatorial regimes, on the other hand, are psychotic, living out the dramas of political philosophies and intolerance that are the hallmarks of European history. I am being facetious for a reason, which is to dispel stereotypes. In the same way American society is not exempt from its own disorder—social critic Tom Wolfe argues that American lives "have become chaotic, fragmented, random, discontinuous; in a word, *absurd*," meaning, America, as its daytime television programming demonstrates, is now a schizophrenic society—Latin Americans are stereotyped as immature and childish, or Frito Banditos. Latin American countries are viewed by Americans as ridiculous places, where governments fall as readily as autumn leaves and currencies are as worthless as Monopoly money. But if Latin Americans see Americans as crazy and fear American culture to some degree, there is some veracity to the views Americans hold of the peoples and cultures of Latin America. To a degree, core countries display social neurosis and periphery countries psychosis.

These different patterns of social deviance present the rather insidious, but inevitable, conclusion: marketing strategies have to consider the frames of mind of these different societies, and they must consider the nuances engendered in the business environment. It is not uncommon for core countries, so obsessed with race, to engage in genocide as public

policy. It is very evident how the philosophical struggles of European tragedy—fascism versus communism—unfold in periphery countries in violent ways. It is now compelling to witness how America has lost her
innocence, for an America where car bombs go off in the heartland is no
longer the place the founding fathers envisioned.

3

The Mexican Meltdown in Perspective

We are not the first, who with the best of meaning have incurred the worst.

—Shakespeare

THE IMPLICATIONS OF THE MEXICAN MELTDOWN

The optimism that was evident at the conclusion of the Summit of the Americas suffered a blow when the Mexican Meltdown sent shock waves around the world. If this was the harvest of free trade, then a market economy is a bitter fruit, critics around the hemisphere pointed out. The enthusiasm at the conclusion of the Miami meetings was now forgotten as panic and fear swept the corridors of power throughout the hemisphere, thinking that Mexico's fate would also be theirs.

But a reversal of fortune is nothing more than a temporary setback. That is, of course, if one is capable of moving forward and learning from mistakes. As Mexico emerges from its current economic difficulties, it is doing so unconvincingly. It has damaged in fundamental and structural ways its middle class, brought ruin upon the private sector, and mortgaged its future. Its leadership is lacking, both in talent and in its ability to persuade. The credibility gap continues to increase. Throughout much of 1995, watching Ernesto Zedillo speak was a painful experience. In Oscar Wilde's *The Importance of Being Earnest*, a main character is in an unusual predicament. Caught in a deception, he is forced to tell the truth, and he is clearly uncomfortable doing so. "It is very painful for me to speak the truth," he explains, continuing, "It is the first time in my life that I have ever been reduced to such a painful position, and I am really quite inexperienced in doing anything of the kind." Ernesto Zedillo, likewise, has little experience with being truthful, and this was very much in evidence as the poor man struggled, forced by the consequences of economic disaster to do so. Nevertheless, Ernesto Zedillo served in Carlos Salinas's cabinet, and prior to becoming Salinas's hand-picked successor, he was the campaign manager for the doomed presidential candidate, Luis Donaldo Colosio. It is impossible for Zedillo to distance himself from the disastrous policies of his predecessor, to say nothing of his own miscalculations and ineptitude.

"The truth," Mexico's beleaguered leader said as an international rescue package was being prepared, "is that we are in an emergency." The truth is that Mexico was in an emergency in 1982, when Miguel de la Madrid became president. It was still in an emergency when Carlos Salinas assumed the presidency in 1988. It remains in an emergency as Ernesto Zedillo takes his turn at bat. What is disturbing is that Mexico has, for eighteen years, been under the supervision of the IMF and the World Bank, who have, along with the White House and the U.S. Treasury Department, assured everyone that everything was coming together *pronto*. Indeed, the implementation of NAFTA was Mexico's official "coming of age," as it became a welcomed member of the First World.

The implications and lessons are of tremendous importance, for they stand to shape how hemispheric integration envisioned by the Summit of the Americas will unfold. If the mistakes encountered integrating Mexico into the North American economy are to be avoided, then the origins of the Mexican Meltdown must be analyzed. There are, of course, two elements involved here. The first are the mistakes and miscalculations the Mexican leaders have made. That discipline and intelligence are the stuff of politics is an argument few put forward. There is no reason to believe that politicians in Mexico City are any more responsible than politicians in Washington, D.C., or Ottawa. Mexicans are responsible for their own problems and spectacular failures. But they had some help. The other area of inquiry surrounds the issue of economic integration. The Mexican Meltdown, in many ways, is but a grotesque manifestation of the problems encountered by Canada when the U.S.–Canada Free Trade Agreement was first implemented in 1991. As with Spain, which encountered significant economic dislocation as it was incorporated into the European Community, smaller economies experience turmoil and convulsions as they are integrated or absorbed by larger ones. The challenge, therefore, is to learn from the Mexicans in order to avoid making the same mistakes as other countries become members of NAFTA.

A LOSS OF CONFIDENCE

The implementation of NAFTA was to be the crowning achievement of the Salinas administration, a defining moment in Mexican history when it would use its privileged access to the world's largest consumer market as the basis for sustained economic development and democratization. It is not without irony that on January 1, 1994, the first day NAFTA took effect, an armed insurrection in the southern state of Chiapas reminded the world that Mexico remained very much a Third World country. The Zapatist rebellion, and the Mexican government's inability to quash an insignificant band of armed peasants, cast doubts on the competence of the Salinas administration. Within a short time, the widening trade deficits demonstrated that, in a market driven economy, Mexico was unprepared to compete in world markets; Mexico was importing vast quantities of goods and services, and not selling much more than it had without the free trade agreement. The result was the erosion of investor confidence in both the political and economic prospects of the Mexican economy.

The erosion of political confidence was composed of several components.

Political Instability

The Zapatist insurrection was quickly followed by the assassination of Carlos Salinas's heir apparent, convulsing Mexico into a state of uncertainty. That the ruling party would prevail in the summer's presidential elections was cast into question, and the probability that electoral fraud would be used by the government undermined prospects that the Carlos Salinas regime would do much for Mexican democratic aspirations. The question of turmoil loomed in the minds of investors, which increased the political risk of Mexico. The reassurances from Washington and Ottawa did little to calm fears, particularly given the inability of the Mexican government to put an end to the political violence throughout the country. That the escalation continued, with stalled peace talks, other political assassinations, and the climate of fear created by a wave of abductions, only fueled investor fears.

Lack of a Macroeconomic Development Model

The uncertainty of the political climate, as is the case in Colombia, created a distorted image overseas. It was difficult for the Salinas administration to explain away the widening trade deficits, which began to deplete the government's dollar reserves. While it is not uncommon for an economy that is expanding to incur deficits, the nature of these deficits is important. If Mexican deficits reflected capital formation and investment in industrial facilities and infrastructure, it would not be cause for alarm. In fact, however, these deficits reflected consumption. The monetary expansion adopted by the Mexican government in an election year eased credit, unleashing a wave of consumer spending. The opening of the Mexican economy to free trade highlighted the absence of an industrial policy by revealing not only how uncompetitive Mexico remained in the world economy but also how dependent the nation was on the export of raw materials (oil) and services (tourism). If not for the in-bond industry, which in analytical terms represented nothing more than the export of labor through rote work, Mexico would have virtually no industrial exports at all.

Politicization of the Exchange Rate

Throughout the spring of 1994 U.S. institutional investors exerted tremendous pressures on the Salinas administration, reeling from political chaos within the ruling party immediately after the assassination of the ruling party's presidential candidate, Luis Donaldo Colosio. Mexico acquiesced to the interests of foreign investors and agreed to maintain the peso overvalued in order to maximize return on the peso-denominated *Cetes* instruments that were being converted to dollars. Thus, Mexico City ignored warnings from the White House and the Treasury Department to "correct" the unsustainable exchange rate. At the same time, Carlos Salinas was determined not to have a devaluation during an election year. The frailty of confidence was evident in the increased volatility of the Mexico City stock market, known as the Bolsa, and rumors of imminent devaluation, even when most investors believed Carlos Salinas wanted to avoid a devaluation on his watch. The overvalued currency, of course, only encouraged more imports, while the central bank's reserves were being depleted by capital flight.

Dependence of Short-Term, Dollar-Denominated Instruments

The spending spree and expansionist monetary policy were financed by short-term debt, highly leveraging the economy and further exposing the Mexican development scheme. Mexico's central bank was committed to defending the exchange rate and therefore supplied the pesos required to purchase the instruments being sold—Mexican Treasury certificates, known as *Cetes*, and other assets—by Mexicans and foreigners alike. The extension of credit throughout the economy made it possible for the dramatic decline in the nation's reserves. Had the Bank of Mexico adopted a different policy by refusing to ease credit, interest rates would have climbed and the Mexican Bolsa would have declined. Sellers would have found fewer buyers. Instead of selling at discounted prices, the increase in interest rates, to offset the interest rate hikes in the United States, would have provided an incentive to hold on to Mexican investments. But as American institutional investors demanded, the exchange rate had to be maintained at a time when the threat of instability prompted investor flight to dollars. Of equal importance to the Salinas administration, had the Bank of Mexico taken these measures, there would have been a marked contraction in demand, which would result in a recession. In an election year, this option was politically unacceptable. The deteriorating economic circumstances also undermined investor confidence.

Specifically:

Interest Rates in the U.S. Rose. The U.S. dollar experienced significant reversals throughout 1994 and 1995, falling to record lows against the Japanese yen and German deutschemark, prompting central bank intervention on several occasions. The dollar's devaluation in fact caused much consternation throughout the developed world. At one point the IMF admonished the Clinton administration for failing to support the dollar. In consequence, U.S. interest rates climbed steadily, not only to arrest the dollar's decline, but to ease inflation fears. The effects on Mexico were of greater consequence, however. In the face of heightened political risk and higher returns in the United States, the opportunity costs of remaining in Mexico proved ever greater, and many investors shifted their holdings away from Mexican assets to American ones. The result was a further deterioration in the central bank's reserves, which accelerated in the fall of 1994 amid political violence and allegations of electoral fraud in the presidential elections.

Disparate Inflation Rates Reduced Mexican Competitiveness. The explosive growth in the trade deficits exacerbated fears that the peso was highly overvalued. Observers believed that the Salinas administration would devalue in the fall during his lame-duck period. With his successor safely elected, he could take the fall for a devaluation prior to Ernesto Zedillo taking office on December 1, thereby allowing the new president to take office with a clean slate. That Salinas did not do this further aggravated the disparity; Mexico by the end of 1994 was "expensive" given the disparate inflation rates between the United States and Mexico. It was now evident, furthermore, that Mexico was unable to increase nonoil and nonagricultural exports. Mexican businessmen who had anticipated new markets in the age of free trade instead encountered frustrations occasioned by the overvalued peso. Industry was unable to compete and exports stagnated. Mexico by October 1994 was hopelessly priced out of international markets.

Emergence of Capital Flight. When Ernesto Zedillo took office in December 1994, Carlos Salinas had left office without devaluing the peso, leaving the problem for his successor. International and domestic investors were alarmed at the lack of experience of the members of Zedillo's cabinet. Indeed, many questions lingered about the ability of the men now in charge of the government. There were, however, grave problems throughout the country by this point. The failure to devalue in the summer of 1994, when it would have been opportune, resulted in an alarming depletion of the central bank's reserves. Had Carlos Salinas devalued promptly, he would have reduced the risk of a future devaluation, thereby bolstering the expectations of return on peso investments and given a much-needed boost to Mexican exporters, thereby increasing the nation's dollar reserves. The risk of fueling inflation was there in the summer of 1994, but it was mild compared to the disaster unleashed in December. This course of action, however, was improbable given Mexico's dependence on U.S. dollar-denominated Mexican Treasury notes, known as *Tesebonos,* which would only increase the government's peso debt should a devaluation occur. From a political perspective, the Tesebonos and the domestic climate in a tense election year made it impossible for Carlos Salinas to devalue.

Imminent Devaluation. Within two weeks after Zedillo taking office, Mexico was in a crisis. This was as much financial as it was political. The confusing situation was made worse by conflicting statements from Mexican officials. The crisis of confidence exploded a few days before Christmas when the Bank of Mexico withdrew from the markets, propelling the peso into a free fall. In a matter of days, Mexico was confronting the same specter it faced only twelve years previously: defaulting on its dollar obligations. In August 1982 Mexico suspended payments on its foreign debt, heralding an international debt crisis. As the peso plummeted in 1994, the Tesebonos—some $30 billion US came due in 1995—weighed heavy on the minds of American and Mexican officials alike. A frantic Zedillo administration was besieged on all fronts. Guillermo Ortiz, who was familiar with the Weston Forum and other American institutional investors, was named finance minister and flew to negotiate with officials in New York and Washington, where Mexico's fate would be determined. In the negotiations that followed the peso fluctuated wildly, from 3.45 to the dollar days prior to the devaluation to a record low of 8.1, before settling around 6.2, after months of turmoil on the foreign exchange markets. The fumbled handling of the devaluation only reinforced perceptions that Ernesto Zedillo lacked the expertise necessary to address the challenges confronting the nation.

THE POLITICS OF DISASTER

The political aspects of economic collapse also proved catalysts for disaster. That 1994 was an election year in Mexico, and it was at a time when the ruling party was facing stiff competition from the opposition, represented pressures Salinas was unable to resist. The economy of Mexico became an instrument through which the ruling party would ensure electoral victory. As in the past, the state was the means through which the ruling Institutional Revolutionary Party, known as the PRI, amassed power and privilege. Mexico in the twentieth century is not unlike Russia in the nineteenth. The Marquis de Custine made the observation about Czarist Russia that, "The political state of Russia may be defined in one sentence: it is a country in which the government says what it pleases, because it alone has the right to speak."[1] So it was in the last two years of the Salinas administration. There was no political debate about NAFTA, there was no political debate about the democratization of the country, there was no debate about the expectations and realities of free trade. Thus, politics drove economics, and disaster ensued.

Politicization of Fiscal Spending

The origins of the Mexican Meltdown reside in the politicization of the Mexican political economy throughout 1994. The authoritarian nature of the Mexican political system concentrates power in the presidency. The political hegemony that has ruled over this nation without interruption for over seven decades makes the PRI the longest-governing political party on earth. By 1994, however, the dichotomy that confronts all core countries—striking a balance between educating a work force capable of participating in a modern economy and fostering sufficient ignorance to allow the manipulation of voters—became a more elusive goal. Mexicans were too educated to remain satisfied with a status quo that failed to provide the opportunities and choices they now demanded. However, the archaic rulers of the past, mocked by Mexicans as "dinosaurs," remained (and still remain) unwilling to relinquish the power they have accumulated over the past seventy years. For Carlos Salinas, the problem was to win over an electorate ever more dissatisfied with the monopoly the PRI enjoyed in the nation's life. That Mexico was finding out that it was woefully unprepared to compete in an open market made matters more difficult for the Mexican government. The implementation of NAFTA, which was the advent of free trade, was heralded as Mexico's coming of age and entering the ranks of the developed world. The truth, however, was that once NAFTA went into effect on January 1, 1994, Mexico confronted an avalanche of imports without a corresponding surge in exports. Indeed, trade patterns throughout 1994 only demonstrated how underdeveloped Mexico was in fact: exports consisted of primary goods, such as oil, agricultural products, and the intracompany movement of goods between U.S. factories and Mexican assembly plants. That the Japanese investments upon which the Salinas administration was counting did not materialize only aggravated matters. On top of these problems there were growing perceptions that disrupted Mexican plans. The Zapatist uprising in the impoverished southern state of Chiapas stunned the Mexican people who, for better or for worse, had always found solace in the fact that, if nothing else, civil violence was virtually unknown in Mexico. The prospect of civil disorder within Mexico paralyzed the Mexican electorate. The sight of an armed rebellion shocked foreign investors, who became jittery at the thought of political instability in Mexico. But appearances had to be kept up, and the Salinas administration embarked on an aggressive program to stimulate the economy for election-year purposes. To accomplish this, the Mexican government politicized the economy and in a matter of months became overleveraged on dollar-denominated Tesebonos. These short-term instruments not only created enormous dollar debt for the Mexican government, but were expensive vehicles that, as it turned out, were susceptible to the volatile nature of the daily headlines, and not the long-term picture. The reliance on "hot" money made the Salinas administration hostage to the capricious whims of forces outside its control, such as foreign perceptions and not Mexican realities. When an economy is rendered political, so is a nation's fate.

Consumption Versus Investment

The infusion of vast quantities of funds through the emission of Tesebonos proved problematic for two reasons. The short-term nature of these liquid instruments meant that "hot" money was now inundating the Mexican economy. These funds, which would leave as easily as they entered, undermined sustainable growth and proved disruptive. Of greater consequence, this "hot" money was being used to finance government spending in an election year, and not in the long-term development of the nation's economy. Since his banishment from Mexico, documentation suggests that former president Carlos Salinas used this "hot" money to finance populist schemes. The Salinas administration embarked on a grandiose spending spree through "*Solidaridad*," designed to disperse money throughout the economy. The glorified pork-barrel projects reached the far corners of the country. Considering that the Mexican peso was already overvalued, the effect of these populist measures made it possible for Mexicans to increase their discretionary spending throughout 1994. The natural consequence was an explosion in demand for consumer goods, mostly imported from the United States. The irony lay in that official reserves were depleted to pay for consumer goods imported to satisfy an artificial demand. To further complicate the economic panorama, it now appears that the Salinas administration illegally diverted significant government funds to the PRI. Furthermore, these funds were used to ease credit to consumers throughout the economy, further increasing consumption. The natural low savings rate of the Mexican consumer, distortion in prices arising from exchange-rate disequilibrium, and the revealed preference for consuming foreign products precipitated unexpected pressures. It was an inopportune policy, in part affected by the escalation of violence in Mexico throughout much of 1994. The PRI was facing the toughest election in its history at a time when Mexicans' expectations about the speed with which NAFTA would transform their lives grew. The ruling party confronted dissension within and a hostile public, tired of authoritarianism and the oppressive federalism through which their lives were controlled by Mexico City. Desperate to stimulate a stagnant economy, the Salinas administration relied on more and more "hot" money, hoping for the best. In fact, over the course of the year, to offset dependence on capital inflows through Tesebonos, the Salinas administration was relying on Japanese investments to materialize in 1994. These expectations were perhaps unrealistic, given the reluctance of Japan to move forward with investments in Mexico under Salinas, and under the existing circumstances. In a series of meetings held in the United States on a state visit, an angered Salinas confronted recalcitrant Japanese officials. The image remains vivid of the Lilliputian Mexican leader pacing in his suite, arguing for greater Japanese investments, particularly now that Mexico was poised to be an economic powerhouse straddling the United States, with effortless transportation access to its enormous consumer market.

Short-Term Versus Long-Term Investments

The dollar-denominated Tesebonos created an infusion of capital, which was diverted for a public spending spree of unprecedented proportions. The fresh money made it possible to minimize the political repercussions of the violence and turmoil unfolding throughout 1994. Revelations made after the Mexican Meltdown suggest how extensively these monies were used to finance the PRI's presidential campaign and stimulate the Mexican economy through easy credit. The absence of an adequate domestic savings rate, however, made it necessary for the Salinas administration to resort to these Tesebonos instruments with greater abandon in order to finance its fiscal programs, and prop the peso, thereby guaranteeing the profits of the peso-denominated Cetes. This is an enduring problem for Latin American countries. Chile, whose savings rate approximates that of some Asian countries, is the only Latin American nation that enjoys significant domestic capital formation. The absence of sufficient domestic savings, however, rendered Mexico dependent on the demands of foreign investors and governments. That this debt was assumed is not an issue in and of itself. How it was used, however, is another matter. "Hot" money has no staying power, unlike capital investments in plant and equipment. Unlike periphery countries, like Brazil, no long-term investments were being made, but the nation was assuming enormous liabilities. In 1995 alone, for instance, $30 billion US in Tesebonos came due, but where was the infrastructure, factories, plants, and capital goods? There was little to show for it, since the money was spent on consumption—media blitzes for the PRI's presidential campaign, tortillas for peasants. Core countries historically consume more than they invest, whereas periphery countries invest more than they consume. Mexico assumed enormous debt that had to be repaid in a matter of months, and in the end had nothing to show for it. The Zedillo administration is continuing on this disastrous path, adding more and more foreign debt with nothing to show for it. If Mexico is to reduce its foreign debt it will be forced to privatize the remaining state-owned enterprises and increase foreign exchange earnings. A credible, rational plan for achieving these goals has not been forthcoming from the Zedillo administration in 1995.

Overvaluation of Currency and Peso-Denominated Securities

The dependence on Tesebonos presented two problems. Foremost, these were short-term instruments that did not contribute significantly to capital formation in the domestic economy. It was "hot" money that was being used to subsidize a bankrupt political system, and not help a developing economy mature. Second, the way in which these instruments were used held the Mexican government hostage by its assumption of all the risk in the event of a devaluation. The majority of buyers for Mexico's Tesebonos were—and remain—American mutual funds. Not a few of the managers and underwriters feared that the disparate inflation rates, the widening Mexican trade deficit since the implementation of NAFTA, and political instability would result in a devaluation of the peso. The Weston Group, which alone had brokered almost $5 billion in peso securities the previous year, took the lead in seeking reassurances from the Mexican government that the peso's slide would be halted. In what became known as the Weston Forum, the Weston Group headed a consortium that included Salomon Brothers, Trust Company of the West, Scudder Stevens & Clark, Oppenheimer Management, Fidelity Investments Company, and Soros Fund Management. This consortium sought to pressure the Salinas administration to prop the peso. In a series of meetings in April 1994, a few weeks after the assassination of Salinas's heir-apparent, while Mexico remained engulfed in turmoil, it became clear that the American mutual fund managers were adamant about not devaluing the peso. Current Finance Minister Guillermo Ortiz, who was finance undersecretary at the time, participated in these meetings, and acquiesced to the demands of the U.S. investors. The pressure exerted by the Weston Group, one participant reported, was tremendous. One Mexican official complained that, for a while, Weston Group President John Liegey was as important in deciding monetary policy as was Miguel Mancera, the president of the

Bank of Mexico, the central bank. The suggestions pushed forward were virtual instructions for Carlos Salinas, who capitulated to the interests of foreign investors and propped the peso to ensure that maturing peso-denominated securities, known as Cetes, would prove themselves a handsome investment in dollar terms. The priority for many buyers of Cetes was to guarantee that their investments, when converted back to dollars, would not be affected by changes in the exchange rate. The Salinas administration capitulated to American interests and assumed the entire devaluation risk, further depleting Mexico's reserves. Of course there are ethical issues surrounding the fiduciary responsibility of these managers to their investors that need to be examined, as is the open-ended question of the appropriateness of foreigners dictating terms to a foreign government, particularly when these rulers display a lack of judgment.

Lack of Accurate Figures

Disaster struck, and Mexico had to be rescued in the single-largest bailout in the history of the world to date. The recovery of the Mexican economy, however, is difficult to measure because the statistics provided by the Mexican government are inaccurate. As discussed below, firms in the private sector have not shied away from manipulating numbers through creative accounting. What alarms, however, is that Mexico's Finance Ministry, the Bank of Mexico, and Office of the President publish misleading and false reports. Of equal concern is that officials in the U.S. government, as well as the IMF and the World Bank, connive in this deception. Without accurate figures, neither investors nor the Mexican public are able to make informed judgments about the austerity measures in place. The Bank of Mexico, for instance, distorts the true inflation rate by manipulating the basket of goods whose prices it monitors, and how it calculates the prices of the goods and services included in its measurements. The President's Office continues to make misleading statements about the extent to which Mexico is accumulating foreign debt, and how it is calculating the effects of the increase in the national sales tax on both government revenue and the nation's economy. The Finance Ministry figures on Mexico's growth in exports is duplicitous in its inclusion of intracompany movement of goods between assembly facilities in Mexico and U.S. factories. In published reports, for instance, Mexican government figures indicate that in 1993 nonoil exports totaled $42 billion US, but when intracompany activity is subtracted, Mexican exports are reduced to a mere $15 billion US, which is quite a difference. Mexican nonoil and nonagricultural exports have not increased substantially—or as much as the enormous devaluation would suggest—and despite the undervalued peso, Mexican goods remain uncompetitive on world markets. The deliberate fabrication of figures is problematic, for it makes it more difficult to analyze how Mexico is reacting to the recovery program in place. This, then, is nothing less than the continuing politicization of the nation's economy, which is actively encouraged by Washington. The Clinton administration continues to face harsh criticism for the bailout of Mexico's economy, and is only too eager to herald good news, whether or not the good news is true, to vindicate its positions. The IMF and the World Bank also have vested interests in showcasing Mexico as a model nation, in much the same way as when Mexico was a darling of the international community until, like Icarus, the Mexican peso came crashing down.

Consolidation Within the Financial System

The Mexican banking system, already facing structural problems with the disquieting growth of its portfolio of nonperforming loans prior to the crisis, is undergoing significant consolidation. Mexican banks were nationalized in 1982. For almost a decade Mexican banks were administered by political appointees who embarked on an ambitious program to make loans based on political connections, and not economic sense. During this time, questionable loans for improbable projects proliferated in a quid pro quo manner, creating vast distortions throughout the economy and funneling resources in inefficient ways. When the banks were privatized, Mexican investors, believing the banking and financial sectors would be protected in any free trade discussions with the United States and relying on false information provided by the government, paid enormous premiums for these banks. The gravity of the extent to which nonperforming loans suffused their portfolio only became evident after the new owners had taken over, when there was little recourse. Thus encumbered with bad loans and having borrowed heavily in dollars to finance modernization and expansion, Mexican banks were not prepared for a devaluation, which saw their incomes crash at the same time their dollar obligations became more expensive. That the free trade agreement with the United States and Canada envisioned a gradual opening of the banking sector contributed added pressure to become competitive in the global marketplace. This all proved too much for Mexico's banking system. The consolidation now underway, which began when the government seized Banca Cremi, Banca Union, and Banpais unleashed a period of uncertainty. This remains more troublesome, because Mexican banks engaged in rather creative accounting practices throughout 1995 to disguise the extent of their problems. Banca Serfin, as one example, reported $60 million US in profits for the first trimester of 1995 when in fact Salomon Brothers estimates that its actual losses approached $540 million US. That the Mexican government lacks sufficient resources to bail out Mexican banks is the main factor driving the renewed efforts to accelerate the opening of the Mexican financial system to foreign banks. The Zedillo administration plans to allow the merger and acquisition of Mexican banks by foreign ones, as well as to permit foreign banks to enter the Mexican market quicker than envisioned by the NAFTA agreement. While this represents an opportunity for American banks, there is an understandable reluctance to rush in, particularly when Mexican banks are not forthcoming with accurate numbers that portray the true extent of their problems. Bancomer, Mexico's second-largest bank, for instance, has had to sell its affiliate in San Diego, Grossmont Bank, in order to boost liquidity. Other banks are now engaged in desperate attempts to sell-off property that has come into their possession as the number of loans that default surged throughout 1995. These problems, coupled with misleading earnings reports, and American concerns with Mexican banks being used for money laundering activities, are reasons why Senator Alfonse D'Amato, chairman of the Banking Commission in the U.S. Senate, has called for continuing investigations into the activities of the agencies of Mexican banks in the United States, making Mexico's banking crisis into a political problem as well for officials on both sides of the border. Under these circumstances American banks are, understandably, worried about assessing how saddled Mexican banks are in reality with bad loans and dollar debts. The possibility of a Venezuela-style banking crisis is not likely, but it is not impossible either. The consolidation within the banking system now underway, like the one in Argentina following the Tequila Effect, as the economic repercussion of Mexico's crisis throughout the developing world was termed by Wall Street, has the potential to strengthen the nation's financial position in the medium and long terms, but uncertainty will reign for some time. The political implications of the banking crisis are destined to linger far beyond the immediate problems created by the peso devaluation of December 1994.

Imprudent Accumulation of Foreign Debt

In the aftermath of the Mexican crisis, there is concern about incurring additional debt as part of the recovery program. The desperate manner in which the United States mobilized, and coerced, its major trading partners to participate in the rescue of the Mexican economy is discomforting. The unprecedented measures only further burden Mexico in the medium and long terms. The reckless accumulation of the debt by Ernesto Zedillo throughout 1995 may have been necessary to meet the country's financial obligations, but the cost has been enormous: In one year Mexico doubled its foreign debt to over $160 billion US. The privatization program of the Salinas administration, which including the selling of the state-owned telephone monopoly and the banks that had been nationalized in 1982, as well as scores of state-owned firms, made a significant contribution to the reduction of the foreign debt. This represents an enormous step backwards for the Mexican nation. The interest burden now assumed will require a sustained period of extraordinary growth coupled with an increase in the domestic savings rate. These are elusive goals for Mexico. As such, Ernesto Zedillo has compromised sovereignty over economic—and political—affairs. The prospect of further privatizations, which will now have to include seaports, airports, railroads, and the state-owned electrical company, looms as a certainty. Indeed, Petroleos de Mexico (Pemex), the state oil monopoly that is the symbol of nationalism, must, in all likelihood, be privatized in one way or another. The accumulation of billions of dollars of foreign debt now makes it virtually impossible for Mexico to regain economic sovereignty in the short or medium terms. The reason for this lies in the difference between incurring debt for investment in capital goods rather than for consumption. What Mexico has done since the crisis is incur debt to meet Tesebono obligations, which are not reinvested in the country. That this additional debt limits the options of the Mexican nation is also a sign of impoverishment, and is not without political consequences. In essence, Mexico is presently incurring foreign debt to finance capital flight. This is a most peculiar development strategy.

Inadequate U.S. Intelligence

While it is true that U.S. officials warned their Mexican counterparts in the summer of 1994 that the peso was by then significantly overvalued, the United States was caught by surprise by the gravity of the Mexican Meltdown. Nowhere in the intelligence community was the White House warned of the imminent debacle. In the frantic meetings in January 1995 to piece together a bailout of the Mexican economy, one State Department official complained that the United States "shares a 3,000-mile border with a nation of 90 million savages, and the CIA is clueless." The characterization of the absence of adequate information is accurate enough, particularly given continuing integration of the Latin American economies. The U.S. intelligence community also failed to report on the power that U.S. investors exert in undermining emerging economies. The pressures exerted by the Weston Forum, for instance, were designed to maximize short-term gains, disregarding the long-term consequences. To its credit, the CIA did issue a warning in July 1994 about the rapid depletion of Mexican reserves, but it was without alarm, or a policy recommendation. Apart from this brief circular, U.S. officials remained uninformed of the disastrous policies being implemented by the Salinas administration in response to the mounting pressures of Mexico's overleveraged position. In the case of the Mexican Meltdown, the turmoil precipitated by the monetary crisis demonstrates how the national security interests of the United States are not served when chaos reigns at the border. The interests of Mexico are not served if Washington remains unaware of how some

American investors are gambling with the futures of unsuspecting investors, on both sides of the border. The ethical questions surrounding the conduct of some American fund managers remain in doubt. That the U.S. government is unable to rely on the intelligence community to foresee these problems is discomforting, particularly at a time when greater economic integration is increasing the interdependence of the United States in the world community. Neither Mexico nor the United States is served by this kind of poor intelligence, and this should alarm Washington.

Journalist Integrity

A surprising casualty of the Mexican crisis has been the objectivity of the *Wall Street Journal*. Since former Mexican president Carlos Salinas joined the board of Dow Jones, parent company of the financial paper, editorials absolving Salinas have appeared. What astounds is how the editor, Robert Bartley, has allowed his personal friendship with the disgraced president to influence his journalism. The integrity of the entire paper is undermined when revisionist history distorts the underlying fundamentals of Mexico's structural development problems. The politicization of Mexico's federal budget during an election year, the overleveraging of the economy through junk bonds, the disparate inflation rates that kept the peso overvalued, and the instability occasioned by the failure to democratize the country at a time its economy was being opened, all have been forgotten. That current Mexican president Ernesto Zedillo has failed in his first year to demonstrate the leadership necessary to address the fundamental problems confronting Mexico remains a serious concern. So does the ability to obtain objective information. Self-serving editorials and articles, such as those published in the spring of 1995 by Robert Barro that lay the entire crisis on Zedillo, do American executives a disservice. Propaganda has no place in the financial pages of American newspapers. The conduct of the *Wall Street Journal*, however, undermines confidence in the media. This is tragic, given that Zedillo's recovery program, however much applauded by Washington, deserves to be scrutinized. The credibility of the American media is an unexpected casualty of the Mexican Meltdown and underscores how events on one side of the border can have unforeseen effects on the other side. In the Mexican crisis, it now appears, confidence of all kinds has been shaken.

THE POLITICS OF A RESCUE

The complete collapse of the Mexican peso in December 1994—which had been dismissed by the U.S. Treasury Department—sent shock waves around the world. The United States led an international effort, in frantic haste, to prevent an international crisis similar to that of 1992. The price

Mexico would pay, however, would be monumental, for it would be no less than the surrender of its economic sovereignty and the mortgaging of its future. But beggars can't be choosers, the saying goes, and the Mexicans, in the age of free trade, had been reduced to the humiliating position of having to beg for handouts and emergency loans, once again. The political repercussions of Mexico's selling itself into servitude will be felt for the remainder of this century and will have consequences well into the next.

Surrender of Economic Sovereignty

The negotiations themselves were hampered by the desperate state of Mexican officials. Finance Minister Guillermo Ortiz, whose command of the English language is uncertain, was overwhelmed to the point of being a distraction; American negotiators were alarmed about his presence of mind as much as they were about the condition of Mexican finances. Ortiz's composure, or rather a lack thereof, was revealing. It is one thing to be in an emergency, but it is another to lose one's dignity. Mexican officials in New York and Washington had a difficult time maintaining their demeanor. If not literally then at least figuratively, Ortiz arrived in the United States on his hands and knees begging for dollars. The sight made some U.S. officials cringe, and it increased tensions at the IMF. An Argentine official in Washington winced at the idea of his own country's Economic Minister Domingo Cavallo in a similar state of despair. Guillermo Ortiz, stuttering and perspiring profusely, was a vision of pathos, and this affected the humiliation Mexico was forced to suffer when the final terms of its economic surrender were negotiated.

The astounding naïveté of Ernesto Zedillo was breathtaking in scope. In an act more appropriate for a nation defeated on the battlefield, the Mexican government willingly capitulated to the most egregious assaults on its national sovereignty. As conditions for a rescue, the Zedillo administration agreed to have its finances approved by Washington; instructed the clients of Pemex, the state-owned oil monopoly, to make their payments to the Federal Reserve Bank in New York for subsequent posting to Mexico's account; and agreed to have Finance Minister Guillermo Ortiz report back to American officials and investors in New York on Mexico's progress once a month. The final word on Mexico's economic policies would be determined in Washington, D.C., and New York, not in Mexico City. For Mexico, then, the prodigal son of the international community, the clock had been turned back to the nineteenth century, when France invaded and installed Emperor Maximilian when Mexico was unable to repay its foreign loans. This time, however, the pomp and circumstance of an Austrian Archduke on the Mexican throne had been replaced by the push of electronic buttons. Mexico, in both cases, no longer had control over its economic destiny.

No wonder other Latin American nations were terrified at the prospect of suffering the same humiliating fate as the Mexicans. No wonder extraordinary measures were enacted around the hemisphere as Latin Americans tried to defend their economic sovereignty, a sovereignty the Mexicans so easily relinquished. Ernesto Zedillo, however, complied as instructed. The IMF team arrived in Mexico City to authorize Mexican expenditures, Pemex buyers wired their payments to New York, and Ortiz found himself at the St. Regis, reporting back to Mexico's new masters. In uninterrupted negotiations in New York, the details of the rescue plan were worked out at the offices of Nacional Financiera, Nafinsa, as investment bankers worked out the details of the massive bailout. A banker from Chase Manhattan made the wry observation that it was "difficult to respect someone who didn't respect himself."

Zedillo acquiesced to everything demanded of him, especially since opposition to the rescue was growing in the U.S. Congress. The White House dispatched Treasury Secretary Robert Rubin, Federal Reserve Chairman Alan Greenspan, and Secretary of State Warren Christopher on an impressive lobbying effort, trying to persuade recalcitrant lawmakers of the importance of saving Mexico. One condition of the loans was that Mexico would report directly to the New York investment community on the nation's progress. Finance Minister Guillermo Ortiz, however, the quintessential technocrat, reported on Mexican progress in a meticulous manner, even if all the news wasn't good. The same Chase Manhattan official displayed the sardonic irony that comforted many angered Wall Street officers when he joked, "After he'd done with his presentation, have the Finance Minister come to my office to shine my shoes." What was not amusing, however, was the compelling task that lay before Mexico in restoring its credibility among the international community. The assumption of vast new amounts of foreign debt at a time when the Mexican economy fell into a severe recession worried some analysts who did not foresee a recovery until the second half of 1996, if political instability did not further erode confidence. The lingering doubts about the men involved continued to grow, this time extending to the Clinton administration as well. Throughout the first year of the Mexican crisis, the comforting words of Clinton officials provided solace, particularly when Mexico's performance was weighed against that of other Latin American nations that averted difficulties with a much greater ease and assurance. As the first-year anniversary of the Mexican Meltdown approached, doubts were raised about the veracity of claims the administrations in both Washington, D.C., and Mexico City were making when the amounts of monies drawn upon from the IMF and the World Bank were scrutinized. Mexico was once again borrowing to finance consumption—in this case, the redemption of Tesebonos—and not investment.

Privatizing Pemex

What was clear by the end of 1995 was how compromised Mexico had become. To begin to address the problems the Zedillo administration had created by crushing the private sector during a time when it assumed greater dollar debt, the question of national patrimony now came into play. Ernesto Zedillo has no choice but to implement an aggressive privatization program if he hopes to reduce Mexico's now-enormous foreign debt. The austerity measures implemented, however, have ruined much of Mexico's domestic private sector. Privatization now has to entail the *foreign* private sector. The specter facing Mexico as the century ends, in essence, is to transfer vast quantities of its national patrimony into foreign ownership. Of the four state-owned areas left—electric power generation, railroads, airports and seaports, and oil—only the last area tantalizes foreign investors and buyers. However reluctant Mexicans may be to the idea of privatizing, if not in name then in practice, the state-owned industry, if Mexico is to enjoy sustainable economic growth, it has no choice.

The Mexican crisis in the face of free trade has far-reaching consequences for the nations of Latin America. The ability of Mexico to subsidize its socialist policies by transferring oil revenues to public spending is no longer possible in an economy driven by market forces. Pemex was founded in 1938 when the government of then-president Lazaro Cardenas nationalized foreign oil companies. These firms, mostly British and American companies, were formed into a state monopoly which, by the early 1990s, had become the eighth-largest oil company in the world with sales exceeding $20 billion in 1991. Pemex had become, perhaps, the most corrupt and inefficient oil company on the planet. It has also served Mexico poorly; Mexico is expected to become a net importer of oil by the year 2000. The inefficient nature of Pemex is best shown by how it has contributed to the retardation of the development of the economy. One way economists measure an economy's lack of development is to analyze its exports and imports. An economy that exports raw materials and imports finished goods is at a marked economic disadvantage. In the case of the Mexican energy sector, Pemex exports oil to the United States, only to buy it back in the form of unleaded gas. The export of oil, a raw material, and the importation of unleaded gasoline, a finished product, vividly demonstrates how Pemex has impoverished the Mexican economy.

To be sure Pemex plays many other roles. In 1991 it provided almost $14 billion to the Mexican government, which was used for social spending and to keep the ruling party in power through pork-barrel programs such as Solidaridad. It has been a galvanizing force that embodies Mexican nationalism; oil has been politicized as a symbol of sovereignty. It has been administered as a private fiefdom between the powerful oil workers' union and the party bosses, who have helped themselves to the largess oil wealth represents. Taken together, then, Pemex has afforded Mexican politicians the privileges of plunder, which is inconsistent with the proper administration of a modern corporation.

The consequences are obvious. Mexico is unable to refine its oil into unleaded gas; Mexico has become more dependent on the United States for its energy requirements; and Pemex, instead of propelling the nation's development, has been fundamental in undermining Mexico's aspirations for economic prosperity. These constitute compelling testament to the misguided policies of the past sixty years. The fundamental facts are irrefutable, and thus alarming. Mexican domestic demand now outstrips Pemex production capacity. The December 1994 crisis has further reduced investment capital. Known reserves continue to decline, recent findings in the Campeche Sound notwithstanding. Inept and corrupt management has undermined efforts to transform Pemex into a modern firm capable of operating within the parameters of world standards for enterprises of this size. Mexico is expected to become dependent on the United States for its energy needs within the next three years.

The administration of Ernesto Zedillo, reacting to the rapid deterioration in the Mexican economy, and to increased foreign demands that Pemex be "rationalized," if not privatized outright, and the acute financial crunch prove instructive. Weaker economies, when integrated into mature ones, are forced to sacrifice political objectives for economic ones. Throughout 1995, in a seeming frenzy of decrees and pronouncements designed to appease foreign interests, the Zedillo administration embarked on a program to "redefine" Pemex to lay the foundation of the privatization, in all but name, of Pemex. By revamping how it defines primary and secondary products, by trying to rationalize Pemex into an efficient company, and by opening up the oil sector to foreign investment, the Mexican government has now embarked on the historic reversal of the oil nationalization. This, ironically, not only conforms to the objectives envisioned by the requirements of NAFTA, but it demonstrates the ultimate price emerging economies must pay to be integrated into larger goals. It is clear, then, that Mexico is selling, as MIT economist Richard Dornsbusch puts it, "the family jewel." Mexico, to diminish the crushing burden that its foreign debt represents, is forced to sell off what has, for more than half a century, represented a national symbol of identity. For Latin American nations, the processes now underway in Mexico portend the future of state-owned enterprises. In a world of market forces, the poor cannot indulge their vanity.

If Pemex were privatized and Mexico leased exploration of its oil fields, the Mexican treasury could stand to reap an estimated $120 billion US.

Pemex itself is worthless as a company; encumbered with high labor costs, inefficient managers, and outdated equipment, it is a primitive enterprise. That Mexico is forced to export oil to the United States and then buy it back in the form of unleaded gas demonstrates how underdeveloped both Pemex and Mexico are in fact. At present, the Mexican government has been redefining how it envisions the oil wealth of the nation. While modest advances have been made, including liberalizing conditions for foreign participation in the oil sector, the constitutional barriers have yet to be overcome. It is, however, only a matter of time before an accommodation of some kind is reached that allows private capital to revitalize Mexico's moribund and primitive state-owned oil monopoly.

CONTAINING THE TEQUILA EFFECT

Two weeks after all agreed on a hemispherewide free trade zone, Mexico crashed, sending billions of dollars fleeing from Latin America for safe havens in the United States. It was not surprising, nor without irony, that Latin American nations, which had been comparing themselves to Mexico at the Summit of the Americas in Miami, now wished to distance and differentiate themselves from the troubled nation. In December 1994 in Miami, everyone praised the Mexican Miracle. In January 1995, in every capital of Latin America, there was no shortage of reasons why each nation was different from the disgraced Mexicans.

Preventing 1982 Redux

Establishing a distance from the Mexicans was of tremendous urgency for the Argentines. As the Latin American nation most adversely affected by the "Tequila Effect," the Buenos Aires stock market was jolted and mass withdrawals threatened the liquidity of the nation's banking system. Within days after financial markets began to plummet, Argentina's Economic Minister Domingo Cavallo was in New York reassuring that his nation "was not a Mexico waiting to happen." The concern expressed by Argentine leaders was understandable. Carlos Menem was running for reelection in May, and the outcome was far from certain. Of greater concern, Argentina's recovery was only in its fourth year; 1990 was the first year of positive growth since 1987, and while inflation was decreasing, the trade deficit was not. Indeed, on the surface, Argentina faced problems similar to Mexico's. The concern among investors, Argentine as well as foreign, resided in the question of a forced devaluation. While the trade deficits in Argentina were small, and dollar reserves higher, the crucial difference was in the convertibility plan in place. The Menem administration established parity in an ingenious voucher system in which every Argentine peso in circulation was backed, one-for-one, with dollars in reserve. That a deficit, in essence, resulted in a reduction in money supply by withdrawing money from circulation, created tremendous concern: It reduced the liquidity of the financial system.

For Argentina, loss of investor confidence would lead to a recession. This was unacceptable in an election year. The risk of plunging the economy into a recession proved minor compared to the banking crisis massive withdrawals occasioned. The peso-dollar parity had established a stable currency, something sorely lacking in Argentina for a long time. Economic Minister Domingo Cavallo was not prepared to destroy the cornerstone of the prosperity Argentina was enjoying under Carlos Menem. The question, then, remained how to convince skeptical investors throughout the country and around the world of that. It was not easy, nor did it come quickly. What prevented a crisis, however, was negotiations for emergency loans and lines of credit totaling $11.5 billion. With these funds at their disposal, Argentine leaders were able to ride out the storm; panicked investors who withdrew their money from the economy would be offset by equal amounts of funds injected by the central bank, thereby keeping the money supply stable until nerves were settled. In addition, plans were announced for further privatizations, including electric and nuclear power plants, designed to raise another $3 billion. It worked. The Argentine banking system, battered, has emerged the stronger, with weaker banks merged or closed and those remaining enjoying stronger positions. But a currency crisis was averted and Carlos Menem was reelected.

The same story was played out around the world, from Turkey to Thailand. Mexico would not be the catalyst for another international disaster, another "lost decade." The Mexican Meltdown, while its repercussions were undeniable, was destined to be a regional economic conflict, one that betrayed the shortcomings of the international financial systems in place, but not one that would upset the new world order.

The Periphery Countries' Saving Grace

It is clear that the Mexican Meltdown affected developing countries around the world. The possibility of the world being plunged into financial chaos galvanized the United States to do whatever was necessary to save the Mexican economy, and with it the notion of free trade. If financial ruin, the reasoning in Washington went, was what free markets would bring, then the nations, particularly those of the former Soviet Union and the Americas, that were turning away from the despair of their misguided socialist economies had little incentive to press forward with their reforms. That Mexico collapsed less than two weeks after all the leaders of the New World, with the exception of Cuba, met at the Summit of the Americas in Miami and agreed to establish a hemispherewide free trade zone made matters all the more urgent, for it was the worst possible timing imaginable.

In no uncertain terms it was clear that the success of Mexico's integration into the North American economy would shape the political dialogues across the continent. But the experience of an authoritarian core country is far different from those of periphery countries, however much they may be predisposed to lapse into dictatorships. The Tequila Effect had to be contained, especially in the fears foreign investors—in this case, Americans—felt at the prospects of economic collapse elsewhere. The flight to quality—the U.S. dollar and American stocks and bonds—accelerated, precipitating frantic activity as Latin American finance and economic ministers scrambled to extend lines of credit and secure loans to counteract the capital flight and restore investor confidence as evidenced by the falling stock markets of the region. The leading periphery countries—Argentina, Brazil, and Chile—managed to prevent similar chaos from unraveling the significant economic progress all three countries had made in the 1990s. While Argentina and Chile have been more successful, for different reasons, in containing the Tequila Effect, Brazil remains on sound footing, and enjoys enviable prospects that its historic pattern of hyperinflation can be relegated to the past as the new century approaches.

Argentina

The response to the Mexican crisis in Argentina was swift. When Carlos Menem took office in Buenos Aires in 1989, he faced an economic crisis precipitated by hyperinflation approaching 5,000 percent in that year alone. In what was called the "Argentine Miracle," a shock program reduced public spending, replaced the almost-worthless austral with the peso, whose parity remains one-to-one with the U.S. dollar, and implemented policies that produced approximately 7 percent annual growth in 1994, 1993, 1992, and 1991. The ambitious privatization program made it possible to get the nation's finances in order, and the policy of having the Argentine peso function, analytically, as a voucher for the dollars in reserves, has worked to successfully control money supply.

The memories of economic chaos, under both military and civilian rulers, made Argentines nervous that their bubble would also burst. As 1995 began, there were runs on banks throughout Argentina, as money fled to banks in Uruguay and safe boxes at home. The redemption of Argentine pesos for American dollars in essence reduced the money supply, not only threatening to plunge the nation into a recession, but also betraying a lack of confidence in the policies that had, for half a decade, brought stability and prosperity. The reduction in the money supply rendered the banks illiquid, causing extreme problems for the national economy. The Merval, the Buenos Aires stock market, lost 40 percent of its value as investors fled Latin America en masse in the wake of the Mexican Meltdown. It recovered, but it still suffered a significant reversal throughout 1995. The Tequila Effect threatened both the reelection of Carlos Menem and the progress his program had brought to Argentina and its 33 million people. In the first months of 1995, for instance, almost 35,000 Argentine businesses went out of business, when commercial sales plunged over 30 percent. Economic Minister Domingo Cavallo had to negotiate several lines of credit totaling $11.5 billion to guarantee liquidity in the Argentine economy and restore confidence, which included $2 billion from Japan's Export-Import Bank.

That Argentina was able to negotiate loans without the agony of the Mexicans quickly brought back confidence, so much so that Carlos Menem won reelection in May 1995. The continuity of his reform policies were guaranteed, not without the able leadership of Cavallo. For the Argentine banking system, ironically, the Tequila Effect has proved to be a blessing in disguise. The strain of early 1995 resulted in a shake-out of the banking sector. Inefficient banks were suspended, others merged with or were acquired by stronger banks. The number of banks in Argentina declined by about 25 percent, which strengthened the entire banking sector by eliminating weaker, inefficient banks that were common in the provinces. In fact, the nation's two largest banks, Banco de Galicia and Banco Frances del Rio de la Plata, emerged in much stronger positions by the end of 1995. And the confidence provided by the lines of credit—and the refusal to alter monetary policy—avoided the need to devalue the Argentine peso, which would have entailed abandoning the voucher system in place, something that would have sent the currency into a free-fall. The prudent and confident manner in which the potential problems were addressed restored confidence among the Argentine public, which returned an estimated $5 billion from abroad, thereby restoring the nation's liquidity. That Argentina stands to emerge from the Tequila Effect strengthened has done much to bolster confidence in the ability of Carlos Menem to extend his previous success in this present term. If not miraculous, then at least Argentina's performance under its current leadership is responsible.

Brazil

The least successful periphery country in abating the fallout of the Mexican Meltdown has been Brazil. Fernando Cardoso, who took office on January 1, 1995, was immediately confronted with the turmoil the Mexican collapse was having throughout the region. Despite having successfully implemented the Plan Real—which reduced inflation to single digits for the first time since the 1950s—Cardoso's popularity was tested. The real came under tremendous pressure as the Brazilian stock market plummeted. The trading band within which the real fluctuates had to be widened, creating a flight for dollars. To bolster confidence—and reverse a widening trade deficit—the Cardoso administration slapped "temporary" tariffs, which angered its Mercosur trading partners. The measures aimed at protecting the central bank's dollar reserves and ensuring a more manageable and less volatile role for foreign capital in the Brazilian economy.

The strategy to stay the course centers on two fronts. First, the Cardoso administration hopes for constitutional reform to downsize the bloated—and bankrupt—social security system. There is tremendous opposition to these measures, and it is not clear if the Brazilian Congress will go along. A complementary strategy is to accelerate privatization, chiefly by allowing the private sector to play a role in Petrobras, the state-owned oil company, and Telebras, the state-owned telephone giant. This would bring much-needed revenue for the government without having to raise taxes, or forcing the devaluation of the real. The second part of the strategy is to redefine the role foreign capital plays in Brazilian economic development. While the nation's politicians define the role the private sector will play in the oil and telecommunications sector, the Cardoso administration has made tremendous strides in limiting the role "hot" money plays in the economy. Ford, General Motors, Volkswagen, and Fiat, for instance, have plans to invest over $10 billion in Brazilian facilities by the year 2000. This kind of investment, which stands to make Brazil the major supplier of vehicles for the entire South American market, first through Mercosur and then through trade pacts under negotiation, is precisely the kind of investment that has proven so elusive for Mexico.

However successful the economic policies of the early 1990s have been, the enduring question of currency stability lingers for Brazil. The Plan Real has proved successful, even when it was subject to the Tequila Effect. The challenge for the Cardoso administration is to keep inflation under control, for if it fails to do so, it will face a slide in the value of the real, which would begin the familiar cycle of hyperinflation. That Brazil unilaterally raised tariffs proves of concern, for it reveals the lack of commitment to the success of Mercosur. Argentine and Uruguayan officials, particularly, were surprised by these moves. The privatization efforts for 1996 should include a broad-based approach, such as Companhia Vale do Rio Doce, a mining company, and Banco Meridional. This would buy time for Cardoso, who faces a $3 billion deficit in Brazil's social security administration. At the same time, the confidence of its neighbors has been shaken by the seeming withdrawal of support for Mercosur. The unilateral tariff measures enacted in March 1995 were widely seen as a partial withdrawal from Brazil's commitment to market-driven reform. The success of the Cardoso administration—and whether or not Brazil can break free of its legacy of hyperinflation—will be determined by the ability to stay the course so hopefully undertaken in 1994. The mixed signals thus far have proved confusing, and, in the aftermath of the Tequila Effect, it is unclear if Brazilians have the resolve to demonstrate the discipline required.

Chile

The fall in stocks that befell Brazil and Argentina was not as severe in Chile. This has more to do with the impressive capital formation of the Chilean economy than with investor confidence. This is very revealing. Chile, unlike most Latin American nations, has benefited from a savings rate approaching 30 percent. This is unprecedented in the Spanish-speaking world and approximates the savings rates seen in the some Asian countries, such as Korea and Japan. While not without critics, including those who are not happy with the way the government intervenes in the foreign exchange market, Chile remains insulated from the volatility that engulfed Latin America subsequent to the Mexican Meltdown. This disciplined and conservative use of discretionary money has allowed Chile to enjoy internal capital formation, thereby limiting the role capital in-flows play in the nation's economic development.

This prudent approach, far from betraying xenophobic tendencies, is consistent with a development model designed to deliver long-term sustainable growth. Whereas stock markets throughout Latin America fell up to 50 percent as a consequence of the Mexican Meltdown, the Chilean stock market fell only 7 percent—before recovering. Chilean officials, known as the "Chicago Boys," first under the dictatorship of General Pinochet and now under civilian rulers, have maintained a restrained approach. Thus, by limiting the role foreign capital plays in the economic development of the country—and with existing foreign capital mostly in long-term investments, not liquid instruments—the risks and volatility have been reduced. This approach is not without critics, who point out that while the economic model pursued in Chile has brought a sustained period of growth, it has been slow in raising the standards of living of the Chilean people. This is true, and Santiago de Chile lags far behind Buenos Aires and Rio de Janeiro in developing a consumer market, but Chile's approach lessens risk. It also lessens the turmoil brought by the whimsical nature of foreign confidence. For Chile, there was much vindication in being spared the panic that consumed its neighbors.

ADMINISTERING AUSTERITY

The crisis precipitated by the collapse of the Mexican peso in December 1994 resulted in an international emergency package designed to restore confidence not only in Mexico but also in emerging markets around the world. For the United States it was imperative to ensure that NAFTA would survive, no matter at what cost. Declaring that it was in "America's economic and strategic interests that Mexico succeed," U.S. president Bill Clinton announced that the United States would be a lender of last resort, in essence pledging however many billions of dollars the Mexican rescue would require. Within days, teams from the IMF and the World Bank descended upon the Mexicans, as if they didn't already have enough problems. The usual restrictive monetarist austerity program was adopted— and implemented—as a condition for the emergency aid. The sense of panic that swirled throughout Mexico City was intensified when peace talks with the Zapatist rebels collapsed and the finance minister was fired. That former president Carlos Salinas was touring world capitals as part of his campaign to become the secretary general of the World Trade Organization only worsened the situation. The White House, to its shock, was forced to distance itself from Mr. Salinas, who, up to a few weeks before, had been hailed as the architect of the "Mexican Miracle." The Mexicans themselves sought nothing less than Mr. Salinas's head, demanding he be tried for "crimes against the nation." There was nothing happy about this new year in the Aztec capital.

The Power of Authoritarianism

Without the benefit of public debate, the authoritarian core country of Mexico implemented the IMF-approved austerity measures, revealing once again how undemocratic America's second-most important trading partner was in fact. The Zedillo administration unilaterally adopted an austerity program that undermined the long-term interests of the Mexican nation. Nowhere was this more visible than in the failure of the Mexican government to secure the backing of business and labor. In the past Mexico had gone through the motions, putting up a democratic facade by coercing the private sector and the irrelevant national labor unions to back the government's economic plans. The gravity of the situation as 1995 began, however, made it impossible to indulge the vanity of maintaining such farcical appearances. In a market ruled by emotion, particularly fear, the situation became dire as the Zedillo administration assembled a Draconian program to arrest the economic crisis.

While there was little public debate in Mexico over the government's surrender of economic sovereignty, the crisis highlighted the failure of Mexican leaders to implement the reforms promised during the last crisis. It also opened a debate about the role of the IMF and the World Bank and whether these institutions helped developing nations—or if in fact they made matters worse. Mexico, after all, had committed itself in 1982 to implement a series of reforms as a condition for being rescued, making it possible for Miguel de la Madrid to meet Mexican financial obligations. These reforms, officials just about everywhere, hailed as successful. These same reforms were continued in 1988 when Carlos Salinas became president. And these were the reforms that were supposed to usher in an era of prosperity as a consequence of the creation of the North America free trade zone. The Reagan White House, the Bush White House, and the Clinton White House all praised Mexico's progress.

Now, however, after twelve years of "reforms" under the auspices of the IMF and the World Bank, Mexico was in shambles. Worse still, further massive "reforms" were required to ensure future "progress." Critics— within Mexico and abroad—began to wonder what reforms were to be reformed. Was reform necessary to reform previous IMF-approved reforms? Or were these reforms to replace the reforms that had been agreed to but never implemented? If the former, what guarantee did anyone have that these new IMF-approved reforms would not need to be reformed subsequently? If the latter, why did both Republican and Democratic administrations cover up for the Mexicans, giving praise when none was due? And why did people the world over have to foot the bill?

To complicate these debates, the growing political turmoil in Mexico raised the question of the limits of authoritarianism. In Mexico the National Action Party (PAN) was coming to ascendance, as voters registered their discontent with the government by abandoning the ruling party. The cohesion of force was being challenged, weakening Ernesto Zedillo as no other president has been in modern Mexican history.

Mexico as a nation-state is a mosaic of peoples and ethnicities held together by the bureaucracy of authoritarianism and the authoritarianism of bureaucracy. The industrialized, forward-thinking northern states that straddle the U.S.–Mexico border are spearheading a backlash that champions a states' rights movement that seeks to limit the role Mexico City plays in the lives of the Mexican people. And in the impoverished southern states, Zapatist insurrection in Chiapas and illegitimate governors in Tabasco and Yucatan polarize the states in opposites directions: the future versus the past. This polarization of Mexico parallels the process of nation-state disintegration going on in other parts of the world. In too many instances, the introduction of democratic reforms in authoritarian countries, rather than bringing about a positive new unity, has had the opposite effect of unleashing divisive forces.

The United States, aghast at the prospect of chaos, watched with a stunned weariness. Historic American isolationism manifested itself in a new xenophobia in the voices of men like California Governor Pete Wilson and North Carolina Senator Jesse Helms who called for greater controls at the borders and a reevaluation of the nation's immigration laws. The opponents of the free trade agreement were galvanized, an empty satisfaction in their voices. The crisis, moreover, gave greater credence to the ethical questions of doing business with countries like Mexico. There was a certain distaste for engaging in such an intimate way with a country that was not a democracy. The crisis—which caught most of corporate

America by surprise—underscored the close bonds being forged. American executives, who found soothing the idea that a market of 90 million consumers across the border had entered into the ranks of the developed world, were rudely surprised to find out that this was not the case. Mexican businessmen, who had become smug in their confidence and prospects, were devastated by the economic ruin visited upon them.

That teams of supposed experts descended upon Mexico City by the planeload only highlighted how whimsical it all had been. The statistics proudly showcased by officials in Washington, D.C., Ottawa, and Mexico City were but wishful thinking. Corporate American giants, including Kimberly-Clark and Chemical Bank, suffered losses. Only a few companies, such as G.E. Capital, were prescient enough to hedge against a devaluation. It was clear six months into the crisis precisely how dependent each nation's fate lay in the other's. That made it all the more troublesome to be dealing with authoritarian rulers. Carlos Salinas was suspected of being involved in the political assassinations that rocked Mexico in 1994, and current president Ernesto Zedillo oversaw the deterioration of the education of Mexico's indigenous peoples, facilitating electoral fraud in the countryside. That politics attracts opportunists is true the world over, but the proportion of scoundrels in Mexican politics is greater than in the United States.

What made things different is that, according to the understanding reached in 1982, Mexico should have already become a democracy by 1994. Carlos Salinas wanted to avoid Mikhail Gorbachev's "mistake." Both leaders embarked on massive programs to salvage their respective revolutions, but whereas Gorbachev concentrated on political reform, Salinas concentrated on economic reform. That Gorbachev let the Soviet economy languish as he struggled to democratize the Soviet system proved his undoing. The Soviet Union no longer exists and the successor states are in tatters. The Salinas approach has proved more successful—or so it seemed—but economic reform was not accompanied by democracy. In the wave of violence that swept over Mexico, it was clear that authoritarianism had its limits, and an enormous price. Washington officials, disgusted with the character of their Mexican counterparts, were as embarrassed at having to deal with these kinds of men (and women) as they were about having to explain away the mess Mexico had become. It proved cumbersome and awkward, but necessity makes certain demands with which career politicians are comfortable; soothing words of praise were made in both capitals, insincere and trite, but none of that really mattered provided disaster was averted.

Loading on More Debt

The immediate priority for the Mexican government was to halt the collapse of the peso and to ensure that it could meet its dollar obligations when the Tesebonos came due. In 1995 a total of $29 billion in Tesebonos would become due. The Treasury Department and the Federal Reserve announced a $6 billion line of credit on December 22, 1994. This was increased to $9 billion on January 3, 1995. On January 11, 1995, the new line of credit was extended to "whatever would be required," as an administration official characterized it, explaining that a portion of the money would come from the Treasury Department's Exchange Stabilization Fund. This fund, which is not under congressional oversight, was used because the Clinton White House wished to maintain order in the foreign exchange markets; the U.S. dollar was falling in response to Mexico's problems in European and Japanese markets. The total worldwide loan package jumped from $18 billion to almost $50 billion, once central banks from the G-7 nations announced their own contributions to the rescue plan.

Within days, Mexico began to draw from these funds in a effort to stabilize its currency. The frantic pace of activity intensified as other lines of credit from the IMF and the World Bank were extended. The volatility of the exchange rates decreased, marginally, throughout January as austerity measures were announced. In tense negotiations, an exchange rate of six Mexico pesos to one U.S. dollar was assumed. That the exchange rate had been approximately 3.45 Mexican pesos per dollar days prior to the devaluation meant that the American dollar was assumed to be stable if it cost 75 percent more in peso terms. Because the Mexican economy is dollarized to a great extent, this exchange rate would unleash a round of inflation, throwing into disarray the economic program envisioned by Mexico's new president.

The conflicting reports on the Bank of Mexico's reserves made stabilization more difficult. Throughout the first half of 1995 officials downplayed the amount of funds Mexico was drawing on to meet its Tesebono obligations, while hailing the speed of the recovery. What was clear, however, was that six months into the currency crisis, Mexico's foreign debt had exploded to an alarming $160 billion, wiping out all the progress that had been made in the previous six years; Mexico owed more in 1995 than it did in 1982, when it almost defaulted on its foreign debt. This greatly compromised the domestic policy options of the Mexican government. While other countries, such as Italy, carry a greater foreign debt in relation to their national output, the burden this new debt would exact on the Mexican economy would, in and of itself, be recessionary. The debt-servicing demands now intensified an already precarious financial position. The true standing of Mexico's reserves remained unclear, and for most of 1995 it was difficult to determine precisely to what extent the Zedillo administration was drawing on its lines of credit. The impact of the exploding debt on the ability of Mexico to recover was likewise left an open-ended question.

Credibility of Information

A casualty of the Mexican crisis has been the ability to rely on governments to provide accurate information. Both Mexico and the United States have manipulated figures to give the appearance of a smoother recovery than has been the case. The Bank of Mexico's figures on exports, for instance, have been inaccurate since the spring of 1995. Wishing to lend credibility to the political argument that exports are booming, a duplicitous accounting of exports is being used to inflate export figures. The cross-border traffic between assembly facilities in Mexico and parent firms on the America side constitutes intracompany movement of goods, not Mexican exports to the United States.

It remains unclear whether Ernesto Zedillo's failure to be forthcoming with accurate information is deliberate. His time in office can be best characterized as a reign of chaos. It is difficult to determine if he is in control of the government, or whether the more recalcitrant of the authoritarian elements within the ruling party are manipulating the government. What is certain is that the level of confidence in Mexico remains weak, particularly when civil disturbances and political anarchy have rendered some Mexican states virtually ungovernable. Within the parameters of the Mexican political economy, a president who appears weak is weak. In the case of Zedillo, who is charmless and dull, his failure to inspire his countrymen only serves to undermine further the chances he will be able to carry out his reform program, however ill-defined that happens to be. In the economic realm, there is no room for debate: Mexico has conceded the administration of its economic affairs to the United States, but the process of democratization appears a more difficult matter. Mexicans, who have never had the benefit of living in a democracy, do not understand it very well. Zedillo thus far appears to believe that democracy is the same thing as anarchy.

THE LIMITS OF ECONOMIC DEVELOPMENT MODELS

For American executives charged with operations in Latin America, the turbulence of the boom-bust cycles is a disruptive force. It is also frustrating, because officials from governments and international lending institutions are always issuing reassuring statements that do little to alleviate worries. If classical economic theory is correct, then why are these countries trapped in endless cycles of booms and busts? The inability to establish sustainable economic prosperity undermines the business climates throughout the Americas. Since the Mexican Meltdown, for instance, orthodox economic policies have been implemented—and praised—but the cost has been enormous. The Mexican private sector and middle class, which are the foundations of modern democracies and market economies, have been devastated by the austerity measures in place.

The Problem with Devaluations

The concern with currency fluctuations in developing economies borders on obsession. Unlike in the United States, where Americans are insulated from fluctuations in the value of the dollar, people in the developing world are very much affected by foreign exchange fluctuations. The American economy is immune to wild fluctuations because of two factors. First, almost 90 percent of what Americans consume, whether in haircuts or real estate fees, is produced in the United States. Second, foreign investors and central banks are happy to hold U.S. dollars. The U.S. trade deficit represents less than 3 percent of the nation's $6 trillion economy. To be sure, foreign investors, such as the Japanese, have been less willing to reinvest in Treasury notes in the 1990s, but this reflects developments in Japan and not concern about the American economy. In the 1990s, the American dollar was sharply devalued relative to the Japanese yen and the German deutschemark, but it became stronger against the Canadian dollar and the Mexican peso, the nation's largest trading partners. That the international price of oil and gold is quoted in dollars further insulates the American consumer from fluctuations in the exchange rate.

For Latin American economies none of this holds true. The central bank reserves of these countries consist primarily of gold—and the U.S. dollar. The strength of their currencies, to a large extent, depends on the level of their reserves. It should depend on the confidence of what their economies produce, but such is the nature of the lack of confidence born out of underdevelopment. In the case of Argentina, the reform program implemented by Carlos Menem requires the central bank to back the number of Argentine pesos in circulation with an equal amount of U.S. dollars in reserves, thus assuring parity, if not guaranteeing liquidity to the financial system. But when these nations agree to hold U.S. dollars in their reserves, they are essentially financing the U.S. deficit, and are at risk when the dollar devalues. This has been an ongoing concern. For example, if Mexico holds $25 billion in reserves, only to see the dollar plummet against the German deutschemark, and then it sees its own currency crash against the American dollar, it has suffered a double devaluation.

The central bank reserves of scores of countries have been affected by the plunge in the American dollar of the past decade. A dollar, for instance, was worth 250 yen in 1985; a decade later, it is worth only 85 yen. This represents an enormous loss vis-à-vis the Japanese yen. The picture, of course, is more complicated because this is not evidence of weakness in the American economy. It could also represent a ridiculous valuation of the Japanese yen that may be unsustainable—it is certainly undesirable from Tokyo's point of view—in the long-run. But the absence of stability of the American dollar places at risk the economies of Latin America, which traditionally remain at risk. Michel Camdeussus, managing director of the IMF, admonishing the Clinton administration for failing to defend the dollar when it plunged to record lows against the German and Japanese currencies as a consequence of the Mexican Meltdown in the first half of 1995, was expressing the concerns—and frustrations—felt by central bank officials in capitals around the world.

The Mexican Meltdown highlighted the interdependence of the economies to the developing world to the American dollar—and the need for the United States to defend the value of the dollar. In the same way that for some countries of the former Eastern bloc, such as the Czech Republic, the German deutschemark has become the de facto legal tender; the Japanese yen is now poised to eclipse the American dollar in some Asian markets. These developments pose no immediate problems, but they raise issues for the medium and long term. Specifically, these currency developments raise the likelihood that central banks in Latin America will begin to diversify their reserves, holding the German and Japanese currencies in greater quantities in order to hedge their exposure to fluctuations in the U.S. dollar. A currency crisis is possible in the United States. The stubborn trade deficits have put a great number of dollars and dollar-denominated securities in foreign hands, and these foreign investors have watched with concern the value of their investments plunge along with the value of the dollar. This, in turn, could affect the ability of the United States to finance its trade deficit. In the new world order there are pressures shifting power relations, with Germany and Japan now competing directly with the United States in unexpected ways. For the countries of Latin America it is easy to see how vulnerable they are to capital flows, not only directly related to their national economies, but between the United States and the community of international investors who hold dollar-denominated securities around the world. With this in mind, an understanding of the tumultuous developments in Mexico and Latin America since December 1994 can be placed in proper perspective.

Unnatural Business Cycles

The Latin American boom-bust cycle is the result of several factors. The immaturity of the markets of the region, the substandard infrastructure, weak political institutions, an uneducated populace, and dependence on foreign capital and technology converge to undermine sustainable economic growth over time. What are natural business cycles throughout the industrialized world here become reversals of fortune on a wild scale, convulsing entire nations to the depths of depression and then to the heights of spectacular growth. This holds true for the entire region, regardless of the individual characteristics of a given nation. With this unfortunate state of affairs, the extremes are aggravated by the agencies whose purpose it is to ameliorate the negative effects of these boom-bust cycles. The myopic view and duplicitous impact of the IMF and the World Bank wreak havoc on vulnerable economies by throwing the variables of economic distortions and boondoggles of corruption into these nations' economic equations.

To understand how these unnatural business cycles work, the experience of two core countries proves instructive. Both Mexico and Peru are presently at opposite extremes. Mexico has been convulsed into a severe recession, while Peru is experiencing tremendous prosperity, the highest growth rate of any nation in 1994. These two authoritarian core countries are similar in the composition of their political structure. The majority of the people of these nations are mestizos, meaning people of mixed Native American and European ancestry, both also have large indigenous populations, and both lack credible democratic institutions. Mexico and Peru, for almost two decades, have been caught up in their own boom-bust cycles that reveal not only how these cycles evolve, but the important roles foreign capital and lending institutions play in the lives of Latin American nations.

Examining the Curious Contrasts Between Peru and Mexico

In 1982, Mexico announced it could no longer meet its obligations on its foreign debt, ushering in the international debt crisis. Within a matter of months, developing countries around the world encountered the same problems, and crisis management was the order of the day as these economies collapsed one after the other. Miguel de la Madrid, then Mexico's president, sought the assistance of the IMF and the United States, swallowing the bitter medicine of austerity and recession. While Mexicans endured a period of sacrifice, Americans enjoyed the largesse of the Reagan years, when foreign debt, irresponsible tax cuts, easy money, and widening federal deficits gave the appearance of prosperity. The 1980s were Mexico's "lost decade" and America's "go-go" time, when "yuppies" entered the lexicon. The discipline de la Madrid exhibited made sense, for he was laying the foundation for a period of sustainable growth provided his reform programs remained on track once he left office.

In contrast to all of this, Peru was governed by Alan Garcia, whose lack of understanding of economic affairs was inversely proportional to his personal ambitions. Garcia sought the glory of men such as Fidel Castro and Saddam Hussein. To harbor such aspirations is bizarre in and of itself, and so was Peru during this time. With great fanfare, Garcia—defending the dignity of humankind, allegedly—suspended all payments on Peru's massive foreign debt. Announcing that Peru was prepared to budget only 10 percent of its income to servicing its foreign debt, the South American nation was shunned by the IMF, the World Bank, the Inter-American Development Bank, along with scores of other private and public institutions. Thus a martyr in the Third World's struggle, Garcia became a legend in his own mind, at the expense of the Peruvian people. It is easy to understand what he hoped to accomplish. He wanted to lead a Third World revolt against the West, leading other developing countries in a boycott of their payments on their foreign debts. In theory, had a significant number of nations defaulted on their loans, it would have caused havoc in the world's financial systems, transferring significant purchasing power from the First to the Third World. It is also clear that not all European nations would have stood by idly, and the threat of war, or at least foreign occupation—and a return to colonial rule, would have loomed as a real policy option in some Western capitals.

The madness of such a scenario was clear to all; only Fidel Castro, Cuba's resident madman, was warm to Garcia's ambitions. Thus, while Lima and Havana forged closer ties, the international isolation of Peru plunged that country into a seemingly bottomless fall. The Peruvian economy crashed, and in response Garcia let the printing presses run around the clock, ushering in a period of such hyperinflation that it took a million Peruvian *soles* to buy lunch. Indeed, by the end of his term in 1989, inflation was running at almost 7,700 percent. Foreign investment came to a complete halt, and thousands of Peruvians fled their homeland, or sought hope anywhere, even if it meant supporting the Shining Path, a Maoist guerrilla movement that engaged in terrorism throughout the country. The results were not without dark humor. The cozy relations between Alan Garcia and Fidel Castro prompted a great deal of activity at each nation's embassy in the other country's capital and a flurry of cables and communiqués back and forth. Cubans, starved for concrete facts and who subsist on rumor, interpreted all the activity and commotion at the Peruvian Embassy in Havana as a deterioration of Lima-Havana ties. In one astounding incident, hundreds of Cubans stormed the Peruvian embassy seeking political asylum, thus creating a delicate situation for these mindless heads of state. It was clear to everyone that Peru under Alan Garcia was not well.

While Mexico City stayed on the recovery course under the capable leadership of de la Madrid, chaos reigned supreme in Lima under Garcia. As is the case the world over, a nation has reached the depths of hopelessness when those with altruistic intentions seek public office. Indeed, when literary writers are forced to seek public office, one can imagine the state of despair that prevails in that country. Vaclav Havel, the persecuted Czech novelist, governs the Czech Republic, once part of the former Czechoslovakia. Mario Vargas Llosa, Peru's eminent man of letters, ran for office in Peru in the late 1980s. The presidential elections took on a surreal aspect as Peruvians, on the brink of national suicide, sought desperately to find anyone to replace Alan Garcia, their child prodigy, more child than prodigy.

Mexico by the end of the 1980s was growing. Carlos Salinas succeeded Miguel de la Madrid, and the hard work was beginning to pay off. Impressive growth rates were recorded as foreign capital inflows accelerated economic activity. Negotiations for a free trade agreement were well underway and, for the first time in a decade, the standard of living of the Mexican people was rising. Peru, meanwhile, was in the throes of a mad presidential election where the winner was an unknown, Alberto Fujimori. The new president inherited a mess of a nation. The year was 1990. During the previous year inflation reached ridiculous levels, the economy shrank over 12 percent and terrorism prevailed throughout much of the countryside. To make matters worse, Peru was in arrears in its foreign debt and had an enormous public relations problem with officials around the world. To top everything else, the United States was furious at the lack of cooperation on Peru's behalf in the war against the drug trade. Fujimori faced enormous problems, which were only made more difficult by a splintered Congress unwilling to implement the harsh medicine required.

But Peru is an authoritarian core country, and Fujimori had choices other leaders, such as American presidents, do not. After consultations with the military leaders, Fujimori disbanded Congress, assumed ultimate authority, and suspended the constitution. It worked. In a series of military offensives, the Maoist guerrillas were neutralized and their leader was captured. An austerity program was implemented, the currency was replaced, and Peru negotiated its outstanding obligations with its international lenders. A series of market-driven reforms were implemented, liberalizing trade and investment laws, and dollar holdings were permitted. A relentless privatization program dismantled the statist economy Garcia had created, ending a system of patronage that had permitted the previous administration to become wealthy as the nation became impoverished. The state's share of the economy exceeded 40 percent when Fujimori took office. In 1994 this had been reduced to a mere 5 percent, which has been pivotal in bringing responsibility back to public finances. Growth returned as inflation yielded. That civil liberties were suspended proved problematic, but unlike other Latin American countries, Fujimori distinguished himself by refraining from state-sponsored terrorism. No death squads roamed the streets of Lima "disappearing" opponents, which in and of itself constitutes progress. Other Latin American leaders have been impressed with the Peruvian approach, to the point of imitation. Guatemala's Jorge Serrano, for instance, taken with how easily one's economic program moves along through Congress once Congress is arrested, attempted to do just that, but was less than successful.

A sense of normalcy began to return in Peru. When new elections were held, Fujimori was rewarded with reelection. In only four years, the annual inflation rate had dropped to 15 percent, the lowest since the mid-1970s, and Peru had the highest growth rate of any nation in the world. Foreign investment more than doubled to almost $6 billion, and the country was on sound economic and political footing. Tourism, which had virtually ended with the spread of terrorism, was once again booming. A record half million foreigners descended upon the Andean nation, creating a boom in hotel construction and revitalizing Lima's airport, which had long languished, filled with empty counters. More promising still are reforms designed to foster the interests of the middle class while, like Chile, creating the conditions for internal capital formation, lessening Peru's dependence on foreign capital. Sustained growth is more possible now that over $300 million in pension funds, belonging to over one million Peruvians, are entering the Lima Stock Exchange. The emergence of democracy is only possible with protection of the middle class. The transformation throughout Peru astounds. It is difficult to think that this country—where passengers were routinely forced off buses by terrorists along highways—is now safe and prospering. Indeed, Alan Garcia became just a bad dream as Peruvians eagerly anticipated the progress and prosperity the 1990s would bring them as they catch up to where they would have otherwise been. It will take six or seven years of 7 to 9 percent annual growth rates to erase the horror Garcia delivered to his nation. In Mexico, on the other hand, the situation was different. For a variety of reasons already discussed, Carlos Salinas committed the cardinal sin of politics: He believed his own press releases. In a series of blunders, which would only be surpassed by Salinas's hand-picked successor, Ernesto Zedillo, Mexico squandered its privileged position, straddling the world's largest consumer market, and crashed.

The Inevitability of Crisis in Economic Integration

There is no denying that Mexican presidents Carlos Salinas and Ernesto Zedillo have made significant mistakes. But the question remains of whether economic dislocation—and a turbulent business environment—are inevitable consequences when disparate economies engage in free trade. The United States dwarfs all other economies of the Western hemisphere. Even Canada and Brazil are minor economies compared to that of the United States. It would be unfair, although far too tempting, to blame Mexicans exclusively for their crisis. It already has been argued that the IMF and the World Bank unleash forces that do more harm than good for developing economies around the world. At the same time, emerging markets are submerged by mature ones. "The truth is rarely pure and never simple," Oscar Wilde wrote. So it is with the Mexican Meltdown. The collapse of Mexico is an inevitable part of economic integration. Consider the case of Canada.

In 1991 the United States and Canada entered into the U.S.–Canada Free Trade Agreement. Within two years of this accord Canada experienced a currency crisis not unlike Mexico's peso woes. The Canadian dollar collapsed from a high of 89.29 cents to the U.S. dollar on November 1, 1991, to about 67 cents by the end of 1995. This represents a devaluation of almost 20 percent. The interdependent nature of the North American economies is nowhere more in evidence than in the financial jitters that rippled through Canada in early 1995. As Mexico collapsed, so did the Canadian dollar, which had to be propped by a hike in interest rates. On January 23, 1995, a month and a few days after the Mexican Meltdown commenced, the Bank of Canada had to raise interest rates to stop the fall of the Canadian dollar. While the markets were reassured, the Canadian currency languished at near-bottom lows for most of 1995, still suffering from the sharp devaluation free trade has meant for the nation.

That the Canadian dollar experienced such a significant depreciation offers insights. Canada is greatly dependent on foreign capital. The depreciation of the Canadian dollar increases the cost of servicing the nation's foreign debt. In the 1990s, almost 35 percent of total government revenues are required to service the foreign debt. A weaker Canadian dollar only adds to the cost of servicing the nation's obligations. Canada, after all, owes about $490 billion US ($700 billion Canadian), and since the Mexican Meltdown, the pressures on the Canadian dollar have meant that an additional $3 billion US was required in 1995 to service the foreign debt. Such figures are staggering; Canada is the most heavily indebted nation on earth on a per capita basis. Indeed, Canada's foreign debt roughly equals its annual GNP, something only Italy approximates. Even the highly leveraged economies of Latin America are well beneath this level of indebtedness.

The figures are surprising. They are also misleading. Free trade, while convulsing the Canadian dollar to record lows, has done much to improve the Canadian economy in the medium and long terms. In the first year of NAFTA, for instance, exports to the United States and Mexico increased 21.3 percent and 22.7 percent, respectively. During the same period, imports from the United States and Mexico rose 19 percent and 21.7 percent, respectively. All this trade activity across Canada's borders created over 400,000 new jobs and pushed the unemployment rate down, and among the G-7 nations, Canada boasted the highest growth rate. For Canadians, who were skeptical of entering into a free trade agreement with Mexico, the benefits have been as tremendous as they have been unexpected. The devaluation of the Canadian dollar, insofar as Canada has been able to contain inflation, has in fact boosted the nation's economy.

This is a far cry from the experience of Mexico. The reason lies, as argued before, in the nature of the indebtedness. Canada's foreign debt is used for economic development—investing in the future. Mexico's foreign debt has traditionally been used for consumption—spending to keep the ruling party in power. While the service requirements of Canada's enormous foreign debt are not inconsequential, the prospering economy offers options for the nation. The need to reduce the foreign debt is great, but only because doing so would free up additional revenue for other purposes. In contrast to Latin American nations, the Canadian economy is resilient enough to withstand the turbulence free trade entails. At the same time, just as the Canadian currency came under attack as a consequence of free trade, it is evident that the repercussions for other Latin American economies will be as severe. Mexico is not an isolated case; it is a Latin American version of Canada's woes. This is true the world over. When Spain was integrated into the European Community, the Spanish peseta was so volatile for a while, there was fear it would, along with the Italian lira and the British pound, wreak havoc on the European currency system.

It is evident, then, that smaller economies suffer extensive economic dislocation as they enter into free trade with larger nations. The experience of Canada first, and the subsequent more extreme version in Mexico second, is evidence of the convulsions other Latin American nations are destined to experience as they enter into free trade with the United States. The structural resilience against such adverse effects is virtually nonexistent. This turmoil, however, is short term, and quite necessary if these countries are to benefit from the economies of scale regional integration offers. That there are social consequences associated with economic dislocation cannot be denied. That the business environment becomes more volatile is also well documented. This may offer some comfort for those caught up in the madness of the Mexican Meltdown. What offers reassurance, however, is that both Canada and Mexico stand to emerge the stronger for having entered into free trade, short-term turmoil notwithstanding.

LESSONS OF THE MEXICAN MELTDOWN

The Rule of Lawlessness

Foremost among the lessons of the disaster in Mexico is that in authoritarian core countries, where the systems of government offer few checks and balances—or checks that don't balance out—it is possible for one individual to engulf a nation in chaos. The nature of civility in these countries—which includes a stable business environment—is tenuous at best. These are also nations where economic sense plays a marginal role. Even in countries as large as Mexico, for instance, the patrimonial system in place undermines the rule of reason, to say nothing of the rule of law. Indeed, Mexican president Carlos Salinas attempted to create a cult of personality while he was in office, but he failed to realize that in order to have a cult of personality, one must first have a personality. Alan Garcia, on the other hand, was able to fill plazas and stadiums, so full of passion was his rhetoric and so telegenic his gesticulations.

From Extreme to Extreme

It is also instructive to understand the forces that push these countries to the extremes. Peru's economic collapse in the 1980s was far worse than it would have been without the loony policies of Alan Garcia. Between 1988 and 1992, for instance, the Peruvian economy contracted by over 25 percent. This sort of thing usually only happens during warfare when cities are blown up. Therefore, the spectacular growth rates under Fujimori reflect the frantic economic activity associated with recovery. In the same way that exceptional economic activity took place in, say, southern Florida after Hurricane Andrew or in California after major earthquakes, in Latin America similar patterns are in evidence. The nature of this comparison— that the business cycle in Latin America approximates only a major natural disaster in the United States—is not lost on Latin American businessmen, the more successful of whom operate in a disaster mentality as modus operandi. Indeed, the most compelling consequence of the Mexican Meltdown is the enormous sense of betrayal corporate Mexico feels. If nothing else, NAFTA, to many Mexican businessmen, had a spiritual element to it. NAFTA represented deliverance from savagery. Mexico, henceforth, would be a "normal" country, by which Mexican meant Western, industrialized, modern. The instability of underdevelopment was supposed to have been banished from their business plans. Instead, Carlos Salinas has been banished, and Mexico is now more than ever an impoverished nation on the brink of bankruptcy, subsisting on emergency loans and negotiating generous terms for restructuring its foreign debt, pleading for mercy.

Catastrophic Remedies

Of equal importance is the sinister role the IMF and World Bank play in these processes. In bad times, IMF-imposed austerity turns recessions into depressions. In good times, it fuels unsustainable growth rates that precipitate disappointment, not unlike a balloon that is pumped too fast and bursts. In good times and bad, it promotes, finances, and supervises development schemes that benefit a small elite, while impoverishing the majority of a nation's people. Nothing is ever delivered on time, or within budget. All decisions are political moves, something that frustrates the capable career economists and engineers on staff, who stand aghast at how political considerations dominate these bodies. This is not to absolve the professional staff, for they are far too inclined to implement policies that propel nations from one extreme to the other. In the Mexican austerity program adopted in 1995, for example, the monetarist policies were so extreme that hundreds of thousands of Mexican companies went out of business as the millions of Mexicans who had only recently reached middle-class status slipped back into poverty. To destroy a nation's private sector is incompatible with sustainable growth. To destroy a nation's middle class undermines democratization. It is immoral to destroy people's lives and call it progress, as Mexican president Ernesto Zedillo characterized his "recovery" program. Indeed, in Mexico, at the hands of the IMF, the seeds of Mexico's next crisis were being planted.

A Culture of Mismanagement and Corruption

The monetarist policies implemented during austerity programs, however, are only part of the problem encountered by the developing nations of the world. Of greater concern is the process by which schemes are approved. Consider for a moment the rather curious career of Jose Cordoba Montoya. An intimate associate of former Mexican president Carlos Salinas, Cordoba Montoya was dispatched to Washington, D.C., to represent Mexico at the Inter-American Development Bank in the spring of 1994. The former chief of staff settled in his new post, happily waiting for Salinas to leave office at the end of November 1994. That Cordoba Montoya would bridge two Mexican administrations would, in some ways, put him in the position of allowing Salinas to influence the direction of Mexico's future abroad, while Salinas remained at home, wielding the influence amassed during his presidency. Had Mexico not crashed, it would have been easy to see how Cordoba Montoya could have used his position to lobby for the approval of projects that would have been administered by his associates in Mexico, facilitating overruns, and delays and the other kinds of expensive incidents that characterize the projects financed by these international lending bodies. It would not have been difficult for the Mexicans to do what the Argentines did in the waning years of the military dictatorship with the Yacyreta Dam project, $7 billion over budget and half a decade behind schedule, enriching those involved with this boondoggle. But Mexico did crash. The much-despised Salinas crony Cordoba Montoya was forced to resign, but ever a resourceful man, he safely landed at a comfortable job—at the World Bank. No wonder furious American congressmen seek major reforms at these bodies, as well as the

United Nations. No wonder professionals at these lending bodies fume at their impotence in the face of a stream of politicians with the final word over projects. No wonder environmentalists and human rights activists denounce the activities financed by these lending bodies that only serve the interests of the authoritarian governments and oligarchies of the recipient nations. Indeed, in the aftermath of the Mexican Meltdown, even Michel Camdeussus, managing director of the IMF, conceded that there was something amiss and admitted that there was a "global problem with the culture" of the Washington, D.C.–based international lending body. It is not clear if Camdeussus believes that the problem referred to is economic or political, or why he believes institutionalized theft should be considered a culture. The global nature of the problem confronting the international lending bodies is that ultimate decisions are made by politicians who have vested interests in the projects financed, and at the professional level, often the medicine administered is worse than the affliction, for it convulses developing economies from periods of hypergrowth to middle-class–destroying recessions. For American executives, these problems undermine the stability on which sustainable growth can take place. The Foreign Corrupt Practices Act constitutes an ambiguous terrain through which to travel. The self-serving nature of government contracts further complicates matters.

Ideological Inconsistencies

In analyzing the differences between Peru and Mexico, finally, the issue of stability is an important one. In the course of these boom-bust cycles, it is apparent to see how these countries swing across the political spectrum from nationalistic socialism to monopoly capitalism. This is inherent in the authoritarian nature of the core countries. As easily as Alan Garcia seizes everything in sight, Miguel de la Madrid becomes Mexico's president with the banks nationalized months prior to his taking office. This philosophical zigzagging betrays the impoverished nature of these societies, where the lack of self-confidence makes it impossible for the insecure to hold convictions. In many cases, as with Alan Garcia and Fidel Castro, it is all about survival: Men of few convictions become trapped by ideologies they are forced to embrace but in which they do not believe. It is this absence of conviction that is the reason for their failures. Fidel Castro became a Communist only after the United States rebuffed him, and the Soviets saw an opportunity. Alan Garcia saw the international debt crisis as his ticket to international fame, and his goal was to be a self-styled leader of the developing world, even if it meant the destruction of his homeland. It is, without a doubt, an unusual business environment.

Taken together, these factors demonstrate that in Latin America, the boom-bust cycle and extreme volatility that characterize the political economy of the region are proportional to the perceptions investors have of the prevailing stability. It is easy to examine the sequence of events from a theoretical viewpoint. A loss of investor confidence does not automatically lead to capital flight. The increasing loss of investor confidence throughout 1994 in Mexico encouraged investors, Mexican and foreign alike, to seek safer havens. The rising interest rates in the United States and the widespread belief that there would be a devaluation sometime between the presidential elections in August and the transition of power in December prompted anxious sellers to cash in their peso-denominated Cetes and purchase U.S. dollars. The understanding between the Salinas administration and U.S. institutional investors known as the Weston Forum resulted in stability in the peso-dollar exchange rate, even if this meant the central bank's reserves were being depleted. The collapse of the Mexican peso prompted a crisis of unprecedented proportions. The United States orchestrated a historic bailout, cajoling recalcitrant European allies and international lending bodies to extend loans and lines of credit. As frantic negotiations took place in New York and Washington, the curious, if not bizarre, element of homophobia was thrown into the Mexican equation, complicating an already complex situation. The Europeans, particularly the Germans who had bailed out East European economies, complained that there was a double standard at work; if Mexico merited bailing out, why wasn't this the case with Russia? These concerns were also voiced by the Japanese. At the same time, the U.S. Congress was hostile to the Clinton administration about the terms of the Mexican rescue package. There is equal concern about the effects of the Mexican Meltdown on the rest of Latin America. Brazil and Argentina, particularly, were hard hit by a shaken international community. Mexico, the darling of Wall Street for much of 1992 and 1993, had stumbled badly, which was not expected especially with the free trade agreement coming on-line. The Tequila Effect, however, was real, and other Latin American economies faced tremendous pressures that required emergency loans and lines of credit to bolster central bank reserves, and assure investors that Mexico's mistakes would not be repeated elsewhere throughout the continent.

In the aftermath of the crisis, valid criticism was made that Carlos Salinas tried to have the best of both worlds: a stable exchange rate and low interest rates. The political situation and Salinas's own vanities prevented a prudent course of action. His capitulation to the Weston Forum and the recalcitrant elements within his own party who were pressuring for spending to guarantee an electoral victory that would reverse the gains of the opposition party, known as PAN, exacerbated economic conditions. The political instability that gripped Mexico during 1995 was ameliorated by an unrelenting stream of fresh money. The peso stabilized and Mexico was able to meet all its Tesebono obligations. That was the easy part. The difficulties then were found in the domestic realm. While Mexico piled on debt, the Mexican economy was convulsed into a recession, threatening the very existence of the middle class, and with it, prospects for the democratization of the country. Political violence continued as before, as did political abductions of businessmen at a time when prices soared, unemployment skyrocketed, and the standard of living collapsed. The private sector was brutalized by the surge in interest rates and money vanished from the Mexican economy, where demand ground to a halt. It will take years for the private sector, which had been encouraged to incur debt, both in pesos and dollars, to recuperate from this crisis. The same can be said of the Mexican people. Indeed, by the summer of 1995 the Mexican government itself acknowledged that half the population lived below the poverty line and that over 60 percent of Mexican children suffered from malnutrition. The business and social price Mexico continues to pay for the December debacle is enormous, if not criminal.

Ineptitude only made the macabre spectacle more painful. Zedillo stumbled from one fumble to another. His lack of credibility continued as Mexico only saved itself by mortgaging its future. In political terms as well he proved incompetent. The stalled peace talks and the growing polarization of the country—the northern states were won by the opposition and the southern states descended into ungovernability reminiscent of "banana republics"—was more than evident in the elections at the end of May 1995. Relying on false information provided by his interior minister, Ernesto Zedillo congratulated a PRI crony on "winning" the governorship of the southern state of Yucatan, when in fact there was massive electoral fraud. That there was widespread coverage of this fraud in the international media only eroded the little credibility Zedillo had left concerning his democratic intentions. Then, within days, peasant militants occupied the offices of the Interior Ministry, an unprecedented display of weakness, suggesting that the Zedillo administration was out of control. Thus embarrassed in such fundamental ways, Zedillo fired his interior minister, which only served to underscore the idea that he was neither capable nor in control of his own government. For the Mexican people, the empty promises of their leaders were compounded by murderous scandal, for it appeared that the highest ranking members of the government, including family members of the Salinas family, were involved in the political assassinations that brought instability to the country and destroyed investor confidence. As for Ernesto Zedillo, the hapless man struggled through the rest of the first of a six-year term, as much by the deep pockets of Uncle Sam as by the grace of God.

NOTE

1. Marquis de Custine, *Empire of the Czar: A Journey through Eternal Russia* (New York: Doubleday, 1989), p. 531.

4

THE PERSISTENCE OF POVERTY IN LATIN AMERICA

The most frustrating aspect of doing business in Latin America is to witness, and become involved with, the volatile nature of these countries' economies. Medium- and long-term business plans are all but impossible, given the instability of the business environment. To make matters worse, from an American perspective, there is no reason for this to be this way. The Americas are blessed with vast riches, and the orderly development of economies should be feasible. But if the objective is to create sustainable economic growth and democracies, it cannot be dismissed that these goals are inconsistent with the advice and recommendations the policymakers throughout the hemisphere receive. Mexico, after all, has been obeying the dictates of the IMF and the World Bank for almost two decades, and it remains a mess, now more than ever. American executives loathe the boom-and-bust cycles that afflict Latin America. But to a great degree Latin American nations go from crisis to crisis precisely because of the nature of the institutional structure of the international lending bodies that are designed to help them. The natural business cycle common in the industrialized world is perverted into these boom-and-bust cycles that wreak havoc.

The economies of the developed world are characterized by natural business cycles. Periods of growth are followed by economic slowdowns that become recessions, at times depressions, then corrective measures begin a cycle of growth before another slowdown appears. This cyclical pattern unfolds over a period of years, and adjustments are transitory. Seldom are disturbances abrupt or prolonged enough to cause social disruptions; the greatest casualties tend to be the political parties in power who are voted out, or at minimum lose support. In Latin America, how-ever, the natural business cycle is largely unknown. Developing economies here are characterized by extremes; stupendous periods of growth and economic activity are followed by spectacular crashes that suffuse the whole of societies, wiping out virtually all gains made. The challenge is not to generate growth—any idiot can stimulate an economy armed with $50 billion in foreign debt—rather, it is to create an economy whose fundamentals allow for sustained growth over several generations. In the 1990s, a few Latin American economies are on the verge on achieving these, but they are the exception. The vast majority of Latin American economies languish in the boom-bust cycle, with all the social and political chaos inherent in these reversals of fortune that plague the region. This is a far cry from other regions of the developing world. Asian economies have managed to enjoy sustainable growth over several decades and are now almost fully industrialized, while the economies of Africa languish in unspeakable poverty and ineptitude bordering on hopelessness. Latin America is somewhere between the extremes of promise and despair. That "somewhere" can be called "frustration."

The frustration of the Latin American nations is based on ineptitude at home, and from abroad. The IMF and the World Bank are bastions of incompetence that have, on balance, impoverished the nations they have attempted to help. The boom-and-bust cycles that torment Latin America, for instance, are exacerbated by the IMF and the World Bank, whose lending practices funnel money into economies faster than it can be re-sponsibly assimilated, and then impose Draconian austerity programs that prolong recessions and deepen depressions. All at once an economy be-gins to experience enviable growth rates, and consumerism skyrockets as a middle class begins to proliferate, but the short-term loans and ill-advised capital infusions do not create the fundamental structure for sus-tainable growth. Then, when the bubble bursts, these international lending bodies impose austerity programs that wipe out the newly arrived middle class and intensify the economic consequences of the bust. Natural business cycles become boom-and-bust cycles because of the IMF and the World Bank; social unrest and the familiar disruptions in business rela-tionships are directly linked to austerity programs designed in Washing-ton, D.C.

Consider two brief examples. In the 1980s, Argentina successfully im-plemented structural reform programs that had admirable results on a macroeconomic level. The Menem administration eliminated the federal deficit, export earnings grew, and the regional trading bloc with other Cono Sur countries was negotiated. The austerity program in place, how-ever, contributed to a widening of the gap between the haves and the have-nots; Argentina's poor became poorer as the distribution of wealth became further distorted throughout society. These problems remain hidden through lending programs that funnel enormous amounts of money throughout the economy. The World Bank, for instance, subsidized health care and housing programs in the second half of the 1980s, to the tune of $328 million. This off-the-books capital infusion for direct social programs lessens the impact of the true effects of the Argentine government's policies on the nation's economy, and the Argentine people. To these kinds of distortions, add long-term loans characterized by mismanagement and corruption. Over a period of fifteen years, the Yacyreta Dam project, financed mostly by the World Bank, and which is supposed to supply electricity for Buenos Aires, is over $7 billion over budget and half a decade behind schedule, and has destroyed four fragile ecosystems while displacing over 50,000 Argentines. These loans ameliorate the short-term problems of the Argentine economy and mask the distortions that would otherwise be apparent. The IMF and World Bank have been politicized, under the guise of internationalization. Officials of these bodies approve loans and programs, then return home to "manage" these projects directly or through cronies in an old-boys sort of way, facilitating corruption and theft, as seen in mind-boggling cost overruns and delays. What does flow to these economies then creates distortions, as short-term capital infusions often do. These fundamental problems—corruption and short-term macroeconomic distortions—at a structural level contributed to the pressures Argentina came under in the wake of the Mexican Meltdown in early 1995. At the same time, there are lingering social problems—a growing underclass at a time when the economy is moving ahead—that portend challenges as the 1990s draw to a close. The pressure on the Argentine peso, the need to have sustainable growth at a time when the Mercosur common market with Brazil, Uruguay, and Paraguay is fully implemented, and the need to bolster foreign reserves are aggravated by the self-destructive policies of the IMF and the World Bank. The impoverishment of the most disenfranchised members of Argentine society looms ominously over the Menem administration in its efforts to create the foundation for long-term sustainable growth, a goal that has proved ever so elusive for Argentina.

From one end of Latin America to the other, when disaster falls, the IMF and the World Bank make a bad situation worse. The duplicity of Mexico's Carlos Salinas, for instance, was made possible only by continuing loans from these lending bodies. Mexico's Solidaridad boondoggle federal programs in which monies—a great deal from foreign loans—were dispersed in inefficient programs around the country, essentially to deceive and bribe the Mexican working classes, rural peasants, and urban poor, did much to disguise the ineptitude of the Mexican development scheme for much of 1993 and all of 1994. Heralded as evidence that the Mexican government "cares" about the poor in academic journals in the

United States, this glorified pork-barrel program was nothing more than the dispersing of patronage funded by loans. Spending money is neither good nor bad in and of itself. Spending money for investment is better than spending money for consumption. Solidaridad spent fortunes on consumption, which, unlike investment, offers little in return. The politicization of the national economy, designed to allow for the election of Mexican president Salinas's hand-picked successor, made it possible for the Salinas administration to cultivate foreign investor confidence by manipulating official figures on the Mexican economy. When the bust came in a spectacular way—the Mexican peso lost half its value in a week and over $15 billion of wealth vanished when Mexican stocks, on both the Mexican Bolsa and the New York Stock Exchange, crashed—an economy lay in ruins, investors in Mexico, the United States, and Europe were stunned, and a mad frenzy of activity around the world was necessary to assemble a rescue package of unprecedented proportions. For American investors it was shocking to see Telefonos de Mexico, "Telmex," plummet from $75 a share to less than $25 and recuperate only to around $30 well into Mexico's so-called recovery. To clean up the mess they helped create in Mexico, the IMF engineered an austerity program. Within the first six months of austerity measures being implemented by the compromised— and weak—administration of Ernesto Zedillo the consequences were all too clear. The Mexican middle class was destroyed, two million Mexican workers lost their jobs, over half a million Mexicans had to flee the country, mostly as illegal aliens to the United States, and the nation was in the throes of a severe recession. In less than twelve months, Mexicans went from thinking they could afford to buy a new car, to worrying about losing their homes and feeding their families.

This constant swinging back and forth from one extreme to the next is the most frustrating aspect of doing business in Latin America. And it is easy to see in sublime ways. Miami International Airport is a barometer of how Latin America is doing. When the check-in counters for a Latin American airline have long lines, that country is experiencing tremendous growth. When those same counters are unmanned, there is a bust. The counters for Aeromexico and Avensa, for instance, were crowded in 1994 and now languish. Mexico and Venezuela are in turmoil, obviously. The counters for Varig and Aeroperu in 1995 were doing brisk business. Brazil and Peru are booming. Thus, there are never-ending crowd control problems for the management of Miami's airport, where this game of musical chairs is relentless.

This turmoil, however, promises to continue as long as the IMF and the World Bank engage in insidious lending programs of tremendous duplicity. In the case of Mexico, it is difficult to see how any of the loans made between 1988 and 1994 made Mexicans' lives better. In 1995, the standard of living of the Mexican people, in real terms, had descended to the 1976 level. Almost two decades of potential progress vanished into thin air, the lives of a generation were destroyed, and a new generation of Mexicans is condemned to poverty. Since the Mexican Revolution, over 10 percent of the Mexican people have been forced to flee, and this flight now accelerates as the century draws to a close, with chaos spilling into the United States, feeding isolationist sentiments throughout America. In Argentina, the same social problems that earlier this century gave rise to Juan Peron, an opportunist fascist who appealed to populism and became a ruthless dictator, are now spreading throughout the whole of society like a virulent weed. Argentina's Carlos Menem, with the assistance of the IMF and World Bank, is laying the foundation for political turmoil early next century, thereby undermining the prospects for democracy in this country. What makes this all the more insidious is how officials connive to disguise the truth. In the second half of 1995, for instance, officials were hailing Mexico's recovery as "rapid" and "ahead of expectations." But the figures boasted were deceptive. If, for instance, a country exports $100 and imports $300, then it has a $200 trade deficit. Let us now say an economic collapse virtually destroys demand. It still exports $100, but now it only imports $75. True, it now has a $25 trade surplus, but at the cost of an economy in tatters. Worse yet, if the nation's exports are, as in the case of Mexico, oil—a raw material—and tourism—a defining element of an underdeveloped economy—the national economy is further impoverished. This is all the more true if the remaining demand, however meager it may be, exists only through the accumulation of greater and greater amounts of foreign debt, as is the case with Mexico's recovery program under Ernesto Zedillo. The austerity program in place in Mexico is destroying much of the Mexican middle class, rendering this country into islands of wealth surrounded by oceans of poverty. Democracies only flourish when a middle class matures and spreads through the whole of society. The destructive nature of the austerity program implemented in Mexico in 1995 undermines the medium-term future of the country—not only its economic development, but also the process of democratization. Thus, whether in Washington or Mexico City, embarrassed officials will do whatever is necessary to cover up their incompetence and poor judgment, even if it means undermining the futures of generations yet unborn. Indeed, most tellingly of all, the failure of the IMF and the World Bank, pillars of the Bretton Woods system, is nowhere more evident than in the simple fact that after half a century of existence, there is not one country on the face of the earth they have helped break from the shackles of poverty to become prosperous. Watching the IMF and World Bank "rescuers" scurry about Mexico City in the spring of 1995 was like watching firemen attempt to extinguish a fire by dousing gasoline: Up in flames went Mexico's private sectors, middle class, and democratic aspirations. The extremism of these lending bodies condemns millions to misery throughout Latin America and the developing world.

PART II

Strategies for Turbulent Markets in the Age of Free Trade

5

THE PERIPHERY COUNTRIES:
ARGENTINA, BRAZIL, CHILE,
PARAGUAY, URUGUAY

A man arrives as far as he can and not as far as he wishes.
—Vasco Núñez de Balboa

The identity crisis confronting core societies is absent in periphery countries. Thus, while Mexicans anguish over who they are, for instance, Chileans have no misgivings about their origins. This is not to say that transplanted societies are not without insecurities. Argentines, Chileans, and Costa Ricans, among others, are prone to feel unsure of themselves. Regardless of how successful societies of immigrants or exiles happen to be, there is a lingering stigma that haunts them. Witness Americans who, despite their privileged position and power in the world, nonetheless are easily intimidated by someone speaking with a British accent and fawn over aristocracy. So too Latin Americans are intimidated by Spaniards and Frenchmen and servile to nobility. There is nothing to be done, other than to be aware of these predispositions and to use them: American consumers are suckers for spokesmen with British accents, and Latin Americans cannot resist the sound of Spanish spoken with a Castilian accent. These insecurities vary, and in the case of Brazil rarely exist; Brazil has been so successful that it eclipses Portugal—the roles have been reversed, and Portugal looks to Brazil. (The British would probably look to the United States if they weren't so burdened by the weight of their antiquated and irrelevant class consciousness.) In Latin America it is therefore imperative to abstain from being critical. The honesty with which Americans deal with one another is inappropriate where feelings must be spared and manners are the hallmarks of civility. In Mexico, for instance, the elevators at the Maria Isabel Sheraton will be annoying, and the shirts will be improperly starched at the Hotel Nikko, and even at the Four Seasons room service is slow, but make no mention of any problems; Mexicans will take negative comments about anything as personal affronts. The inability for critical self-examination undermines the prospects of advancement. It is tragic to see the Mexican people, for instance, who work so hard and sacrifice themselves to languish in perpetual drudgery; Mexicans do not lead enviable lives. But the fragile psyches and humbled self-esteem result from a litany of misfortunes and setbacks that fill the landscape of Mexican history. Foreign businessmen are not allowed the luxury of honest criticism; Everything is fine, Everything is splendid, is the only thing a prudent foreign businessmen tells his hosts. In fact, only Mexicans are allowed to be critical of Mexico, and then only within a narrow range. The accusation of "malinchismo," which refers to the belittling of Mexican things in favor of American ones, among Mexicans is roughly analogous to an American accusing another American of being a "Benedict Arnold," the difference being that the former is common while the latter is almost never heard.

But it is worth remembering that there are strong rivalries among the periphery nations. Brazilians resent how few Americans understand that Portuguese is not Spanish, and many prefer to speak to Americans in English rather than Spanish. That Brazil is the largest nation in South America gives them the confidence to demand, however ill-advised it may be, to be treated on their own terms. American businessmen who attempt to speak Spanish in Rio de Janeiro or Sao Paolo are not only guilty of a faux pas, they are also offending their hosts. The same is true in North America; Canadians are adamant about not being confused with being Americans, and they bristle when they learn that most American high school students, for instance, think Canada is part of the United States.

These rivalries extend to the Spanish-speaking nations of the Cono Sur. There is competition, both economic and cultural, between Argentines and Chileans. Chileans think Argentines are lazy and irresponsible spend-thrifts who take life too carelessly. Argentines, on the other hand, think Chileans do not understand how to enjoy life, and are dreary. There are elements of veracity in these perceptions. Chile, which enjoys the highest savings rate in the New World, has been successful in forming capital, while Argentina has a considerable foreign debt. When I praised the impressive savings rate in Chile to an Argentine businessman in Buenos Aires once, he huffed, replying that, "Of course they save their money in Santiago—there's nothing to spend your money on, it's so boring there!" This exchange took place as we prepared to go to dinner and the theater, after which, at midnight, we had a meeting over after-hours drinks that ended at two in the morning. In Chile, in contrast, one is back at the hotel by 10:00 P.M. As an American businessman, being aware of, and sensitive to, these sensibilities is enough. Of greater concern is the indifference with which American businessmen blindly wander about Latin America. One of the most peculiar feelings about doing business in Latin America is the realization of exactly how privileged Americans are in fact. What we take for granted in our own lives are luxuries throughout Latin America. For instance, whereas I am accustomed in the United States to participating in a wide range of activities with American business colleagues, from playing golf and squash to going skiing, scuba diving, horseback riding, or mountain biking, it is rare to find Latin Americans who are able to do almost all of these activities. Their life experiences are diminished by the circumstances of their societies, and therefore they have difficulty relating with American executives in less formal settings. Thus, it is imprudent to take sides, make comparisons, or render judgments.

ARGENTINA

Background

With a population of Native Americans numbering fewer than fifty thousand, Argentina constitutes a transplanted European nation on the American mainland. This is not to say that Argentines are Europeans in exile. Rather, they are a nation that is New World, but without influences of indigenous societies. Indeed, well over half of Argentines are of Spanish and Italian immigrants, with considerable numbers tracing their lineage to Britain, Germany, and other European countries. There are also half a million Argentines of Middle Eastern descent, with the current president, Carlos Menem, among them. The absence of Native Americans, most of whom died in the colonial period from their inability to resist European diseases, has allowed Argentina to develop as a European nation, without the conflicting notions of identity that plague the core countries. For Americans this is welcome news, insofar as dealing with Argentina is comparable to dealing with a nation in Western Europe; the connection on a commercial level is made quicker and the currency of business intercourse is more "rational." Argentines, however, are not European in two intriguing aspects. This first is their insecurity. Unsure of their own identity as a nation, they have misgivings about their place in Latin America, where they are somewhat out of place. While Buenos Aires is a cosmopolitan and sophisticated city, Argentines are not unlike Americans who also feel somewhat taken by the pretentiousness of the Europeans. The second is in the language spoken in Argentina. Although it is Spanish, there are enough vernacular expressions derived from Italian— as well as a distinctive accent—that makes it not-quite-Spanish. Other

Latin Americans are quick to make derisive comments about how Argentines speak, and at times some archaic usages are surprising, but the evolving Argentine version of Spanish is charming.

Discovered by Juan de Solis in 1516, Argentina formally declared independence from Spain in 1816. In 1823, formal diplomatic relations within the United States were established. The United States and Argentina have engaged in constructive relations throughout their histories. A successful coup in 1946 by Col. Juan Peron resulted in the militarization of the country, both in terms of economics and politics. Radical socialism, bordering on fascism, was the foundation on which Peron's power rested. Worker unions were consolidated into the General Confederation of Labor (CGT), which was used to pursue a policy of nationalization and industrialization. With the assistance of his charismatic wife, Eva Peron, Argentina was seen as a refuge for the vanquished ideals of those defeated in World War II. The European traumas—and neurosis—as well as a certain predisposition for barbarous zealousness characteristic of Europe, played itself out in a series of dramas in Argentina.

Peron's programs were wildly popular, and he was reelected in 1952, only to be ousted by the military in 1955. A series of subsequent military and civilian governments managed and mismanaged the economy for about a decade. When the military government of Juan Ongania failed to deliver on both economic growth and political reform in the late 1960s, Peronism regained its appeal among the disenfranchised. Juan Peron, safely in exile, was barred from participating in the election held in 1973, but his stand-in, Hector Campora was elected. The Peronists swept into both houses of the National Congress, Campora promptly resigned and was replaced by Raul Lastiri, who called for new elections. Later that year Juan Peron, permitted to return from exile and run for office, won a decisive victory and assumed the presidency in October 1973. Peronism was back on top.

The return of fascist government in Argentina caused much concern, as much in Argentina as elsewhere. In the 1970s Argentina became swept up in a madness, as the emergency decrees were announced, which resulted in the suspension of fundamental human rights. The fascist government declared war on its own people and a "dirty war" unfolded, which left thousands of people dead. The knock on the door in the middle of the night, people being swept into unmarked cars, the terror of living in a police state gripped Argentina, much the same way that Europe had been gripped by nazism and Stalinism. In a riveting display of how cultural predispositions and habits move along with people, in the 1970s Argentina lived the worst of Italy under Mussolini and Spain during the Inquisition; Argentina is very European.

Upon his death in office, Peron was succeeded by his wife, who was herself overthrown in a coup on March 24, 1976. From then on, generals ruled in an unforgiving military state that exercised power through a military president and three-man military junta. The generals continued in their campaign to silence their critics, combat so-called "terrorists," meaning university students and housewives, and tried to establish control throughout society. None of this was good for business. None of this was sustainable over a long period of time. It was not, however, until Argentina declared war on Britain over the Falkland Islands, known in Latin America as the Malvinas, that the generals relented. Their humiliating defeat at the hands of the British in June 1982, the deterioration of the nation's economy, stunning revelations about corruption throughout the military, continuing denouncements of human rights abuses, and the Argentine nation's complete exhaustion at living through a nightmare, discredited the military in no uncertain terms.

A gradual transition to civilian rule was implemented—bans on political parties were lifted, censorship was reduced, basic civil liberties were restored—which culminated in free elections in 1983. Raul Alfonsin became the first democratically elected president in a generation, and the hard work of restoring democratic institutions was begun. Alfonsin did a credible job of assuring civilian control of the government and restoring the democratic institutions that had long languished. His successes at addressing the economic problems confronting the nation were less spectacular. In May 1989 Carlos Menem was elected president. Although a Peronist candidate, Menem abandoned the socialist and statist model long associated with his party and embarked on a program of market-driven reform and privatization. Inflation was brought down through conservative monetary policies, state expenditures were slashed, taxes were increased, and an ambitious privatization program was undertaken. He won reelection in May 1995 and his success at preventing Argentina from following the disastrous steps of Mexico—there was no Tequila Effect in Buenos Aires—is primarily responsible for his reelection.

Economic Model

When Carlos Menem took office in July 1989, Argentina recorded an inflation rate for that month of 198 percent—a record even by Latin American standards. A series of emergency measures was announced to reduce import duties, privatize public sector firms, reduce public outlays, and slash state subsidies. The market-driven reform program was further strengthened by the Deregulation Decree signed on October 31, 1991. Argentina's historical development model of import substitution was formally at an end. The developmental strategy now lay in establishing a free market economy, instead of the closed economy that had collapsed from the limits inherent in such a model. Under Carlos Menem an ambitious program to do away with nontariff barriers, rely on free trade, and minimize government regulation in the economic life of the nation began to bear fruit. Critics pointed out that similar progress was not being made on the political front; the military was granted a general amnesty for its crimes and even today thousands of "disappeared" people remain unaccounted for. Critics also point out the fascist tendencies lurking beneath the surface of the Argentine nation; the most savage terrorist act outside the Mideast against Jews occurred in Buenos Aires in 1994.

The success on the economic front, however, cannot be denied. The privatization program continued, and unlike other countries like Mexico, proceeds were used to balance the nation's fiscal accounts. Argentina eliminated debt and saved, whereas Mexico used its insidious Solidaridad as a massive pork-barrel program to squander most of the income from the sale of state enterprises. For Argentina, however, the overhaul of its tax laws and its prudent finances allowed it to do almost the unthinkable: back its currency with an equivalent amount of U.S. dollars. Thus, perhaps the most stunning move was the Convertibility Law, which took effect in April 1991. The austral would be replaced by the peso and parity would be imposed with the U.S. dollar the first of the following year. Since 1992 the Argentine peso has remained stable.

This is very instructive for corporate officers to understand. Argentina has, in effect, surrendered control of its money supply. By adhering to a policy in which the amount of Argentine pesos in circulation has to be backed one-to-one with American dollars in reserves, analytically, the Argentine peso is nothing but a voucher for the American dollar. Anyone can redeem an Argentine peso for an American dollar at any time, without restrictions. Of course no Argentine official can come out and admit that this is what they have done, but from an analytical point of view, the effect is the same. This is one reason why in 1995, in the wake of the Mexican crisis, Argentina faced an emergency. To maintain its one-to-one parity, it had to ensure that there was an ample supply of American dollars in reserve while at the same time convincing the Argentine people—and foreign investors—not to redeem their Argentine pesos for American dollars.

The reason for this is that since Argentina has to ensure that all Argentine pesos in circulation are backed by American dollars in reserves, a trade deficit, or people redeeming pesos for dollars, will reduce the money supply. For Argentina, the loss of investor confidence is the same as a trade deficit: It reduces the money supply and exerts a recessionary pressure on the economy. The challenge for Argentina, then, was to ensure sufficient credit lines from international sources to ensure that its one-to-one parity could be sustained as the Tequila Effect manifested itself throughout Latin America. For the government, however, it is ill-advised to admit that control over the money supply has been relinquished through a voucher system. The politically acceptable euphemisms used are "currency boards" and "currency parity." Much of Argentina's ability to avoid a collapse similar to Mexico's resides in the capable management of Finance Minister Domingo Cavallo, who successfully negotiated an $11.1 billion US line of credit from various international lending organizations and central banks. This liquidity stabilized international markets and restored confidence in Argentina.

Regardless of how Argentina wishes to disguise it, it is important for a corporate officer to understand that, the natural business cycle notwithstanding, as long as Argentina remains committed to its Convertibility Law and to adhering to its policy of limiting the supply of Argentine pesos in circulation to the number of American dollars available, the one-to-one parity will be maintained. Provided discipline is maintained, so will the economic order. In the past, sound programs have been undermined when they have been politicized. Argentina has done a credible job of exercising restraint and prudence. But not unlike Italy or Germany, there remains the predisposition to let the sensible become senseless, and chaos reign supreme. Business plans do not fare well under such conditions. This, however, does not discount the possibility that even in turbulent times business cannot go on as usual; the Italian government seems to be collapsing all the time, but that has not prevented Italy from surpassing Britain in economic output. The short and medium terms for Argentina, clearly suggest continued stability, as democratic institutions are strengthened and the economy enjoys sustainable, robust growth.

Political and Market Conditions

A democracy, Argentina is engaged in a program to assert in a definitive manner civilian control of the states. Since its dispute with Chile over Beagle Channel was resolved in 1984–1985, and diplomatic relations with the United Kingdom were restored in February 1990, Argentina has become a member of the international community in good standing. Relations with the United States, first strained in the 1970s in the wake of the fascist government engaged in state terrorism against its own people, and then exacerbated by the United States siding with Britain in the Falkland War, are now well on the mend. The United States lifted sanctions immediately at the conclusion of the Falklands conflict, and Argentina gained Washington's favor when Argentina backed the U.S. position in the Persian Gulf War.

Argentina is a member of Mercosur, the common market among Argentina, Brazil, Uruguay, and Paraguay. A program of biannual tariff reductions has hurt some American exporters to Argentina, who cannot compete with the lower tariffs and the higher transportation costs. There is, however, a significant benefit for American companies with production facilities in Argentina; from Buenos Aires, the markets of Brazil, Uruguay, and Paraguay are now accessible. Conversely, U.S. exporters stand to benefit from economies of scale; one importer in Argentina can receive, process, store, and ship to customers in any of the four countries. As Mercosur unfolds, the most challenging problem will be the coordination of macroeconomic policies among the four nations, particularly Argentina and Brazil, which have disparate inflation and interest rates. Another concern for Argentina stems from its inability to reform bureaucracy and upgrade infrastructure as quickly as desired. Argentine goods remain uncompetitive for most other South American nations but more attractive to Europeans, in part due to the continued devaluation of the U.S. dollar.

Argentina has in place a customs program that includes thirteen trade zones. These are used exclusively to store and assemble transshipments, not only to the other Mercosur members (Brazil, Uruguay, and Paraguay), but to Bolivia and Chile. The trade zones are applicable for goods whose final destination is an authorized destination. Additional information is available from the Argentina Trade Office in New York.

Trade Zone	Export Country
Barranqueras	Bolivia
Buenos Aires	Bolivia, Paraguay, Chile
Concordia	Mercosur Members
Empedrado	Brazil
Jujuy	Bolivia, Chile
La Quiaca	Bolivia
Mendoza	Bolivia, Chile
Monte Caseros	Brazil, Paraguay
Paso de los Libres	Bolivia
Pocitis	Bolivia, Paraguay, Chile
Salto	Bolivia, Chile
San Juan	Bolivia

For American firms, there is a decisive competitive advantage in using a free trade zone while establishing a presence in the Argentine market. Argentine consumers hold a favorable opinion of American goods, and the disparate inflation rates between Argentina and the United States make American goods a bargain. The burst in domestic demand in the 1990s has outstripped the capacity of Argentine producers. American exporters of capital goods have seen sales rise; there is a lag time in getting increased productive capacity on-line, particularly when investor confidence has not been fully restored. The intricate demand of the Argentine business and consumer communities, moreover, has seen a marked increase in the demand for services companies to increase sales, as well.

Argentina is in the process of achieving a sustainable economic prosperity, if present trends continue. The stability brought by Carlos Menem is remarkable; in the short term, capital, technology, and services companies have ample opportunities to establish a significant presence in the Argentine economy.

The greatest opportunities reside in telecommunications, computers, petroleum, and electronic components.

- The privatization of the national phone companies has resulted in a boom as the antiquated telecommunications sector modernizes. With annual growth at a robust 25 percent, there is now a massive program to upgrade, not unlike that seen when Mexico's telephone monopoly was privatized. The market for state-of-the-art transmission stations, switching gears, satellite equipment, and telephone equipment, inclusive of the pen-up demand for cellular and cordless phones, is estimated at $150 million US.

- The economic growth now underway depends on the computerization of Argentine business. A market estimated to surpass $100 million US, Argentine business is introducing computers across the board as part of market-driven reforms designed to make the nation competitive internationally. The small Argentina computer market is growing more than 10 percent annually, in hardware, software, and related accessories and support services.

- The energy demands of Argentina are increasing, and the development of the nation's oil resources are a high priority. The Argentine oil company, YPA, already trades on the New York Stock Exchange, and is expected to experience 15 percent annual growth. The exploration and development of offshore reserves are now underway. A priority for Argentina is the ability to develop adequate refining and transport facilities and distribution networks to market efficiently its oil production.

- The electronic component market is expected to represent a market valued at $75 million US as Argentines refurbish their homes after years of neglect. The harsh conditions of economic life here under a statist military government has long deprived people of modern conveniences. Consumer electronic goods and appliances are growth market sectors.

Argentine consumers are demanding. Years of import substitution have contributed to a preference for local producers, which is only accentuated by a chauvinistic pride born of insecurity. This means that American products can expect to find savvy and demanding consumers who expect value. The opening up of the Argentine economy, and the creation of Mercosur, now afford Argentines what they have seldom had in the past: a choice. They must be courted in a sophisticated manner. But it is worth the marketing effort, for Argentines, among the most well-educated and affluent consumers in Latin America, are loyal and good customers.

Direct investment opportunities are significant as well. The privatization program continues with great enthusiasm. The national airlines, telephone company, and oil leases have been successfully privatized. The government is expected to sell its interests in the petroleum company itself. Information on current privatizations can be obtained by contacting:

> Mr. Juan Carlos Sanchez
> Executive Director, Privatization Administration
> Hipolito Yrigoyen No. 250, 9o Piso
> Buenos Aires, Argentina
> Tel.: (54-1) 331-2823
> Fax: (54-1) 331-5653

Once these stakes are sold, the fiscal current account is expected to be balanced, and the surplus generated can be used to boost reserves, allowing Argentina to increase its money supply in accordance with its current monetary policy. As the century draws to a close, Argentina is well poised to capitalize on its achievements and take a leadership role in South America. It will use Mercosur as the foundation for acquiring a competitive advantage in anticipation of a hemispheric free trade agreement.

Quick Facts on Argentina:

Population: 33,023,000

Ethnic Groups: 97% European, mostly Spanish and Italian

Religions: 92% Roman Catholic, 2% Protestant, 2% Jewish, 4% other

Urban: 86%

Language: Argentine Spanish

Business Language: Argentine Spanish, English

Work Force: 36% industry and commerce; 20% services, 19% agriculture, 25% other

For further information, contact:

> Argentine Trade Office
> 900 Third Avenue, 4th Floor
> New York, NY 10022
> Tel.: (212) 759-6477

> Randy Mye
> U.S. Department of Commerce
> 14th Street and Constitution Avenue, N.W.
> Washington, DC 20230
> (202) 482-1548

BRAZIL

Background

There are two Brazils. The northern and western parts of the country, where the Amazon is located is a vast landscape, where Native Americans, primarily the Tupi and Guarani peoples, live. These are vast territories, mostly uninhabited, filled with amazing natural resources. It is also where the poorest Brazilians live. The other Brazil is the southeastern portion of the country, wedged near Uruguay and Argentina. This is European Brazil, cosmopolitan, industrialized, productive. Brazil is increasingly polarized; the southeastern area would rather split away from the rest of the country, which it perceives as backward and a financial burden. The remainder of this vast country resents the contempt in which it is held. There are also racial lines; southeastern Brazil is Western, and white, while the rest of the country is "Indian" and nonwhite.

This is a far cry from the Brazil of yesteryear. It is easy to forget that in the 1960s Brazil saw itself imperially. Brazilians then were convinced that they would only achieve superpower status if they, like the United States, had access to both the Atlantic and Pacific Oceans. That Bolivia, Peru, and Ecuador stood in the way of this bold vision was a minor detail to be worked out at a future date. Brazilian imperialism—and its strong military—caused alarm among its Spanish-speaking neighbors. In sharp contrast, Brazil is now much more humbled. It has come to know the burden of growth, the demands of a welfare state, the necessity for peaceful coexistence of various peoples in a multicultural environment, and the requirements of a complex governmental and bureaucratic apparatus, and these problems have created divisions among Brazilians. The growing tax burden on the productive southeast has political repercussions; industrial Brazil has tired of subsidizing rural Brazil.

Three cities, Sao Paolo, Rio de Janeiro, and Belo Horizonte, are the industrial engines of the economy. With over 160 million people, Brazil ranks the sixth most populous nation on earth. Two-thirds of all Brazilian people are urban dwellers. Four major ethnic groups constitute Brazilian society: The Native American Tupi and Guarani peoples; the descendants of the Portuguese who settled the country; the Africans who were brought over as slaves and raised the nation through their labor; and waves of mostly European and some Asian migration. The Portuguese and Africans intermarried with Native Americans, and waves of Europeans have intermarried with the Brazilians, which has transformed this country into a rainbow of hues, a nation of intriguing and beautiful people unlike any other. The diversity of the Brazilians astounds, as does the vitality of immigrant cultures. The largest Japanese community outside Japan, for instance, is in Sao Paolo.

The result is spectacular. Brazil has evolved into a truly American society, with achievements in the arts and music, literature and theater, cinematography and religion. The intermingling of cultures and races has given rise to a dynamic society, which stands in sharp contrast to some of its neighbors, which in comparison are stagnant. Nowhere else on earth have European and African traditions coexisted in such harmony. The segregation found in other societies is markedly absent; tolerance is greater, although class and social differences remain profound and far-reaching. The recent manifestations of intolerance and tension have as much to do with latent racism as with the perceived differences among Brazilians and the contributions different segments of the population make to the nation.

Conflict, however, is part of Brazil's history. Although settled by the Portuguese rather than the Spanish, the tragedy of turmoil is the same as throughout Latin America. Brazil lived under a constitutional democracy for about forty years until a military coup in 1930 brought General Getulio Vargas to power. He ruled until 1945, when civilians regained control of the country. The period of civilian rule, however, lasted fewer than twenty years. In the early 1960s Brazil, under Joao Goulart, experienced a period of increasing inflation rates, economic stagnation, and political unrest. These problems led a group of military officers to stage a coup, and on March 31, 1964, Army Marshal Humberto Castello took over the country. Brazil then entered into a period of military rule—Castello was succeeded by Army Marshal Arthur da Costa (1967–1969), who was succeeded by General Emilio Garrastazu (1969–1974), who was succeeded by General Ernesto Geisel (1974–1979), who was succeeded by General Joao Figuei-redo (1979–1985). The military leaders displayed little tolerance for op-ponents: Brazilians were expelled, banned, and arrested. The military attempted to instill discipline throughout the whole of society. Not sur-prisingly, Brazil, whose national motto on its flag reads "Order and Prog-ress," enjoyed consistent economic growth. It might not have been a fun place to live, but Brazilians were too busy working to think about com-plaining.

There are limits to everything, including excess. After an entire gen-eration, the limits of what a military regime can do had been reached. General Figueiredo began a process of national reconciliation. Political parties were allowed to organize, and banished leaders were permitted to return. A process to return the country to sanity—and civilian rule—was begun. In 1985, Tancredo Neves became president. When he fell mortally ill soon after taking office, his vice-president, Jose Sarney, succeeded him as president. The military slowly returned to the barracks during this time, and the return to civilian rule was complete when Fernando Collor be-came president in 1989, after the first direct presidential elections in Bra-zil in twenty-nine years. The return of civilian rule was accompanied by the return of the kind of shenanigans that alarmed the military two de-cades previously: scandal, corruption, and disorder. Brazilians, it seemed, were eagerly making up for all those years of having behaved themselves. The Collor administration was marked by scandal after scandal, tabloid news story after tabloid news story. It all ended rather sadly for Fernando

Collor. Charged and tried for corruption, he has been largely discredited and is the object of ridicule among his countrymen.

Fernando Cardoso, who became president in 1995, on the other hand, has made it the centerpiece of his government to demonstrate to the Brazilian people—particularly those who live in barracks—that civilians are capable of managing the affairs of the nation in a responsible manner.

Economic Model

Between 1968 and 1973 the Brazilian economy grew at an average annual rate of 11 percent. This period of economic expansion and industrialization is referred to as the "economic miracle" that the military leadership was able to mastermind. After 1973, growth slowed until the country stagnated in 1981. Nevertheless, the achievement was real and remarkable. In less than a decade, industrial development transformed the southeastern portion of the country, allowing for the systematic improvement in the standard of living of the Brazilian nation. The most notable shortcoming, in fact, lay in the inequitable distribution of income. A few Brazilians were becoming incredibly wealthy while the vast majority remained in dire poverty.

The success of these military governments also lay in Brazil's unbelievable natural resources. Half of Brazil, which is equivalent in size to almost the entire United States, is covered with forests, the Amazon being the largest tropical forest habitat in the world. Fully a third of Brazilians are employed in agriculture and, with the exception of wheat, Brazil is one of the few countries in Latin America that is self-sufficient in food. Indeed, Brazil is the worlds' leading exporter of some commodities, such as coffee and orange juice concentrate, while being an important supplier of cocoa, soybean, sugar, and cotton. Another area where Brazil takes a leadership role is in hydroelectric power generation. Over 90 percent of Brazil's electricity is provided by hydroelectric plants, most notably the Itaipu Dam on the Parana River and the Tucurui Dam in Para. At the same time, in cooperation with Germany, Brazil is developing a nuclear program; the first power plant, Angra I, began operation in 1982. The nation counts on vast mineral resources, including tin, chromite, bauxite, cooper, zinc, nickel, lead, tungsten, and gold. There are also vast deposits of low-grade coal. The development of Brazil's oil reserves continues to lag; Brazil is a world leader in alternate fuel sources, such as the development of sugarcane-derived alcohol fuel.

The return to civilian rule has reinvigorated efforts to develop sustainable growth through a market economy. This has proved elusive. Periods of hyperinflation undermine confidence in the economy, and currency—several currencies—has had to be replaced. The effects of the Mexican crisis in 1995 sent shock waves through Brazilian markets. The political turmoil shook confidence in the prospects of Brazilians. Nevertheless, the transition of power was able to take place and Brazil's monetary policies have, in the past two years, been sound. The confidence of the nation, as well as in the Brazilian Real, continues to strengthen, and foreign capital is returning.

Political and Market Conditions

Brazil became independent from Portugal on September 7, 1822. The United States is Brazil's largest trading partner. Since the 1960s the Brazilian economy has diversified and its trade relations are extensive, including Europe, Japan, the Middle East, and Latin America. Because of its economic position, Brazil has been at the forefront of fostering relations among the countries of Latin America and in promoting greater economic integration. The United States, however, remains Brazil's crucial commercial partner. While relations have been friendly, the area of greatest conflict between these two countries stems from Brazil's unwillingness to extend intellectual property protection to some products, specifically computer software products. This, coupled with cumbersome import licensing procedures and a system of quotas for computer hardware, has created tensions that culminated in 1988 and 1989 when the United States implemented retaliatory steps against Brazil. Trade negotiations addressed these concerns, including Brazil's own complaints against high U.S. tariffs encountered by Brazilian products, such as orange juice. A series of agreements resolved most issues, although negotiations on outstanding bilateral matters continues on an ongoing basis.

The scandal under Fernando Collor, however, created so much tension within Brazilian society that he was forced to resign. Vice-President Itamar Franco assumed the presidency at a time when the economy continued to be unstable. A familiar pattern of hyperinflation gripped the economy and it appeared that Brazil would be unable to escape the boom-and-bust cycles so common in Latin America. Fernando Cardoso, a sociologist and member of the Franco cabinet, designed an anti-inflation program. The Plan Real would replace the currency, realign fiscal and monetary policies, and deliver a shock to the economy. Implemented in June 1994, when inflation for that month alone stood at 45 percent, the Plan Real proved successful. By December of that year inflation was down to 2 percent for that month, and Brazilians counted on a currency with purchasing power.

It is no surprise that in that fall's election Fernando Henrique Cardoso won. On January 1, 1995, there was a peaceful transition of power. In his address to the nation President Cardoso declared that with the "opening of the Brazilian economy, we are leaving behind xenophobic attitudes." It came at an opportune moment, for on that same day tariffs among the Mercosur countries were eliminated on over 95 percent of the goods traded. Brazil now has virtually unlimited access to markets in Argentina, Uruguay, and Paraguay, consistent with Mercosur agreements. The Cardoso administration has been quick to signal to the international community its commitment to open markets. In March 1995, Brazil announced it would allow private investment in the oil, mining, and telecommunications sectors, thus reversing a half century of control by the state in these areas.

The response has been formidable. The Tequila Effect notwithstanding, Brazil is well poised for a period of sustainable growth. The Cardosa administration is determined not to follow in the steps of Mexico and politicize its monetary and fiscal policies. The opportunities in the Brazilian economy, too, are alluring on their own and difficult to resist. The vitality of the fundamentals of the Brazilian economy are nowhere more in evidence than in the announcements made by General Motors and Volkswagen. In the spring of 1995, in an impressive vote of confidence, General Motors announced plans to invest $1.2 billion US in Brazil to meet growing domestic Brazilian demand. Volkswagen, too, announced a $2.5 billion US program to double its Brazilian production and make Brazil the center for its worldwide truck operations. In 1994 the Brazilian economy grew 5 percent and the Cardoso administration expects growth rates between 4 and 6 percent per annum for the remainder of the century.

The opportunities for American companies in Brazil are enormous. The commitment to a market economy is significant, and the ability of civilians to demonstrate to the military that they are capable of administering the affairs of state is crucial to the strengthening of democratic institutions in Brazil. That an elected president was able to resign and his successor was able to complete the term, and then pass power to another civilian is a remarkable achievement of which Brazilians can be proud. That a viable economic program has been implemented that has arrested runaway inflation and put the nation on a sound economic sounding is promising. The economic integration now under way among the Mercosur countries, coupled with the confidence of the international community and the ability of Brazil to withstand short-term liquidity crises resulting from the Mexican Meltdown, are reassuring. Corporate America has an important role to play in Brazil's future.

Quick Facts on Brazil:

Population: 161,025,000

Ethnic Groups: Portuguese, Italian, African, Japanese, German, Tupi, and Guarani

Religions: 89% Roman Catholic, 11% other

Urban: 75%

Language: Portuguese

Business Language: Portuguese, English

Work Force: 40% services and government, 35% agriculture, 25% industry

For further information, contact:

> Embassy of the United States of America
> Avenida das Nacoes, Lote 3
> Brasilia, Brazil
> Tel.: (55-61) 321-7272
> Fax: (55-61) 225-9136
> Telex: 061-1091 and 61-2318

> U.S. Consulate
> Avenida Presidente Wilson, No. 147
> Rio de Janeiro, Brazil
> Tel.: (55-21) 292-7117
> Fax: (55-21) 220-0439
> Telex: 21-22831

> U.S. Consulate
> Rua Padre Joao Manoel, No. 933
> Sao Paulo, Brazil
> Tel.: (55-11) 881-6511
> Fax: (55-11) 852-5154

> Embassy of Brazil
> 3006 Massachusetts Avenue, N.W.
> Washington, DC 20008
> Tel.: (202) 745-2700

> Larry Ferris
> U.S. Department of Commerce
> 14th Street and Constitution Avenue, N.W.
> Washington, DC 20230
> Tel.: (202) 482-3871

CHILE

Background

Forty percent of Chile's population lives in Santiago, the capital. The Chileans are of Spanish descent, with significant waves of immigration from England, Ireland, and Germany. The southern provinces—Valdivia, Llanquihue, and Osorno—have a marked German influence; the south-central area is where the Native American Mapuche people live, near Temuco. Eighty-four percent of Chileans live in urban centers and are very Westernized in their thinking and customs. The mineral-rich northern provinces have been the object of Chilean expansion, which has resulted in conflicts with Peru and Bolivia. The War of the Pacific (1879–1983) among Chile, Peru, and Bolivia saw the loss of territory by both Peru and Bolivia, with Bolivia losing its outlet to the sea, thus becoming a land-locked country with a navy. Animosities between Bolivia and Chile culminated when, after a century of negotiations proved futile, Bolivia broke diplomatic relations with Chile in 1978. There is also an intense regional rivalry with Argentina; Chileans are quick to make derisive comments about Argentina, in no small part from the fact that Buenos Aires is considered more glamorous and sophisticated than Santiago. A more serious manifestation of this rivalry is seen in the boundary dispute between the two nations, which festered until 1985 when Pope John Paul II oversaw mediation.

These conflicts are part of the familiar pattern we see among the transplanted European nations in South America. As is to be expected, waves of immigrants from Europe in the nineteenth century and the early part of the twentieth resulted in a considerable working and middle class that grew prosperous from the exploitation of Chile's enormous natural resources. The country's oligarchy then confronted an educated—and monied—urban population that was increasingly dissatisfied with the status quo—a status quo that favored an elite. In the 1920s the fragile representative democracy became unstable as reform policies sought to establish a welfare state and assert workers' rights. Not unlike the social reform programs in Europe, Chileans sought to establish a more equitable distribution of wealth and to design a social welfare program for the entire population.

These efforts met with frustration and the country degenerated into chaos, which resulted in General Carlos Ibanez exercising a dictatorship in everything but name from 1924 to 1932. In 1932, a representative democracy and constitutional procedures were restored, and the Radical Party ruled for the next twenty years through a series of coalition governments. It was during this time that Marxist and socialist ideas won favor at a grass-roots level. The role of the state continued to increase in the economic life of the nation, albeit with greater fervency in urban centers than in rural ones, where conservatives enjoyed great influence. The vast mineral and forestry wealth of the nation allowed for a comfortable standard of living for Chile during this period. Populism grew, culminating with the election of Eduardo Frei as president in 1964. A member of the Christian Democrats, Frei embarked on an ambitious program to provide education, expand housing, and reform the agricultural sector. The social programs he implemented pleased no one; the Left believed they were not enough, and lamented the failure to unionize agrarian workers; the Right believed them to be excessive and that they constituted an intrusion of government in the lives of citizens.

Chileans were galvanized, and in 1970 Salvador Allende, a Marxist member of the Socialist Party, was elected president. The Allende administration then launched a series of initiatives that alarmed many Chileans. It was during this time that private industries, including the banking system, were nationalized. Massive land expropriations followed, as did the nationalization of American interests in Chilean mines. The inability to win majority support in the Congress, coupled with the narrow nature of his election victory, denied Allende a clear mandate for his Marxist program. As a consequence, Chile degenerated into economic and political turmoil. There were mass demonstrations against Allende in the streets, severe shortages of consumer goods arose, food supplies to the capital were disrupted, and strikes virtually shut the country down. The National Congress censured the president as Chile became polarized amid economic crisis.

What proved most destructive, however, was the nationalization of ITT's interests in the Chilean telephone company. Alarmed by the precedent Chile had set, ITT prevailed upon the Nixon administration to prevent "another Cuba" in Latin America. That some in the Nixon White House had close ties with ITT facilitated a dialogue and, in an alarming sequence of events, the United States, through the CIA, engaged in a campaign to destabilize Chile. A disinformation campaign was implemented, secret deals were made, and Allende's opponents were encouraged. This campaign culminated with a military coup on September 11, 1973, that brought General Augusto Pinochet to power.

A wave of violence then descended upon Chile as thousands of perceived enemies were systematically arrested or "disappeared." Not unlike Argentina, Chile launched a war on its own people, terror was used as authority, political parties were banned, press censorship prevailed, and the country became a military state. American officials grew alarmed at the viciousness and extent of violence that swept through Chile. Ironically, when ITT's role in the destabilization of Chile was revealed, it faced a massive public relations problem in the United States. In a desperate attempt to restore its credibility, ITT sponsored an insipid children's television program, "Big Blue Marble," designed to teach American children about children in other countries and how nations should live peacefully. The role the Nixon White House and ITT played in overthrowing the government in Chile set the background for future adventures—and misadventures—in Latin America when Ronald Reagan became president. For Chileans, however, there was little peace in the sixteen years that General Pinochet terrorized his nation.

On December 14, 1989, in Chile's first free elections since 1970, Patricio Aylwin won. A Christian Democrat, Aylwin ran as part of a seventeen-party coalition, and he was permitted to assume office in March 1990 on the condition that General Pinochet remain commander-in-chief of the armed forces. Since taking office, the process of restoring democratic institutions has been underway, and market-driven reforms, introduced by

General Pinochet, continue. Although years of repression have left a noticeable mark in Chilean public life, the economics are the most promising aspect of life in this country. It has now been two decades that Chile
has been dismantling its statist development model and introducing market reforms. The civilian rulers remain cautious, however, for fear that if
they anger the military, their days in office will be limited. Governing out
of fear and not out of moral authority has its own perils, which is not lost
on many corporate officers.

Economic Model

Few countries are as blessed with a combination of natural resources
and small population as is Chile. Throughout most of its history the ruling
oligarchy—and then elite, both civilian and military—has enjoyed a luxurious existence. Under General Pinochet market reforms were implemented that were masterminded by students—and disciples—of Milton
Friedman of the University of Chicago, hence the term, "Chicago Boys."
The economic growth of the past two decades—as much a result of the
Chicago Boys as the efficiency of the military ones—has resulted in a
mature middle class, confident of its place in society and demanding the
right to participate in the economic life of the nation.

The overthrow of Allende led to a period of extreme difficulty. Not only
were the generals encountering problems with the learning curve—running a barracks is far easier than running a country—but this came at a
time when the prices of copper collapsed and the price of oil surged. A
recession followed and it was then that General Pinochet allowed the Chicago Boys to implement an austere monetarist reform program. The object was to reduce inflation and facilitate the dismantling of the statist
economic model. Market reforms were introduced, tariffs were cut, controls on capital goods were lifted, and foreign investors were welcomed
back. Price controls were lifted and a massive privatization program was
implemented. The only exception, which angered the most ardent advo-
cates in the private sector, was that the government retained control of
CODELCO, the large copper mining and refining firm. The process of
creating consensus was facilitated through state terror—those who raised
their voices in opposition soon found their throats slashed.

Lip service support for General Pinochet, however, became real when
these policies began to bear fruit. The Chilean economy began to grow
at an enviable 7 percent annual rate, and inflation was curtailed. Prosperity returned to the country, and so did most middle-class aspirations.
A worldwide slowdown in the early 1980s, however, had severe consequences for Chile. This is consistent with small countries that depend on
exports of raw materials. The prices for copper and forest products suffered a significant downturn, and Chile began to borrow heavily to sup-

port its living standard and the peso-dollar exchange rate. Disparate levels of inflation now made Chilean goods expensive on world markets, and a financial crisis followed. A recession threatened to become a depression in 1982 as the government found it necessary to intervene and take over several large banks and confront mounting discontent with the growing number of unemployed, while renegotiating its foreign debt with international lending bodies. The prosperity General Pinochet brought was unsustainable precisely because it was a prosperity centrally controlled by the government.

The IMF designed an austerity program that included a revaluation of the Chilean peso. The benefits derived from the 1982 devaluation were further magnified by higher worldwide growth rates. That world prices for commodities recovered helped Chile service its foreign debt obligations. General Pinochet's break with the austerity program prior to elections also spurred growth. Chile, in essence, learned that market reforms are only successful if they are complete. It makes no sense to have a market-driven economy if the exchange rate is manipulated for political reasons. This is fundamentally the same mistake that Mexico under Carlos Salinas would make a decade later; it politicized the exchange rate at a time when it was moving toward a market economy.

Chile's Chicago Boys, moreover, proved to be clever and innovative. Chile has been at the forefront of using debt-for-equity swaps to reduce the public debt burden. That the central bank is now autonomous is welcome, for it augers well for the long-term prospects of the country. The continued reductions in the foreign debt has made it easier for the Aylwin administration to continue reforms, which include modernizing the banking system. Chile continues to develop a close working relationship with the IMF, as well as with American officials. As a result, the strong economic growth of the second half of the 1980s is continuing well into the 1990s. It is not without irony that it was precisely this success that made it more difficult for the generals to remain in power; a flowering middle class has greater confidence in its ability to seize its own destiny and dispense with the patronizing nature of military governments.

Political and Market Conditions

Chile gained its independence from Spain on September 18, 1810. Its odyssey since then has been intriguing. The return of Chile to democratic rule in 1990 has been instrumental in normalizing relations between Chile and the United States. The 1976 car-bomb assassination in Washington, D.C., of a former Chilean ambassador to the United States further strained relations between Washington and Santiago. In subsequent years, the resolution of this crime—the United States is adamant about foreign governments engaging in terrorism on American soil—has been pivotal in restoring full bilateral relations between the two countries.

Despite these problems, the United States and Chile have long maintained vigorous trade. Indeed, Chile is scheduled to become the next country included in NAFTA now that Mexico has agreed to Chile's inclusion. This is a welcome development, and evidence of hemispheric integration; Mexico severed diplomatic relations after General Pinochet's coup and only restored them with the return of a civilian president. The volume of U.S.–Chilean trade, moreover, is significant. The United States purchases almost half of Chile's agricultural exports—mostly fruit—while providing over a third of Chile's imports—mostly consumer goods. Chile's mining industry earns about half its foreign currency. With over 20 percent of the world's supply of copper, Chile counts on stable world prices to make its financial calculations. The state-owned CODELCO produces 1.2 million metric tons of copper, most of which is processed into refined or blister copper. These, in addition to exports of gold, silver, iodine, iron ore and natural nitrate, present Chile with a dilemma: The export of raw materials creates uncertainty about foreign exchange earnings.

For this reason, since the abandonment of an import-substitution economic development model after 1973, Chile has been successful in increasing efficiency and spurring industrial development. With a growing middle class and an educated work force, Chile is in a position where its domestic industry is efficient enough—and the exchange rate sufficiently reasonable—to permit it to begin to export. Manufacturing now accounts for almost a quarter of the gross domestic product, and the efficiency of domestic industry has reduced dependence on imports. To attract foreign investors, there are few barriers, and foreign firms with a presence in Chile are afforded the same protection as domestic ones. With the exception of certain agricultural products, most notably wheat and sugar, Chile has fewer nontariff barriers than almost any other country in Latin America.

The openness of the economy, and the prudent course followed by the Aylwin administration, has won the confidence of the international investing community. Chile was the beneficiary of $1.1 billion in foreign investment in 1990 and enjoys a trade surplus. The restructuring of its debt maturities was welcomed by international banks. The continued strengthening of copper prices on world markets has allowed the current government to balance its budget. Rationalization of fiscal policies continues, and transfer payments to Chilean social programs comes from the proceeds of CODELCO, one reason why the privatization of this giant seems unlikely within the short or medium terms.

Chile has efficiently managed its exchange rate for over a decade. A crawling peg between the Chilean peso and the U.S. dollar is adjusted monthly. Differentials between the domestic inflation rates of Chile's major trading partners and the United States are analyzed, and adjustments are made to assure relative parity—the Chilean peso has therefore become neither overvalued nor undervalued, eliminating price distortions or disruptions occasioned by sudden devaluations. At the same time, parallel market and interbank interest rates float between a managed band. The result has been one of tremendous stability. Chile continues to consolidate its growth, strengthen its democratic institutions, and embark on a program of free trade with its neighbors.

The opportunities in Chile are tremendous. While not a member of Mercosur, it is working toward integration into NAFTA, thus suggesting the versatility of that trade agreement for the hemisphere. American firms can also count on fair treatment in the Chilean market, economic stability, and a sophisticated consumer. The problems encountered throughout the years of military rule are being resolved. On a human level, the emotional scars of the "disappeared" victims whose fates remain unknown haunts the Chilean soul, as does the ominous presence the generals continue to play in the background. At the same time, Chileans remain very sensitive to their status in Latin America; they are regretful of their unresolved disputes with Bolivia and Peru, and are envious of the attention lavished on Buenos Aires. This is one reason they remain a nation apart, more eager to forge closer ties with Mexico and the United States than with their own neighbors. If present trends continue, however, all these misgivings should vanish; Chile offers many opportunities.

Quick Facts on Chile:

Population: 13,689,000

Ethnic Groups: 60% European, 40% mestizo

Religions: 89% Roman Catholic, 11% Protestant

Urban: 84%

Language: Spanish (92%), Mapudungun (4%)

Business Language: Spanish, English

Work Force: 34% industry and commerce, 30% services, 19% agriculture, 17% other

For further information, contact:

> Embassy of Chile
> 1732 Massachusetts Avenue, N.W.
> Washington, DC 20036
> Tel.: (202) 785-1746

> Roger Turner
> U.S. Department of Commerce
> 14th Street and Constitution Avenue, N.W.
> Washington, DC 20230
> Tel.: (202) 482-1495

North America–Chilean Chamber of Commerce
220 East 81st Street
New York, NY 10028
Tel.: (202) 288-5691

PARAGUAY

Background

Paraguay offers the most homogenous population of any of the periphery countries. Although a Native American presence no longer remains as distinct, neither does an entirely European one. Paraguay, then, is an entirely American society, emerging from the blending of the Spanish and Guarani Indians. Through intermarriage and centuries of history, Paraguayan society offers an example of the natural evolution of a distinct society. Ninety percent of the people understand the Guarani language, and a smaller percentage are fluent in Spanish as well. Spanish remains the official language of business, with English widely understood.

Paraguay's history is as familiar as it is tragic. The first half of this century was characterized by the Chaco War, a civil war that went on intermittently amid dictatorships, coups, and countercoups. Complete chaos tore asunder this country in waves of violence and madness. General Alfredo Stroessner took power in May 1954 and ruled in a reign of terror until 1989, when he himself was overthrown by General Andres Rodriguez. The brutality of the military regime was complete and devastating for the nation. With little history or experience in democracy, and with weak democratic institutions, Paraguay offers a fragile civilian government, unsure and uncertain. The traditions of the Guarani Indians, as well as Spanish feudalism, however, have given rise to a culture that nurtures communalism and subsistence. With an annual per capita income of just over $1,400 US, Paraguay is a nation of impoverished consumers. That Paraguay remains an economy based on agricultural exports—often characterized by wild price fluctuations—has made it difficult for the government, whether civilian or military, to develop and implement a development program. The average Paraguayan's life is one of hardship and deprivation.

The consistent inability of Paraguay to make progress is disturbing. Indeed, only through cooperative ventures with other countries, as with the construction of the Itaipu hydroelectric project with Brazil, has Paraguay been able to make significant strides. It is expected that when the Yacyreta hydroelectric project, a joint venture with Argentina, is complete, Paraguay will become the largest exporter of hydroelectric energy in the world. The reform program currently underway seeks to establish greater cooperation with Paraguay's neighbors and to nurture a more enterprising culture. The continued dependence on the export of raw agricultural products undermines long-term growth and development. The lack of democratic experience, and the time required to recover from decades of political oppression, render Paraguay the saddest member of the periphery countries.

Economic Model

Apart from ruling through terror, there has not been a consistent policy in Paraguay. Dependent on the world market for its agricultural products, burdened by a significant foreign debt, encumbered by a population lacking in experience in participating in a modern economy, in many ways Paraguay is only now emerging from its Dark Ages. It only became officially independent from Spain in May 1961, while in the grips of a military dictatorship—as Spain was then. Independence has been of little comfort; Paraguay's backwardness is evident in the fact that its capital, Asuncion, was the only South American capital city without nonstop commercial aviation service to the United States until the spring of 1995.

Reform has come slowly, and often by the will of fate. A record harvest of cotton and soybeans in 1989 meant a good year. The elimination of a three-tier exchange rate that same year introduced an element of rationality into the economy. In recent years, debt renegotiations with foreign creditors, particularly Brazil, Germany, and Japan, have lessened Paraguay's foreign debt obligations. Growth in key industries—sugar, cement, and wood products, most notably—has granted the nation breathing space.

At the same time, Paraguayans remain poor. Their purchasing power is minuscule compared with that of their neighbors. The economy still lacks a coherent plan for sustainable development. The people have a long way to go developing the institutions and traditions necessary for a market-driven economy to prosper over a period of time. It is ironic that Paraguay's development has been fast enough to warrant phasing out of the Agency for International Development's bilateral assistance program, but not sufficient to develop a middle-class consumer. A visitor to Paraguay is shaken by the feeling that the people are walking around dazed, not entirely recovered from some trauma. It is an apt description, for Paraguay remains numb from decades of terror. For corporate America, there is little that Paraguay offers, other than a marginal export market for consumer goods, computers and peripherals, electronic components, medical and scientific instruments, and telecommunications equipment. Basic industry is only now developing and only the most fundamental products have a market. That Paraguay is a member of Mercosur further reduces the reasons for establishing a direct presence in the country at the moment; the market can be satisfactorily served from offices in Brazil or Argentina.

Political and Market Conditions

The American Embassy in Asuncion reports that under civilian rule Paraguay is making significant progress in democracy, human rights, and drug interdiction. Progress on the economic front is lagging. This is in part attributable to the role state-owned companies continue to play in the nation's economic life. Almost half of all sales are accounted for by state-run companies, the largest of which are ANDE, ANTELCO and PE-TROPAR, the electric, telecommunications, and oil refinery state-owned monopolies, respectively. As a consequence, the private sector lags far behind, rather liberal foreign investment laws on the books notwithstanding. The mentality of the Paraguay bureaucrat is reminiscent of that of the East European Communist official of the sixties and seventies. There is a culture of lethargy and indifference that is hard to dispel, particularly when there is little incentive to do so.

Not all is bleak. To its credit, Paraguay has a fair system for evaluating bids when awarding contracts. American companies can best participate in the Paraguayan economy by selling to a state monopoly. Paraguay is desperate for new technologies and for improving its technical capabilities. U.S. exporters are actively encouraged to meet with procurement officials and make presentations on their products. International bids are welcome for most procurement contracts and construction work. Following is a list of the state monopolies active in awarding international procurement contracts:

Administracion Nacional de Electricidad (ANDE) (electric utility)
Calle Padre Cardozo No. 360
Asuncion, Paraguay
Telex: 142 PY ANDE

Administracion Nacional de Navegacion y Puertos (ANNP) (National Navigation and Ports Administration)
Plazoleta Isabel la Católica
Asuncion, Paraguay
Telex: 790 PY ANNP

Administracion Nacional de Telecommunicaciones (ANTELCO) (National Telecommunications Company)
Calle Alberdi
Asuncion, Paraguay
Telex: 178 PY ADMGRAL

CORPOSANA (water utility)
Calle Jose Berges No. 516
Asuncion, Paraguay
Telex: 172 PY CORPOSANA

Entidad Binacional Yacyreta (EBY) (Yacyreta hydroelectric plant)
Calle Humaita No. 145
Asuncion, Paraguay
Telex: 268 PY YACYRETA

Entidad Binacional Itaipu (Itaipu hydroelectric plant)
Casilla Postal 691, Calle de la Residenta No. 1075
Asuncion, Paraguay
Telex: 176 PY ITAIPU

American investment in Paraguay is encouraged and welcome. It is based on the principle of national treatment, and Paraguay is taking concrete steps to make itself more attractive to foreign capital. At this time, however, most investments would entail ventures with the Paraguay government. In 1989, for instance, Texaco entered into a joint venture to explore for oil in certain areas of the country. Other American companies have begun to export to Paraguay government entities. There is little direct investment in plant and equipment. The most compelling areas for direct investment are in the agricultural sector and in servicing the growing hydroelectric production facilities. Whether an open market economy can be created that takes advantage of the opportunities Mercosur offers—and whether democratic life survives—remains the litmus test that will win investor confidence. For the moment, therefore, the climate for extensive direct investment remains as tenuous as Paraguay's move to democracy.

Quick Facts on Paraguay:

Population: 5,081,000

Ethnic Groups: 95% mestizo (mixed Spanish and Guarani Indians)

Religions: 97% Roman Catholic, 3% other

Urban: 47%

Language: Guarani, Spanish

Business Language: Spanish, English

Work Force: 44% agriculture, 34% industry and commerce, 18% services, 4% other

For further information, contact:

Embassy of Paraguay
2400 Massachusetts Avenue, N.W.
Washington, DC 20008
Tel.: (202) 483-6960

Randy Mye
U.S. Department of Commerce
14th Street and Constitution Avenue, N.W.
Washington, DC 20230
Tel.: (202) 482-1548

URUGUAY

Uruguay is an intriguing country precisely because it defies the standards seen throughout Latin America. A country with a low birth rate that has seen the emigration of almost 20 percent of the population over the last two decades, Uruguayans are a mature market. Although a quarter of the people of Uruguay are of Italian descent, unlike Argentina, Spanish culture and heritage predominates. There are few Native Americans. Montevideo is the only large city in the country; the remainder of the country is dotted with towns and villages. The population is educated and literate, but this has not prevented a continued decline in the nation's standard of living. While acceptable by Latin American standards, that almost one in five Uruguayans has moved to Argentina or Brazil is compelling evidence of the underdevelopment of the national economy, which is particularly alarming when one considers that it is the youth of Uruguay that continue to emigrate. As a result, the government vigorously supports free trade and market reforms as a way to reverse the continuing decline of Uruguay.

Background

A small nation wedged between the two giants of Brazil and Argentina, Uruguay has been the object of desire by Spain and Portugal during the colonial period, and then by Argentina and Brazil in modern history. The struggle for much of this century has been to defend and preserve a sense of independence and foster a national identity. The civilian governments in the first half of this century implemented ambitious programs to create a welfare state coupled with continuing social and political reform. Import substitution and a statist model predominated at times, which served the country well, to a point. The familiar limits of a centralized program became evident in the 1960s, and Uruguay entered a period of increasing economic and political turmoil.

This culminated with a coup in 1973 when the military closed the Congress and established a military state. A reign of terror descended upon this nation for a decade. Not until 1984, when Julio Maria Sanguinetti assumed the presidency, did civilians return to office. In the following presidential election in 1989 Luis Alberto Lacalle won. Since taking office in 1990 he has concentrated on economic reforms, the centerpiece of which is Uruguay's participation in Mercosur. President Lacalle has implemented a classical reform program: reducing public spending, pursuing a sweeping privatization program, and reforming the state bureaucracies and labor laws.

These reforms have not been universally embraced. This decade in Uruguay has been characterized by significant opposition to President Lacalle's efforts to pass through labor reforms and privatize state-owned enterprises. The abandonment of a statist development model has introduced an element of uncertainty, as is inevitable in market-driven economies, which continues to encounter opposition. Labor protests continue, particularly since the Lacalle administration wishes to end labor's unlimited right to call a strike. That Uruguayans are of an older median age further frustrates reform efforts, given that most voters lived through the Great Depression and remain enamored with the ideals embodied in programs similar to the New Deal in the United States. While minimal, the possibility of military intervention remains credible, more so than in other Latin American countries.

Economic Model

Uruguay's development strategy is to fuel economic growth through exports. Its industry accounts for just under a quarter of the nation's gross domestic product. Agriculture accounts for about 12 percent. Industry, however, is closely linked to its agricultural output. Uruguayan agriculture produces beef, wool, and grains, along with fruits and vegetables. Its industry is centered on its impressive cattle and sheep, which number over forty-five million head. Manufacturing of leather products such as shoes, handbags, and other consumer leather goods; meat and fish processing; textiles; and hides constitute the bulk of Uruguay's industrial base.

Uruguay is presently engaged in a program to foster economic diversification and maximize exports, now that Mercosur has made the markets of its neighbors more accessible. That Uruguay is burdened with the highest per capita foreign debt in Latin America is one reason for the urgency in the Lacalle administration's initiatives to increase exports. A firm proponent of hemispheric integration and free trade, in recent years Uruguay has also begun to pursue its activities aggressively through its trade offices in Europe, the Middle East, and Africa. The government is striving to reduce domestic inflation—which approached 100 percent in 1992—in order to qualify for lines of credits and loans from the IMF and the World Bank. The political realities of the nation, however, have made it difficult to push through proposals to accelerate certain privatization programs and reform labor and social security agreements.

Uruguay is seeking closer ties with the United States, which is made easier by Washington's enthusiastic welcome of the return of civilian rule. That under the military regime Uruguay's strict banking secrecy laws were used for drug trafficking and money-laundering activities has been of special concern to the United States. In recent years Uruguay has steadily cooperated more fully to curtail these kinds of activities, while working with U.S. officials on developing a debt-reduction program. Washington's unequivocal support has been used by the Lacalle administration to persuade critics at home. Uruguay expects to be able to liberalize trade and accelerate economic integration with Washington's full support.

Political and Market Conditions

Uruguay gained its independence from Spain on August 25, 1825. Its economy is largely centered on livestock production. Most service industries, with the exception of insurance, which remains a legal monopoly of the state, face few restrictions. There is a significant offshore banking industry, encouraged by Uruguay's secrecy laws, and there are significant capital in-flows from Brazil and Argentina. The crushing foreign debt, however, has made it difficult to sustain economic growth. The continuing emigration of Uruguay's youth further exacerbates a delicate problem; fewer workers are expected to service foreign debt obligations and provide for a large, aging population.

The average Uruguayan's disposable income fares unfavorably with his American counterpart, which places severe limits on the kinds of consumer products that can be exported to Uruguay. For American companies, the opportunities are interesting, but not compelling. Direct investment in the agricultural and livestock industries, as well as banking, are in order, but the relatively small number of Uruguayans and the accessibility of this market though the other Mercosur members suggest that a more prudent course of action is to export to Argentina or Brazil and serve the Uruguay market from these locations. The structural problems Uruguay encounters are medium term; until the emigration of Uruguay's youth is reversed, there will not be dynamic economic growth in this country. Corporate America can well make a significant contribution to Uruguay's growth, and benefit from active participation in the Uruguayan economy, but it is paramount that the brain drain be reversed. The success of Uruguay lays in reclaiming its citizens living abroad and in further economic integration with its neighbors. The conflicts inherent in shifting the nation's budgetary priorities are common and well understood by most citizens of the industrialized world. The familiar crowding out—public expenditures versus private investment—undermines Uruguayan democracy. But there is no alternative if a market economy is to be availed upon to improve the standard of living of the Uruguayan nation. Labor and social security reforms, although politically risky, are necessary if the foreign debt is to be brought down to a manageable level. Without progress on these fronts, Uruguay faces an arduous task in the years to come.

Quick Facts on Uruguay:

Population: 3,159,000

Ethnic Groups: 90% European, 7% mestizo (European and Native American), 3% black

Religions: 66% Roman Catholic, 2% Protestant, 2% Jewish, 30% nonprofessing or other

Urban: 89%

Language: Spanish

Business Language: Spanish, English

Work Force: 22% industry and commerce, 20% government, 17% commerce, 13% agriculture, 28% other

For further information, contact:

Embassy of Uruguay
1919 F Street, N.W.
Washington, DC 20006
Tel.: (202) 331-1313

Roger Turner
U.S. Department of Commerce
14th Street and Constitution Avenue, N.W.
Washington, DC 20230
Tel.: (202) 482-1495

6

THE CORE COUNTRIES: BOLIVIA, COLOMBIA, ECUADOR, GUATEMALA, MEXICO, PERU

The historical and economic processes that have shaped Latin America represent a differentiation of strategies when conducting business in these markets. The core countries are fundamentally different from the periphery countries, with the mainland Caribbean nations exhibiting elements of both, thus constituting hybrid nations. The subtle nuances should be considered market niches, such as differences in the Spanish used in Chile as opposed to Argentina, or the perceptions of Native American culture in Mexico City as opposed to Lima. Most important, however, are the sweeping differences between core and periphery countries that together constitute structural elements from which the societies of these nations have emerged and presently evolve. These are broad-based general themes running through these societies and, of course, there are many individual variations. Nonetheless, taken together, the four differences discussed below represent philosophical differences that constitute mileposts throughout these countries and alter marketing strategies.

NOTION OF SELF

Latin Americans from the core countries are burdened with inferiority complexes. They are unsure of their origins and do not understand their place in the world. This is a pity, for it is sad to think that so many people fail to understand that their humanity is sufficient; no one need apologize for genealogy. In the core countries, tremendous energy is expended in claiming a European heritage and in looking, dressing, and acting in a

Western manner. The unsure smile, the easy intimidation, the quick apology all betray the continuing insecurities of people plagued by an irrational and lingering inferiority complex. It is very difficult for Americans to understand the psychological repercussions. In the United States, for instance, it is the children of mixed-race couples, such as Amerasians, who in many cases feel it necessary to "decide" about with which race they identify. For Latin Americans of the core countries, however, the choice is more agonizing because of the connotations associated with being "Indian." To lay claim to a European heritage is to distance one's self from the "savagery" of the "Indian." Witness the neurosis of Mexican painter Frida Kahlo. The daughter of a German Jew and a Mexican mother, Frida Kahlo's life represented ambivalence on many levels. Her decision to embrace the Native American heritage of Mexico was the source of scandal in her time, as was her open acceptance of her own bisexuality. She remains the exception; Latin American women aspire to look like New York sophisticates, not Native American peasants. There is nothing an American businessman can do about any of this, apart from being aware of these Latin American preoccupations and sensibilities. Throughout the core countries, a great amount of theater is involved in efforts to assuage the inferiority complexes. American businessmen must therefore be prepared to indulge nonsense, nonsense required nonetheless to soothe fragile egos.

These issues are absent from the lives of Latin Americans from the periphery countries, for the most part. This is due to the absence of Native American people—in Argentina, for instance, less than a fraction of 1 percent of the population has Native American blood—or these societies are entirely New World products, such as Paraguay, where both European and Native American cultures have assimilated to form a new culture, or Brazil, where the marginalization of Native Americans to the vast tropical forest frontiers and the intermingling with Africans have created a singular society. The confidence of lineage in, say, Argentina and Chile, has done much to ensure that the development of these countries began, first as transplanted Europeans, and then as wholly American societies. There is much to the familiar observation that the Mexicans descended from the Aztecs, the Peruvians descended from the Incas, and the Argentines descended from—ships. To descend from a ship is to arrive from Europe. And the baggage of the Europeans weighs heavy on the periphery countries. While Mexican Frida Kahlo manifests the neurosis of an identity crisis, Argentine Eva Peron displays European psychosis. The crusading zealousness, the overpowering fascism—of the Left and of the Right—the intolerance born of competing claims are all hallmarks of the tragic histories of the Europeans. Latin Americans know who they are, but there is little comfort in knowing who one is if one only knows one is predisposed to insanity. I recall sitting at a beautiful outdoor cafe in Buenos Aires adjacent to the Recoleta cemetery—such a juxtaposition betrays the European flair for the morbid—when a thunderous explosion ripped through the city. A car bomb had gone off somewhere. Amid the chaos of sirens swelling the shocked population, that this kind of terror struck Buenos Aires is not evidence of underdevelopment. On the contrary, it occurred to me that being in Buenos Aires was exactly like being in Europe—I might as well have been sitting at an outdoor cafe in Madrid or Rome. As descendants of Europeans—who descended from ships—the madness of Europe is as much a part of their lives as are the refinements of Europe. The periphery countries are New World European societies, which does not necessarily offer much solace to the American businessman.

NATURE OF CIVILITY

The secure act differently from the insecure. The inferiority complexes of the people of the core countries have given rise to a culture of consumerism obsessed with superficial status symbols. The confidence of the periphery countries, in contrast, leaves the people here less prone to fall prey to coarse displays of wealth. Latin Americans from the core countries aspire to civility, not sophistication. Latin Americans from the periphery countries, on the other hand, discern the shades of cosmopolitanism. It is enough for a Mexican to know the fundamentals of dinner wines, but an Argentine is expected to be able to distinguish among dessert liqueurs. Among Argentines, for instance, cosmopolitanism forbids such "vulgarity," as Argentines see it, often looking at Mexicans with condescending attitudes that reside in the fact that Mexicans have Native American blood, and are darker skinned. This is not to be confused with civility, as Americans understand civility, however. This is Argentina, after all. This is a country that, less than a generation ago, had a government that was kidnapping its own citizens, drugging them unconscious, and throwing living people off low-flying airplanes into shark-infested waters as a way of dealing with political opponents. To be civilized does not preclude being immoral or criminal. To be sophisticated does not mean one cannot be corrupt, or evil. That one's aspirations for civility are realized does not preclude betraying decency. Latin Americans of the periphery countries, like the European ancestors that nurtured them, are masters of betrayal.

PHILOSOPHICAL WORLDVIEW

It is one thing to deal with businessmen and businesswomen from periphery countries and quite another to deal with those from core countries. For Americans, the periphery countries, by and large, make more sense. These nations are of European origins, and the European worldview is something with which Americans identify. An Argentine businessman is more understandable to an American executive than a Mexican one. The reason this is so resides in the nature of the historical and cultural processes that have shaped the evolution of the core countries. The presence and incorporation of so many distinct Native American cultures changes the equation by throwing unfamiliar variables into play. Mexico, for instance, remains an enigma to Americans, at times shrouded in romantic idealism, and always feminine, which is to say, mysterious. American executives, time and time again, dwell on the sun-drenched beaches, the splendid fishing, the vibrant and exciting cuisines, all of which seduce: golf, fish, and have pitchers of margaritas amid the lush, tropical surroundings.

The illusion is often a delusion, hiding a certain hesitance about the nature of Latin America. It is with some trepidation that Americans move forward, and often they misinterpret fundamental aspects of the core countries. This kind of culture shock, to use the widespread phrase, is not limited to males. Consider, for instance, the differences between two American women in Mexico, making observations about the same phenomena. In *Mexico,* Alice Adams writes:

In one of our guidebooks, hitherto highly reliable, we came across this intriguing sentence about Merida: "Nowhere else in the country, for instance, do you hear so many men giggling." Quite fascinated by this possibility, Janet and I were both alert for giggling men, but we observed none, nowhere—not in restaurants or parks, nor on the streets, nor on the bus that we took to the Museum of Popular Arts. And we wondered: If this is true, and Merida men indeed do giggle a lot, how did the writer of the guidebook know about it? Where is all this alleged giggling done? In Spanish, *giggle* is expressed by two words, a phrase that literally means "to laugh in a silly way"; I asked the maid in our hotel if many local men did that (feeling very silly myself at the question), and that somewhat somber lady said no, not in her observation.[1]

Alice Adams writes for the *New Yorker* magazine and is by no means an unintelligent woman. But in quoting from the *American Express Pocket Guide to Mexico* guidebook, she betrays an ethnocentric parochialism that is sweet in its naïveté. Not unlike many American executives who first arrive in Latin America, her observations betray a cultural misunderstanding of the forces shaping the cultures of core countries. Contrast her with another American woman, Dorie Reents-Budet:

During the first week of the Cerros project [a Maya site in Belize], the men working with me excavating the temple on top of the largest pyramidal mound began calling me "Na-chem" and "Cayuco," and then commenced giggling. I knew something was going on, yet it took me a while to comprehend their cleverness. Having remembered that punning is an integral part of Maya culture, I realized that they had transformed my name "Dorie" into "dory," the English word for "little boat." From there, they crossed language boundaries to "cayuco," which is Spanish for "little boat," and then moved to Yucatec [Maya] with "Na-chem" or ["]lady canoe"![2]

Here we have someone who, sensitive to the cultural context of where she happens to be, understands the nuances of the reality of the place. When Alice Adams searched in vain for the giggling men, the giggling men found Dorie Reents-Budet. There is a lesson here. And it is about the dangers of appearing naive, which is to say weak, to one's Latin American counterparts.

THE ROLE OF MODERNITY

In societies where there are significant influences from non-Western cultures, there are conflicts, not only within the individuals who make up these societies, but also in the institutions. The presence of "Indians" throughout the core countries is a source of controversy. These peoples are resented, misunderstood, and devalued. They are resented because in their failure to assimilate, they set themselves apart, rejecting the domi-nant societies in which they live. Just as the counterculture movement in the 1960s throughout the United States gave rise to conflicts—If you don't like the American system, then move to Russia, many hippies were ad-vised—in the core countries there are similar sentiments—Take that bas-ket of fruit off your head and get a job, "Indians" are often made to understand. There are many areas of misunderstanding. The number of Native American peoples overwhelms, and their diversity in culture, lan-guage, and customs astounds. Latin Americans who live in the core coun-tries are fascinated by these "Indians" they understand so poorly. The core countries are anthropologists' dreams, and in the same way that Americans spend an enlightening hour in front of the television watching some documentary on some exotic people somewhere far away, Latin Americans in the core countries do the same, only the people in the documentaries are not that far away. The resentment and misunderstand-ings give rise to contempt. "Indians," by not assimilating, are not part of the market economy. The cost of providing, however inadequate it may be, education, health care, and food (through price controls, subsidies to producers, or cash grants to disenfranchised communities, or a combi-nation of all three) are borne by those who are assimilated, who do work, who pay taxes.

The political economy of the core countries requires transfer payments and the transfer of purchasing power from the productive to the nonpro-ductive, as these terms are defined by market economies. Mexican and Guatemalan businessmen, for instance, bristle at the sight of "Indian" women camped out on the sidewalks of the fashionable avenues of their respective cities, and are embarrassed that their efforts to portray their nations as modern to outsiders is undermined in such a devastating way. The notion of progress, to many intellectuals and ordinary citizens alike, is not served by having floating populations of peoples not very much interested in participating in, or contributing to, the nation's life.

But the system of paternalism required to effect these subsidies entails authoritarian hegemonies. In the case of Mexico, the ruling PRI has striven to institutionalize "revolutionary" zeal as a way of ensuring performance of the social obligations required by entire communities who, by asserting their identity, freely choose to become disenfranchised from the modern world. As Richard Rodriguez writes, in *Days of Obligation*, "the Revolution parted to reveal . . . Marx *ex machina* . . . a political machine appropriate to the age of steam. . . . [I]t gave Mexico what Mexico needed most, the stability of compromise."[3]

This is, as seen through the eyes of the West, the fundamental challenge of the core countries: to impose order upon savages by taking care of people incapable of taking care of themselves. The irony, of course, is that there lies within each person some savagery, the darker side of the human nature. For the majority of people—mestizos and whites alike—who live in the core countries, a subconscious issue is that of identity and self-esteem. It is one thing to say one's ancestors brought civilization to the barbarian tribes of Europe; it is quite another to see impoverished "Indians" carrying on as impoverished "Indians" are wont to carry on, and associate one's self with that. The presence of "Indians" in contemporary life is a reminder of a family's black sheep who refuse to be forgotten. Thus comes the enormous identity crisis and frail ego of the Latin American, part conqueror, part conquered, wishing to absolve himself of responsibility by indulging the notion of victimization, and blaming others— the Spaniards once, and now the Americans.

Apart from the issues of economic burden and perceptions from the public, Native Americans are part of the lives of core countries. On an individual level, the vitality of Native American culture flourishes throughout the core countries, while languishing in the periphery countries, including the United States and Canada. The dilemma for Latin Americans of European descent, which is to say Latin American businessmen, is to examine the nature of heritage. Whereas Americans must see an animated film to be reminded of Pocahontas, in Mexico City stepping out of a five-star hotel on Paseo de la Reforma one sees a Oaxacan woman sitting on the sidewalk selling rag Indian dolls in her image. For most Americans, as well as Europeans, the memories of our own origins are distant. All these issues have been resolved across the centuries and with the emergence of what we flatter ourselves by calling "civilization."

For the Latin American of the core countries, however, these issues remain unresolved. The conquest of Mexico, Guatemala, Colombia, Peru,

Ecuador, and Bolivia, for instance, may have taken place half a millennium ago, but there remain many unresolved issues. These revolve around the nature of what civilization means, and questions of race. The Mexican Meltdown of 1995 is evidence of the frail self-esteem of Latin Americans of the core countries. As if confronting a duality within themselves—the Civilized European versus the Savage Indian—the image of self is fragile. Latin Americans equate "savagery" with poverty, thus the relentless obsession with status symbols—cellular phones, European clothes, private schools, luxurious cars, vacations—that give rise to a culture of consumerism. Critics often focus on the immature nature of these habits; Latin Americans do not save because they do not have the discipline for delayed gratification, the argument goes. But this is an incomplete assessment. In the core countries there is an obsession with proving oneself a member of the middle class, which is compelling, given that the specter of poverty lingers on virtually every street corner. Walking past the exclusive boutiques of Mexico City's Polanco district, for instance, offers no immunity from the sight of impoverished Native Americans begging on the street corners. Add to this the negative self-image of the Latin American, and consumerism takes on a perverse air: One may never look like a fashion model gracing *Vogue* magazine, but a diamond-studded Rolex offers some comfort. Latin Americans equate materialism with civility.

History is on their side. Throughout the ages, acquisition—of things, of knowledge, of achievement—is a hallmark. In the nineteenth century, France attempted to install a throne in Mexico. A Hapsburg archduke, Maximilian, who was graced with an intriguing combination of idealism and wisdom, arrived in Mexico City to rule over a land no one had ever been able to rule. The result is often a distorted self-image. The authoritarianism of the core countries, with its multitudes of impoverished, illiterate, and manipulated peasants, is different from the dictatorships that befall the periphery countries. Societies with direct European roots, periphery societies live out the traumas brought over from Europe; old dramas in a new theater where socialism, capitalism, fascism, communism, and so on unfold. That these countries, particularly Argentina, Brazil, Chile, and Uruguay, have duplicated the conflicts of Europe on American soil, makes the differences between core and periphery countries clear. The authoritarian rule in Mexico is fundamentally different from the dictatorships of Chile. In Mexico, authoritarianism is the glue that holds an invented nation together, and therefore becomes the means through which power and force, if not legitimacy, are institutionalized. In Chile, there are democratic institutions and aspirations in places that may be temporarily undermined by the power grab of the military bent on protecting the nation as it deems necessary. But whereas in Mexico the whole political structure is based on institutionalizing force, in Chile dictatorship is an intrusion on the democratic process. Soldiers occupying civilian positions are no longer entirely soldiers but they are not true civilians. There are tremendous pressures on the military hierarchy when the defined roles are altered in unexpected ways. Mexican officials who, before the privatization programs of the early 1980s began, used to run enormous state-owned firms relished their power and the privileges conferred upon them. This is in stark contrast with Chilean military officers who were thrust into civilian posts after General Augusto Pinochet overthrew civilian president Salvador Allende in September 1973. A decade into his rule, the Chilean telephone company was run by General Ivan van der Wyngaard.

In the 1980s a regional Baby Bell wanted to sell some equipment that was too outdated for America but was appropriate for the needs of Chile. It was astounding to participate in the series of meetings held when General van der Wyngaard visited the United States to conclude the deal. A young man who knew little of the telecommunications industry and relied on his advisors, both civilian and military, he was uncomfortable with the task assigned him. The meetings went well, but there was a sense of embarrassment on the general's part, a reluctance to engage in conversation or discussion, perhaps because of his reluctance to engage in these meetings at all. The extent of his discomfort was easily masked by the question of language and the presence of interpreters. After two days of meetings and site tours, we took a break and in informal conversation I found out that the general was a cycling enthusiast. I told him I knew of a number of excellent cycling shops in the city. We made an appointment to spend half a day shopping, rescheduling subsequent meetings. It was quite an experience, driving around town under police escort to various cycling shops, buying bicycles and cycling equipment. It turned out to be a splendid afternoon, and more was accomplished buying helmets and cycling shorts than meandering around the corridors of the telephone company. In that informal setting the general revealed his misgivings about military rule in his homeland. The stiff and awkward man in exhaustive meetings vanished and a charming officer revealed himself. He expressed the desire for civilians to return to power, which is not uncommon among professional military men thrown into civilian posts. He spoke of his dissatisfaction with the interruption this period of military intervention represented for the development of the country, as well as his own career. He was affable, a good man thrust into a difficult situation by unfortunate circumstances. The general's visit continued as planned and he returned to Santiago as scheduled. There is an awkwardness in military dictatorships, an uneasiness about their role in society. The stronger the democratic institutions of a nation, the more professional a military they have. The Chilean general was a well-educated, well-read man of great integrity. This cannot be said of the so-called generals of authoritarian governments, where professionalism is not a priority. The discomfort within the military of periphery countries at exercising authority in civilian positions creates the need for the return of civilian rule. This stands in sharp contrast to authoritarian regimes, where power is the end in itself. The difference between authoritarian core countries and dictatorial periphery ones is that in the former the players wish to retain power and in the latter the military officers wish to relinquish it. In the least developed core countries, like Guatemala, there is an intermingling of authoritarians and the military through oligarchial families; authoritarianism wears the mantle of a military state. In these countries, however, the military is not very professional, but merely thugs with weapons. Periphery country military leaders are aware of the distortions their power grabs inflict on societies; core country authoritarians are not.

The insecurities can be as annoying as they are compelling. It is unfortunate—and not without pathos—the way Latin Americans from the core countries continue to apologize for their existence. An American oil executive with extensive experience in Mexico and Ecuador, two core countries, observed, "My job is to sell pipelines, not conduct self-esteem seminars or provide psychological counseling. And I'm a little tired of being told whose relatives arrived on what galleon in the seventeenth century."

But galleons are important; Latin Americans, for many reasons, discount their Native American heritage and claim Europe as their origin. Emperor Maximilian was bemused by it all, commenting that he had failed to realize that "there are more nobles in the City of Mexico than in the whole of Europe." And this obsession with pedigree continues as this century draws to a close. Richard Rodriguez, a celebrated American writer of Mexican ancestry, reports: "My aunt . . . sent me a list of names, a genealogy braiding two centuries, two continents, to a common origin: eighteenth-century Salamanca. No explanation is attached to the list. Its implication is nonetheless clear. We are . . . of Europe. We are not Indian."[4] But this is presumptuous on his part. His aunt's intentions may reflect the limits inherent in two different traditions. Europe has a written history whereas the New World has an oral one. In the same way the ancient Greeks had oral traditions that transmitted history and mythology from generation to generation, so did the peoples of the New World. It is far easier to hand down pieces of paper than oral stories, particularly when, as in the case with Mexico, for instance, there are fifty-six Native American groups who spoke over one hundred languages. It may very well be that his aunt has records of ocean crossings aboard ships, but has none about land migrations in the distant past. Oral traditions vanish in the wind; written ones can be locked away in a room. That history has been recorded in the Spanish language, and on paper, is an accident of history, and does not necessarily betray the bias Richard Rodriguez infers.

There is no denying, however, that there is a definite shame associated with Native American cultures. The reason for this resides in two perceptions. The first is the assumed savagery of the Native American peoples. The Native Americans were militarily defeated, and in many cases succumbed to disease. For the Europeans of the time this was evidence of weaker constitutions and inherent inferiority. Then there was the shock and horror European sensibilities felt at certain aspects of Native American societies: human sacrifice, cannibalism, and body sacrification (the ritual mutilation [usually scaring] of the body for aesthetic or religious purposes), among other things were not the hallmarks of European civilization, or civility. (That the Europeans engaged in equally appalling practices made no difference; standards are established by the victors.) The second perception is one of physical beauty. For all protestations to the contrary, the classical standards of beauty first celebrated by the ancient Greeks and Romans and then glorified by the Renaissance, hold sway around the world. These Western standards, which do change over time, fill the media, and the minds of people around the world. The waistlines of Renaissance and Victorian females, for instance, have changed with contemporary icons, but the facial features and physical characteristics have not. In the same way that women in the West aspire to unrealistic standards, so do the people of Latin America. But it is one thing to be a blond, blue-eyed American woman with an eating disorder, and quite another to be a Latin American woman with an eating disorder—with non-Western physical characteristics.

Race is a very complicated issue in core countries. It has given rise to peculiar cultural predispositions. Mexicans and Guatemalans, for instance, are obsessed with pedigree. Colombians denigrate the contributions of their Native American peoples. Peruvians and Ecuadorians deny the contributions of the indigenous civilizations. In Mexico, this kind of self-hate has, for instance, given rise to the peculiar Mexican perverse obsession with Europe. The height of Mexican arrogance is to make known, with grand fanfare, that one has just returned from an extended sojourn through France.

For American corporate officers working with Latin America, it is enough to be aware of these problems. In the same way that in the United States I have found it necessary to bring to the attention of an administrative assistant that her bulimia was interfering with her work performance because she was spending too much time away from her desk, so has it been necessary to devise strategies to minimize time wasted in hearing Latin Americans apologize for their pigmentation. One successful strategy is the preemptive strike: Praise the vitality and beauty of your host's nation's diverse cultural legacy and the singular nature of the resulting society. Another is to discount all knowledge of any unpleasant aspects of pre-Columbian history.

No American arrives in London and inquires if his host's ancestors were barbarians who impaled children in the ninth century. No American should arrive in Mexico City and ask if his host's ancestors ripped out the beating hearts of sacrificial victims. "A Berkeley undergraduate approached me one day," Richard Rodriguez writes, "creeping up as if I were a stone totem to say, 'God, it must be cool to be related to the Aztecs.' " Perhaps it is, through American eyes; it isn't to Mexicans. And the Peruvians bristle at being thought of as Incas, as do Guatemalans at the notion of being Mayans. Throughout the core countries to be "Indian" is to be a "savage." For all their protestations to the contrary, and for all the monuments raised to the Native Americans, racism rules throughout the core countries. This is as much a result of open contempt for "Indians" as it is a manifestation of the perceived historical goal of rescuing the landscape—geographic, social, and political—from "savagery."

The core countries have failed miserably to reconcile the antagonism inherent in resolving conflicts found within individuals and within societies. It can be argued that the haunting doubt has been appeased, somewhat, through religion. Richard Rodriguez notes: "The image of Our Lady of Guadalupe . . . is more wonderful election to Mexicans than any political call to nationhood. [Mexico] has no political idea of herself as compelling as her icon."[5] This is far different in periphery countries, especially in Argentina and Chile where Native Americans are so scarce that they are a curiosity. But in countries like Mexico, there is an obsession with the question of modernity. Octavio Paz, the official apologist for Mexico's authoritarian hegemony, explains it this way: "The meaning of traditional Mexico's opposition to the modern world . . . cannot be understood if one forgets that Mexico came into being during the Counter-Reformation. It is an essential difference: the Americans were born with the Reformation; we, with the Counter-Reformation."[6]

The meaning of traditional Mexico's opposition to the modern world cannot be understood if the Counter-Reformation itself isn't understood by Mexicans. This is not to suggest that there are no Mexican intellectuals of stature. Enrique Krauze, arguably, is an intellect of international consequence, but since Mexico is encumbered with anti-Semitism, it is impossible to envision circumstances under which he could be the voice of Mexico, however qualified he may otherwise be for that role.

There is another reason that is more insidious. At times, caught up in the frenzy of the demands of business, it is easy to lose sight of the bigger picture. In Latin America, one of the great themes is the nature of fascism. There are two kinds of fascism. There is fascism of the Left and fascism of the Right. Mexico and Cuba are examples of fascism of the Left, where liberalism gone mad creates nightmare states where human rights are violated and citizens enslaved to the hegemony of the state. Chile and Argentina, when the generals take over, are examples of fascism of the Right, where run-amok military men attempt to live out perverse fantasies, such as genocide against the Jews, with relentless passion. The ideological diatribes of Octavio Paz constitute the framework within which patrimonialism unfolds, and the democratic aspirations of Latin Americans are denied. Both kinds of fascism are best avoided; not only are they morally repugnant, they are also bad for business.

Thus stuck with Mr. Paz, Mexico is relegated to the sidelines of contemporary culture. Indeed, a more profound understanding of the Counter-Reformation is found in the words of Paul Tillich:

> The Counter-Reformation was not simply a reaction, but a real reformation. It was a reformation insofar as the Roman Church after the Council of Trent was not what it was before. It was a church determined by its self-affirmation against the great attack of the Reformation. When something is attacked, and then reaffirms itself, it is not the same. . . . The medieval church [which is to say the Catholic Church] was open in every direction, and included tremendous contrasts, for example, Franciscans and Dominicans (Augustinians and Aristotelians), realists and nominalists, biblicists and mystics, etc. In the Counter-Reformation many possibilities which the Roman Church had previously contained were shut off.[7]

Thus, modern Mexico, blinded by its anger at the "Indians," nurtures tremendous resentment against Native Americans. The role of modernity in the lives of these people is still being defined. For American businessmen, the core countries are the most difficult to truly understand precisely because they are the most exotic nations of Latin America.

BOLIVIA

Background

Bolivia is the poorest country in South America. The majority of the Bolivian people are subsistence farmers who live in poverty. The population growth is kept in check through an appalling method: high infant mortality. It is estimated that a quarter of all children born in Bolivia die before reaching the age of five. This is a nightmare country. Approximately 60 percent of Bolivians are Native Americans, of the Aymara and Quechua nations. An additional third are mestizo, meaning of mixed Native American and European ancestry. Only about 10 percent of Bolivians are of European descent. There are other small communities scattered throughout the country; Japanese and Mennonites near the Santa Cruz area, Lebanese Christians and South Koreans near La Paz.

It is difficult to understand how a country that has so many natural resources—Bolivia is about the size of Texas and California combined—is so desperate. During colonialism Bolivia supplied the world with its silver; the richest mines in the world were located in Potosi. During Spanish rule, Bolivia was governed from Lima, Peru, and called "Charcas." After independence was achieved on August 6, 1825, the country was named after Simon Bolivar, the liberator of South America. Independence, far from bringing prosperity and stability, only wrought destruction. A rapid succession of governments—coups and countercoups—was the manifestation of a desperate attempt to control the wealth from the Potosi mines. Indeed, the whole of the country was in such turmoil that when war broke out with Peru and Chile, Bolivia lost its access to the Pacific. The War of the Pacific (1879–1884) not only rendered this the only land-locked nation in the hemisphere, but deprived it of vast nitrate fields lost to Chile. Continuing disputes between these two countries—water rights over Rio Lauca remain unresolved—contribute to acrimonious relations to this day. A subsequent war with Paraguay—the Chaco War (1932–1935)—served to discredit the then-rulers.

But there is an important lesson here in the nature of wealth. How is it possible that one of the richest nations in the world has come to this? For the people of Bolivia, silver has been a curse, and the greed it inspires has been a damnation. Observers have noted that, in some ways, Bolivia is a moral lesson in the nature of greed—and in the importance of the individual. The lessons in the writings of Ayn Rand seem to be proved out by Bolivia; wealth resides in the human mind, which can create, not in the material, which can be squandered. In the same way that the heirs of Cornelius Vanderbilt have squandered a vast fortune, so too have Bolivians turned to nothing the riches of Potosi, the world's wealthiest city.

It is a sad fact that Bolivia only enjoyed one brief period of stability and prosperity. At the turn of the century, a rebound in the price of silver and the ruling oligarchs protected their interests in the nation's mines. For about thirty years the mine owners ran the country, effectively excluding the Native Americans and working classes from the nation's political and economic life. Bolivia's defeat by Paraguay in 1935, however, undermined the credibility of the ruling oligarchy. So did the worldwide Great Depression. The Nationalist Revolutionary Movement (MNR) began to benefit from increasing support. When it was cheated out of a rightful victory in 1951, Bolivia descended into turmoil that culminated in the 1952 revolution. Victor Paz emerged as president, introduced universal suffrage, nationalized the largest mines, and carried out extensive land reform.

The military intervened twelve years later when it ousted Victor Paz at the beginning of his third term as president. A series of military juntas ruled the country for twenty-one years. One leader during this time, Hugo Banzer, who governed between 1971 and 1974, was successful in bringing economic growth to the country, even though this prosperity was short lived and excluded the majority of Bolivians. When Victor Paz took office—after runoff elections in 1985—Bolivia was in deep economic turmoil. Hyperinflation was running at 24,000 percent—meaning that prices on most items were rising several times *each day*—and it was impossible to print currency with sufficient zeros as quickly as necessary. The incoming Paz administration implemented a shock program.

This brought about stability, but when the prices of tin collapsed on world markets in October 1985, Bolivia confronted serious economic problems once again. Jaime Paz became president in August 1989 and, although a Marxist philosophically, he has approached problem solving in a rather pragmatic way. The classical economic policies consistent with most stabilization programs are embraced by the government, and great strides have been made in making Bolivia if not prosperous, then at least bearable. The elimination of price and currency controls and an anti-inflationary campaign have brought inflation to under 20 percent per annum, a remarkable achievement.

The United States maintains constructive engagement with Bolivia. This is designed to strengthen the democratic institutions, while enlisting Bolivian cooperation in the war on the drug trade. Bolivia accounts for almost 40 percent of the world's coca production and is a major source of the cocaine that flows to the United States. Aid to Bolivia remains dependent on this nation's cooperation with the United States.

Economic Model

It is hard to imagine what kind of development strategy Bolivia has followed for most of this century. The systematic plundering of the nation's mineral wealth by a handful of families is not an economic policy; it is a travesty. The succession of coups and countercoups reveals the viciousness and savagery of human greed. It is only since 1985 that a coherent, cohesive, and rational economic policy has been designed and implemented. Bolivians are eager to join the community of civilized nations, which includes a formal economy.

The results are very much in evidence. Whereas in 1987 Bolivian exports totaled $570 million US, by 1990 they had climbed to over $900 million US. Of American exports to Bolivia, which totaled $190 million in 1991, over half were related to the mining equipment sector. The stabilization in the prices of silver and tin have helped Bolivia enjoy some semblance of stability. Bolivian consumers, however, remain far poorer than their Latin American neighbors and the demand for consumer goods continues to be limited. For corporate America, therefore, the key markets remain those associated with mining, agriculture, and the upgrade of the nation's infrastructure. Telecommunications, electrical energy generation equipment, road and railroad construction, computers, and medical equipment are all vital areas of strong growth in Bolivia.

Political and Market Conditions

The current administration of Gonzalo Sanchez Lozada is committed to market reform. The Sanchez administration enthusiastically endorses free trade and the expansion of regional trading blocs. There are problems, however, with achieving these goals. The Bolivian government accounts for over 70 percent of the nation's economic activity. Given that Bolivian law requires firms submitting bids for government purchases to be legally established under Bolivian laws, it is imperative that American firms either have local subsidiaries or be represented by import firms or sales agents. The laws concerning sales to government entities are complicated. American firms are advised to seek representation from established agents. Following is a list of agents:

> Crown Agents
> Saint Nicholas House
> Saint Nicholas Road
> Sutton Surrey SM1 1EL
> United Kingdom
> Tel.: (44-81) 643-3311
>
> Crown Agents Services Ltd.
> 910 Ponce de Leon Blvd.
> Suite 601
> Coral Gables, FL 33134
> Tel.: (305) 448-9866
>
> Crown Agents
> Avenida 20 de Octubre No. 2475
> P.O. Box 11393
> La Paz, Bolivia
> Tel.: (591-2) 39-0696
>
> C3D International
> 27 Rue Louis Vicat
> 75738, Paris, France
> Tel.: (33-1) 4638-3475
> Fax: (33-1) 4638-3482
>
> C3D
> Calle Hermanos Manchego No. 2571
> La Paz, Bolivia
> Tel.: (591-2) 27-9428
> Fax: (591-2) 39-1614

Opportunities are increasing at a remarkable pace. The Sanchez administration is in the process of implementing an ambitious privatization program; everything from mines to airlines are up for sale. The liberalization in the exchange rates—and the elimination of currency controls—

allows for the free movement of capital into and out of the country. The investment law passed in September 1990 is among the most liberal in the world and has increased the confidence of foreign investors. The American embassy in La Paz can provide the most current information on the reform programs in Bolivia. The address follows:

Embassy of the United States of America
Edificio del Banco Popular del Peru
Calles Mercado and Colon
La Paz, Bolivia
Tel.: (591-2) 25-0251
Fax: (591-2) 35-9875
Telex: AMEMB BV 3268

Bolivia is a medium- to long-term market for consumer goods. American companies in the areas described above can make an immediate contribution to the nation's development, but for most consumer and retailing goods the market is relatively small. Bolivia can be better served from Argentina, which maintains the following free trade zones for the Bolivian market: Barranqueras, Buenos Aires, Jujuy, La Quiaca, Mendoza, Paso de los Libres, Pocitis, Salto, and San Juan. While Bolivia is making significant strides in establishing the foundation for sustainable growth, these are only the first steps on a long road.

Quick Facts on Bolivia:

Population: 7,500,000

Ethnic Groups: 48% Native American, 39% mestizo (European and Native American), 12% European

Religions: 96% Roman Catholic, 4% other

Urban: 50%

Language: Quechua (37%), Spanish (35%), Aymara (24%), other (4%)

Business Language: Spanish, English

Work Force: 50% agriculture, 20% services, 30% other

For further information, contact:

Embassy of Bolivia
3014 Massachusetts Avenue, N.W.
Washington, DC 20008
Tel.: (202) 483-4410

Paul Moore
U.S. Department of Commerce
14th Street and Constitution Avenue, N.W.
Washington, DC 20230
Tel.: (202) 482-1659

COLOMBIA

Background

The two perceptions of Colombia are of coffee and cocaine. A successful advertising campaign in the United States has implanted the image of Colombian coffee as this nation's primary export. The continuing war on drugs, on the other hand, has placed this South American country at the center stage of violence. Drug cartels, whose immense economic power astounds, flaunt their power, undermining Colombian democracy and stability. The vast amount of cash—which is laundered through the international banking system, thereby corrupting the business communities here, in neighboring Latin American countries, and in the United States—is compelling in the power it wields throughout the affected societies. Gabriel Garcia Marquez, Colombia's Nobel Laureate in literature and the unofficial spokesman for the country, lamented that "the notion of easy money is Colombia's worst problem."

The temptations have been hard to resist, and the result has been the accumulation of power and violence in the hands of a small elite. Upon taking office in June 1994, Colombian President Ernesto Samper Pizano argued that the nation "must increase social spending so that there is no Chiapas in Colombia." The articulation of such a priority sent the message that the armed rebellion in the south of Mexico had its origins in the desperate situation of rural people, who are often tempted to enter the drug trade for the promises of easy money Garcia Marquez decried. Such goals, however, remain only goals. In March 1995 the Clinton administration denounced Colombia's failure to be more forthcoming in international efforts to combat the drug trade. President Clinton lamented that Colombia had become "the world's primary cocaine producer." The other image, of Colombia as a coffee exporting giant, remains very much a part of the nation's self-image. Coffee constitutes a symbol of nationalism, which is why its role in the economy is overemphasized. The recent rebound in the international price of coffee masks a structural problem: the National Federation of Coffee Growers dictates a quota system that in effect subsidizes Colombian coffee growers.

Perceptions are misleading. The American view that Colombians are all drug dealers is as inaccurate as is the image that coffee is Colombia's primary export. Behind the headlines lies reality, a reality that is far sounder and more reassuring than would otherwise be believed. Colombia is not a lawless place held hostage by drug lords. It is a sophisticated country, engulfed in a vexing problem, but not at all entrenched in the drug trade. There is a strong industrial foundation, and the prospects for the country are bright. Recent oil finds stand to make Colombia an important oil producing nation. Although democratic institutions are strained by violence—law enforcement officials, including judges, are the targets of terrorism by the drug cartels—it remains a democracy. This alone speaks volumes of the resolve of the Colombian people to stand their ground and not fall to the violence of the drug lords.

Economic Model

In June 1994, Colombia, Mexico, and Venezuela met to continue discussions on creating a free trade zone among the three countries. The incoming Samper administration made it clear that recent market reforms would continue. "The opening has been done, we are not going to review the tariffs, we are not going to close to foreign investment," Samper stated. The move to a market-driven economy is a continuation of policies in place for twenty years. Since the 1970s, Colombia has diversified its economy by moving away from the import-substitution development model that had characterized the country since the 1950s. The diversification of exports—cement, flowers, rice, cloth, coal, yarns, sugar—has contributed to an invigoration of the economy through growth in these nontraditional export markets. While dependent on the export of coffee for foreign exchange earnings, the economy has been characterized by the availability of "narco-dollars," creating a parallel economy of sorts.

This presents its own series of problems for the economy, and it distorts the official figures concerning the income levels of Colombians. The country counts on four industrial centers, Barranquilla, Bogota, Cali and Medellin, which include the textiles, food processing, construction, paper, chemicals, petrochemicals, iron, steel, metalworkings, and cement industries. The nation's natural resources of coal, iron ore, petroleum, copper, and nickel are used to satisfy domestic needs and exported. The diversification of the economy has been successful. Of all Andean nations, Colombia is the most industrialized and prosperous. The distortions, and violence, related to the drug cartels undermine stability, however. This is a consistent pattern since this country's independence from Spain on July 20, 1810.

Political and Market Conditions

Colombia continues to provide American companies with tremendous opportunities. Colombia imports wheat, transportation equipment, electric generators, aircraft, and steel. Recent finds of low-sulfer crude oil now stand to make Colombia a major supplier in the near future. British Petroleum, in a joint venture with three partners, has begun a $7 billion US investment to develop and exploit these reserves in Tauramena. An investment of this size not only strengthens Colombia's ability to develop its economy, it also emboldens civilians to wage the continuing battle to rid Colombian society of the lawlessness of the drug trade.

The elimination of import licensing requirements has increased trade between Colombia and its major trading partners. The initiation of free trade with Venezuela and Mexico—which has been hampered by each of these nation's economic crises—has set the course for greater regional economic integration; fully 98 percent of imports now enter Colombia under the prevailing free import regime. Restrictions do apply in certain areas, most notably in the mining and petroleum sectors, which require the authorization of the Ministry of Mines and Energy. The Colombian government's privatization program presently calls for the sale of ports, railroads, and telecommunications. Investment laws afford foreign firms equal treatment under Colombian law. Of significant consequence are new laws permitting foreign investment in public utilities with the approval of the National Planning Department.

The economics of the country are more stable than the political structure. While Colombia has maintained prudent fiscal and economic policies, it continues to feel the effects of drug-related violence. The 1985 attack on the Supreme Court by the M-19, a terrorist organization, left 115 people dead, including eleven Supreme Court justices. Colombians remain affected by this, as well as other bombings during the past decade, designed to instill fear among the population. The arrests of major drug figures, however, and renewed campaigns against the drug trade, are making in-roads. While the United States would be happy with greater cooperation, the Samper administration is in a difficult position. It must cooperate with the United States, but it cannot run the risk of destabilizing the country should Colombians perceive their government's actions as capitulations to the needs of the United States instead of the needs of Colombia. The majority of Colombians feel trapped, and blame the relentless demand for drugs in the industrialized world. The drug lords in Colombia, after all, are exporters, and not in the business of meeting domestic demand. There lies the crucial conflict between U.S.–Colombian relations, economic and political.

Quick Facts on Colombia:

Population: 35,220,000

Ethnic Groups: 58% mestizo (European and Native American), 20% European, 14% mulatto (European and African), 4% African, 4% other

Religions: 95% Roman Catholic, 1% Protestant, 4% other

Urban: 68%

Language: Spanish

Business Language: Spanish, English

Work Force: 57% services, 23% agriculture, 20% industry and commerce

For further information, contact:

> Embassy of the United States of America
> Calle 38, No. 8-61
> Bogota, Colombia
> Tel.: (57-1) 285-1300
> Fax: (57-1) 288-5687

> Paul Moore
> U.S. Department of Commerce
> 14th Street and Constitution Avenue, N.W.
> Washington, DC 20230
> Tel.: (202) 482-1659

> Embassy of Colombia
> 2118 Leroy Place, N.W.
> Washington, DC 20008
> Tel.: (202) 387-8338

ECUADOR

Background

Not unlike other core countries, Ecuador is characterized by a vigorous evolution over the centuries of Native American and European peoples to form a singular culture. Most Ecuadorians can trace their heritage to both American and European ancestors. The Quechua language survives, and Native American influences are dominant in this Andean country. In the second half of this century, as the country has grown, migration patterns have changed. Ecuador entered this century as a rural country; it ends it an urban one. This migration has been from the mountains to the coast. The concentration of people on the Pacific coast has contributed to a depopulation along the eastern part of the country, where vast rain forests unite Ecuador with the Brazilian Amazon.

In 1830 Ecuador seceded from Greater Colombia, which the South American liberator, Simon Bolivar, had created after the War of Independence in 1822. The newly independent country, ruled by the oligarchy that prevailed at the end of the colonial period, followed the familiar pattern of Latin America: chaos. Ecuador suffered at the hands of rogues-as-presidents and rogues-as-dictators for over a century. It was only in 1948 that the first free, fair elections brought a civilian president to power. It was, however, short lived. From 1960 until 1979 the country descended into disorder once again, as a series of unstable civilian and military opportunists rendered the nation ungovernable.

In 1979, Jaime Roldos became president and ushered in a period of stability through civilian administration of public life. When Roldos died in an airplane crash, Vice-President Osvaldo Hurtado became president.

The subsequent elections brought other civilians to power, first Leon Fe-bres in 1984 and then Rodrigo Borja in 1988. Since 1979 Ecuador has encountered difficulties getting its economic house in order. The most promising development remains fifteen years of peaceful transition from civilian to civilian governments. The market reforms have been slow in coming, given the communal cultural legacy of the Ecuadorian people, along with the instability inherent in small countries dependent upon agricultural economies. Ecuador's uninspired approach to problem solv-ing has undermined economic development, and the instability through-out the 1960s and 1970s has proved detrimental to creating a corporate culture. Foreign investors, save those purchasing Ecuadorian agricultural products, have shown little interest in this nation.

Economic Model

Ecuador's insular economic development has led to a significant com-parative disadvantage in the global economy. With the exception of its primary agricultural exports—bananas, coffee, and flowers—along with its oil exports, there is little else in the form of a formal economy outside the domestic industry involved in import substitution. Ecuador's oil ex-ports, for instance, contribute over 50 percent to foreign exchange earn-ings. The bulk of revenues for the government remain oil exports, not a tax base from a prosperous middle class or business community.

This dependence on the export of primary goods remains the chief reason why the Borja administration's reform program has met with such mixed results. Pursuing an austerity program to combat inflation—reduc-ing public spending, slowing monetary growth—has resulted in some im-provement in the economy, but not much. A country where inflation is considered stable when it is almost 50 percent, is a country with little business sense. The only saving grace for Ecuador this decade continues to be the stability in the oil markets, which allows the government to make reasonable fiscal budgets. For the business community, however, there is little comfort in the move toward trade liberalization, free market reforms and privatization. There is, after all, so little in the way of industry as to be inconsequential. This is made more frustrating by the lack of purchas-ing power of the Ecuadorian people. What can corporate America sell to people with no incomes? And what does Ecuador offer the foreign inves-tor, other than existing exports? The highly restrictive labor laws have discouraged in-bond industry. At the same time, there are other countries where labor-intensive work can be performed in a cost-effective manner closer to the United States, and foreign investors remain weary of investing for the medium and long terms in a country with a fragile record of democratic rule.

At present, Ecuador's development model, sadly, is based on foreign aid. The International Monetary Fund, the World Bank, and the Inter-American Development Bank are all involved in trying to create a development plan for Ecuador. The Paris Club, a group of bilateral creditors, has been actively involved in rescheduling outstanding debt, in addition to ongoing rescheduling negotiations with international commercial banks. There lies the dilemma for a small country burdened by a violent past, an enormous foreign debt, and a population that lacks the purchasing power to interest foreign investors. This is only made worse by Ecuador's continuing objections to the 1942 Rio Protocol of Peace, Friendship and Boundaries, which ended a war with Peru. In 1995, border skirmishes continued and peace talks were once again held under the auspices of Brazil. Despite the peace treaty signed in 1995, lingering resentment between these two nations continues, as does their border dispute. Relations with the United States are friendly, but American interests in Ecuador, apart from commercial, center on Ecuadorian cooperation in the fight against the drug trade. The United States provides multilateral assistance in drug interdiction programs. The only continuing area of friction centers on Ecuador's claim to sovereignty over its territorial waters and the migratory species that transverse through these areas.

Political and Market Conditions

Ecuador clearly is a limited market. High inflation, low growth, and impoverished purchasing power makes for a small market. In addition, Ecuadorians with the means for a middle-class standard of living tend to travel to the United States, Miami primarily, and purchase consumer goods there. For corporate America, this further limits a presence in the Ecuadorian marketplace, other than exports to specific market niches.

The most compelling business opportunities lie in participating in Ecuador's export market. Ecuador continues to subsidize exporters through the advanced sale of foreign exchange, a gimmick to manipulate exchange rates. In essence, it is a transfer of purchasing power to exporters. It remains a market intervention that distorts the Ecuadorian economy even further. Selling to Ecuador is made more cumbersome by complex custom's procedures. Selling to state agencies is further aggravated by the peculiar requirement that such sales must be made exclusively via Ecuadorian flag carriers.

Quick Facts on Ecuador:

Population: 11,252,000

Ethnic Groups: 65% mestizo (Native American and European), 25% Native American, 7% European, 3% African

Religions: 85% Roman Catholic, 15% other

Urban: 55%

Language: Spanish (93%), Quechua (7%)

Business Language: Spanish, English

Work Force: 42% services, 39% agriculture, 11% industry, 8% other

For further information, contact:

> Embassy of Ecuador
> 2535 15th Street, N.W.
> Washington, DC 20009
> Tel.: (202) 234-7200

> Paul Moore
> U.S. Department of Commerce
> 14th Street and Constitution Avenue, N.W.
> Washington, DC 20230
> Tel.: (202) 482-1659

GUATEMALA

Background

Guatemala is the most heavily populated country in Central America. This is an achievement in and of itself, given the government's policy of genocide. Since 1954, when the United States masterminded the overthrow of Jacobo Arbenz, Guatemala's democratically elected president, that nation descended into a period of repressive military rule. American historian Walter LaFeber characterized Guatemala's strategy of "turning a country into a cemetery." The United States has no reason to be proud of how it has cooperated with this nation's savage and ruthless military rulers in what can be considered the last "Indian War" on the mainland of the Americas.

This goes a long way toward explaining the dismal conditions in this country. The vast majority of Guatemalans are related to one of the Mayan peoples. Over two-thirds of the population are subsistence farmers, living in small, family-oriented communities. With one of the lowest urbanization rates in the world, the abject poverty and backwardness of Guatemala mirrors that of Mexico's southern state of Chiapas, where there is presently an armed uprising. Mexico and Guatemala share a 620-mile border, consisting of rain forests and ravines. In the 1980s, when Guatemala was caught up in a massive war against the "Indian" peoples, over half a million Guatemalans fled into Mexico, where the refugee problem became so great that dozens of camps were administered by United Nations refugee programs. The repatriation of these peoples continues, although the process has been difficult.

The incredible pattern of violence continues. In 1992 the Nobel Peace Prize was awarded to Rigoberta Menchu, an outspoken advocate of Native American rights in Guatemala, to remind the world of the campaign of genocide unfolding in that country. When then-president Jorge Serrano attempted a "self-coup," as had Peru's Alberto Fujimori, the country entered into a crisis that was resolved when the Guatemalan Congress elected Ramiro de Leon Carpio president. The 1990s, then, continue the pattern of the unraveling of constitutional rights and political turmoil. In 1994, the Guatemalan crisis intensified when the remains of over 1,000 men, women, and children who had been murdered by the military were discovered in Playa Grande. Soon thereafter, the U.S. State Department issued a travel advisory cautioning against "nonessential travel" to Guatemala after there were intensified attacks on Americans and other foreigners in the country.

The collapse of order and the deteriorating human rights situation continues. Guatemala has made front-page news in the United States after it was learned of American complicity in the terror campaigns in that nation. Evidence that the Central Intelligence Agency and army intelligence officers were involved in the 1990 murder of Michael DeVine, an American citizen, and in the 1992 killing of Efrain Bamaca Valesquez, shocked the Clinton administration. It appears that U.S. government officials contracted with General Hector Gramajo, who as the Guatemalan official with jurisdiction over the highlands populated mostly by the indigenous people, carried out massacres in a broad campaign of terror and genocide. These revelations have created a credibility crisis for the CIA, and many American officials are demanding reforms within the agency to ensure that similar episodes do not happen again in the future. Relations between Guatemala and the United States remain tense, as the Clinton administration has ordered an inquiry into the role American officials played in the systematic human rights abuses in this Central American country.

Economic Model

With the foregoing background, it is not surprising that Guatemala's public sector is among the smallest in Latin America, and a Darwinian survival of the most savage prevails. A continuing privatization program is in place; the government wishes to sell its interest in the telephones, railroads, airlines, and open electric power generation to private capital. Economic projections for healthy growth in tourism are now undermined by the current situation in the country and by tensions between the United States and Guatemala. Efforts to diversify the economic have encountered problems, including protectionist regulations in the aviation and tourism sectors. The economic program of import substitution has been adequate in a country where consumer demand is so low because people are so poor. Guatemala's is largely an agricultural economy with a light manu-facturing sector aimed at the needs of the domestic market. Apart from approaching a market economy in a wishful manner, there is no coherent economic development policy in this country where there is no coherent rule of law.

Political and Market Conditions

There are opportunities in Guatemala, nonetheless. Imports continue to grow steadily, and the greatest opportunities reside in food processing equipment, agricultural chemicals, textile machinery, paper products, household consumer goods, and industrial chemicals. Guatemala imports wheat and feed grains in relatively high quantities. It exports vegetables, mostly broccoli and cauliflower, as well as fruits, mostly melons and straw-berries. There is a light in-bond assembly industry.

Guatemala became a member of the General Agreement on Tariffs and Trade (GATT) in 1991 and has preferential access to the American mar-ket through the Caribbean Basin Initiative (CBI) and the Generalized System of Preferences (GSP). Bureaucracy remains cumbersome. To ad-dress the concerns of foreign investors, the Guatemalan government has created the Fundacion para el Desarrollo de Guatemala, known as Fun-desa, which helps foreign investors become oriented with the business norms and comply with the necessary paperwork. Fundesa may be reached by contacting:

Paul Weaver
Fundacion para el Desarrollo de Guatemala (Fundesa)
Parque Las Margaritas
Diagona 6, 10-65
Zona 10, Ciudad de Guatemala, Guatemala
Tel.: (502-2) 32-7952
Fax: (502-2) 327958

Americans doing business in Guatemala are advised to contact the State Department concerning the conditions in the country. The long-term prospects are sound, provided some semblance of constitutional order is established and human rights abuses are eliminated. While there is no strong anti-American sentiment in Guatemala, many Guatemalans roman-ticize what might have been had Jacobo Arbenz not been overthrown by the United States in the 1950s. This is neither here nor there, for there is no guarantee that he would have escaped making the same mistakes so many other well-intentioned reformers in Latin America have made (and continue to make). For the corporate officer, consideration must be given to the public relations aspect of conducting business in Guatemala. Ex-porting to the country entails little risk exposure, but setting up facilities—

whether offices or other facilities—establishes the perception of complicity with a reprehensible regime. Not unlike objections made to American firms conducting business in South Africa while Apartheid was in place, or in the People's Republic of China, where human rights violations are widespread, American firms in Guatemala run the risk of being accused of being socially irresponsible. The American public, stunned by its own government's complicity in the revelations made in 1995, has made its moral objections about the situation in Guatemala known in a vigorous manner. As this goes to press, Alvaro Arzu was elected president.

Quick Facts on Guatemala:

Population: 9,735,000

Ethnic Groups: 50% Native American, 40% mestizo (European and Native American), 7% European, 3% other

Religions: 97% Roman Catholic, 3% other

Urban: 39%

Language: Spanish (66%), Quiche (13%), Cakchiquel (6%), Mam (4%), Kekchi (4%), other (7%)

Business Language: Spanish, English

Work Force: 65% agriculture, 20% services, 10% industry and commerce, 5% other

For further information, contact:

> Embassy of the United States of America
> 7-01 Avenida de la Reforma
> Zona 10, Ciudad de Guatemala, Guatemala
> Tel.: (502-2) 31-1541
> Fax: (502-2) 31-8885

> Embassy of Guatemala
> 2220 R Street, N.W.
> Washington, DC 20008
> Tel.: (202) 745-4952

> Helen Lee
> U.S. Department of Commerce
> 14th Street and Constitution Avenue, N.W.
> Washington, DC 20230
> Tel.: (202) 482-2528

MEXICO

Background

The past is the refuge of those without a future. Thus, Mexico invoked its historic revolutionary ideals as a way of begging for emergency loans.

The exchange of messages between Washington, D.C., and Mexico City in January 1995 resembled the same set of messages that flowed back and forth in January 1955. At that time, Dwight Eisenhower was the president of the United States and Adolfo Ruiz Cortines was the president of Mexico. At that time, Mexico sought a $75 million loan, payable over ten years, from the United States to help support the peso, which had been drastically devalued in April 1954. In 1995, however, Mexico would require $50 billion, payable whenever, to help support the peso after a drastic devaluation weeks before. Fine wine improves with age; Mexican finances do not. But it was in 1955 that the Eisenhower administration agreed to help the Mexicans, on the condition that the Bank of Mexico and Mexico's Finance Ministry adhere to American standards established by the Federal Reserve Bank in Washington, D.C.

Thus, forty years of tutelage under the auspices of the United States has done little to help Mexico break out of its cycle of currency crises. In August 1976 the Mexican peso suffered a significant devaluation, and then again in February 1982 and once more in August 1982. A wave of inflation descended upon Mexico, with almost daily devaluations for the next six years, when a "managed" devaluation was put in effect after 1988. The currency situation became stable, until it collapsed in December 1994. In each crisis, the pattern is the same. Mexico requests urgent aid from Washington. Conditions are set, aid is given, and obeying instructions, Mexico manages to manage—until the next disaster strikes. Despite forty years of capitulation to the United States, Mexico's problems linger, but with a difference: In each successive crisis, the stakes are higher. From $75 million to $50 billion is an enormous increase, one that is not reflected in the economic growth of the Mexican economy during the same period. This is evidence of an economic model out of control, an economy subservient to the demands of another. It is an affirmation of the failure of the Bretton Woods system to address the specific needs of developing nations.

Economic Model

The North American Free Trade Agreement (NAFTA) took effect on January 1, 1994, with the expectation that this would begin a process of hemispheric economic integration. The United States, Canada, and Mexico would together form the largest trading bloc in the world, with over 360 million consumers in an economy that surpassed $7 trillion. "Fortress America" would then be able to secure a sustainable competitive advantage in world markets. The fifteen-year time frame for fully implementing the NAFTA agreements would be sufficient to address economic dislocation issues arising from the integration of such disparate economies into one cohesive marketplace. Two areas that were not fully resolved were banking and finance, and the oil industry. As a consequence of the Mexican Meltdown, however, Mexico has unilaterally initiated a fast-track plan to open these areas to foreign investment and capital. The unfolding banking crisis has forced the Mexican government to contemplate allowing foreign banks to acquire troubled Mexican banks, letting weak Mexican banks merge with larger ones, and permitting foreign banks to open operations in Mexico. In 1994 the government had to intervene to save Banco Union, Banca Cremi, and Banpais. In 1995, the Serfin, Inverlat, Bital, Confia, Del Centro, and Oriente banks required assistance to maintain their capitalization minimums. That Pemex is in a state of constant turmoil is one reason why, if nothing is done to reverse trends, Mexico will be a net importer of oil by the year 2000. Mexico already is forced to import unleaded gas and other refined products, and the Zedillo administration is attempting to engineer ways to allow foreign capital to rescue Mexico's oil industry by circumventing existing restrictions in Mexico's constitution.

The Mexican Meltdown has thus forced an acceleration of reforms envisioned by NAFTA, but which were not agreed to because of political considerations. The question of politics is crucial in Mexico. To understand the political economy of Mexico, one need look no further than the Mexican Postal Service. In Mexico, postage stamps come without glue. It is not clear whether the technology is too sophisticated or if, with Mexican postal rates higher than in the United States already, it would drive the prices higher still. What is clear is that Mexicans, tolerant of mediocrity, adjust rather than demand better service. Throughout Mexico, post offices have bottles of liquid glue all over the counters and Mexicans stand about, measuring drops of glue onto stamps, before affixing them to their mail. Of course the counters are messy and sticky, and it is a rather cumbersome process. To make matters worse, once one goes through the trouble of doing all this, it is of little use, for there is a great likelihood the mail will not arrive. American residents in Mexico have informal networks in which friends and relatives traveling back to the States are prevailed upon to drop off mail; sending an express package by a commercial delivery service to one's office in the United States filled with nothing but mail is not unusual.

The point of all of this is to suggest how complacent Mexicans are about their lives. NAFTA, in part, is an effort to change this worldview. Economic integration is designed to accelerate the processes of economic liberalization and democratization, fostering a sense of empowerment. Free markets require men and women capable of exercising their free will. The progress made under the Salinas administration cannot be dismissed. The privatization program returned hundreds of companies to the private sector, foreign capital arrived at a remarkable rate, the Mexican Bolsa was opened to foreign investors, and duties and tariffs were reduced as part of Mexico's complying with the terms of GATT. The Mexican people re-acted with tremendous enthusiasm, as if waking from a slumber, and the pace of economic activity increased throughout the entire nation.

The pent-up demand was evident in the frenzy of consumer spending, financed by the ill-advised easy credit policies of the Salinas administration during an election year. For all practical purposes, it appeared that Mex-ico had arrived. The neoliberal economic policies implemented since 1982 appeared to have provided the country with a firm foundation on which to build sustainable growth. Wealth and industrialization, leisure, and democracy were at hand. The truth was somewhat different. Mexico's economic model, which was founded on the twin pillars of the in-bond industry and the nation's vast oil wealth, were poorly managed. The in-bond industry, called *maquiladoras*, creates dead-end jobs, selling the labor of mostly young women at wages that cannot provide for decent liveli-hoods. The institutionalization of poverty, as with minimum-wage jobs in the United States, creates the class of the working poor and confronts the government with a dilemma: If wages rise, then industry is not competi-tive, but at the wages paid, Mexicans remain impoverished. Mexico's vast oil wealth, too, has been a curse. Unlike other countries, such as Saudi Arabia, that have managed their oil wealth in a responsible way, Mexico has squandered this opportunity, creating a stifling bureaucracy within a political structure that has made the nation more dependent and less independent.

Consider how Mexico has gone about building its infrastructure. Years back, while driving to Acapulco from Mexico City in the company of an American executive in the construction industry, we pulled over to see a new highway under construction. This was to be the highway that serves Mexico well into the next century. There it was: Peasants banging on big rocks with little rocks. We gazed upon this site and what appeared as a nightmare on the horizon—modern men using Neanderthal, Stone Age technology to welcome the twenty-first century—now proves to be real. In economic terms the vision before us makes sense. Latin America is capital-poor and labor-rich; employing many laborers is cost effective where wages are low instead of depending on expensive equipment. Nevertheless, it is a ghastly vision, seeing a multitude of men on their hands and knees, working like slaves.

The "new" Mexico, like the "new" Latin America, is being built on the broken backs of men carrying rocks and stones and gravel, crawling on their hands and knees the way Latin Americans are inclined to crawl on their hands and knees, the way the pyramids were once raised and then razed, the way floors are scrubbed in New York skyscrapers and asparagus harvested on California farms. My American colleague turned to me and, shaking his head, said, "This looks like the set for a documentary on how slaves built the Egyptian pyramids or something." There was a pause. As we drive off, I was reminded of the words of D. H. Lawrence: "To the Indian, there is near and far, and very near and very far. There is two days or one day. But two miles are as good as twenty to him, for he goes entirely by his feeling. If a certain two miles feels far to him, then it is far, it is *muy lejos!* But if a certain twenty miles *feels* near and familiar, then it is not far. Oh, no, it is just a little distance. And he will let you set off in the evening, for night to overtake you in the wilderness, without a qualm. It is not far."[8]

The "new" Mexico of Carlos Salinas and Ernesto Zedillo is "not far" from the fifteenth century. The Mexico of tomorrow is being built by men on their hands and knees, not far from Mexico City, not far from the fifteenth century. To these nightmarish images, add tales of corruption, mismanagement, and inefficiency that are legendary. This kind of economic development model inspires little confidence in the ability of the Mexicans to handle their affairs responsibly.

Political and Market Conditions

The catastrophic fall from grace of Mexico stems from its inability to manage the political economy in a responsible manner. As a consequence, the political stability of the country is not guaranteed. Increasing violence and civil disorder within the Zedillo administration characterized 1995. The Mexican middle class, encouraged by the easy-credit election year schemes of Carlos Salinas, went into debt, purchasing homes, cars, and consumer goods. With the devaluation, interest rates soared to alarming levels, making it difficult to make payments. The risk of losing one's cars and homes, or getting into arrears has, in effect, drained the economy of liquidity and constitutes a transfer of purchasing power from Mexico's middle class to foreign investors on a massive scale. This kind of economic dislocation results in structural damage to the political structure of the nation.

The political challenge for Mexico is twofold. It must democratize, by which the world means free elections, where opposition victories are recognized, in both Guanajuato and Yucatan, and everywhere else. The second is to address the public relations problems confronting the country. If investor confidence is to be restored, the nation's image must be restored. Indeed, perceptions are an integral part of investor confidence. How Mexico is perceived by the world is of monumental consequence. A French diplomat, unamused by American pressures to enlist the G-7 to back the economic rescue of Mexico, referencing Emperor Maximilian, noted that had France "prevailed a century ago, the world wouldn't be in this predicament today."

Compare that kind of contempt with another. At a dinner party in southern California the woman with whom I am speaking claims to understand everything about Mexico completely. This is because of where she is from and who she happens to be. This young woman is from Persia and she fled the Islamic revolution and arrived in Mexico as a "long-term" tourist, along with the Shah of Iran and his entourage. She lived and settled in Mexico for a while, but after a few years it became evident that returning to her homeland was not an option, and if she must settle down somewhere, she decided to settle somewhere that made sense. Leaving revolutionary Iran for crisis-ridden Mexico was not the most sensible choice, and she and her family finally settled on settling in southern California. Then I asked her, what of these people, the Mexicans? What did she make of people who passively accept whatever happens? What does she make of people who resign themselves stoically to the whims of the Fates? What does she make of people who are resigned to complete squalor, living beneath cardboard boxes hung between water tanks, with newspapers and rags for beds? What does she think of frantic Mexican officials scurrying about begging for dollars?

I am reminded of what an American thinks. I am reminded of Edmund Wilson's memoirs, in which he writes: "One thing that sometimes makes me rude is discovering that some man has no ambition. I was rude to a young man. . . . [He] said he didn't even care about getting anywhere. . . . I can't bear the idea of anybody so uninteresting and so uninterested just wanting to get along and exist."[9] I am curious of what she thinks of a nation of people who are so uninteresting and so uninterested and who merely want to get along and exist. I am curious if she mourns the same "nothingness" that infuriated Emperor Maximilian. I am curious to know if a lack of ambition is what she blames for Mexico being Mexico. She ponders for a moment and, knowing that I already understand and need not be convinced of anything, forms a catty response.

"Dealing with the Mexicans," this Persian princess, who is not entirely unsympathetic to the Mexicans but who has little grace suffering a people she claims are so completely lacking in sense, says with a smile on her face, "is like dealing with idiots savant—*without the savant.*" Fugitives from revolutionary Islamic justice can be unforgiving in their judgments, which is one reason they are at dinner parties in Beverly Hills and not at dinner parties in Teheran.

Quick Facts on Mexico:

Population: 94,065,000

Ethnic Groups: 65% mestizo (European and Native American), 26% Native American, 8% European, 1% other

Religions: 96% Roman Catholic, 3% Protestant, 1% other

Urban: 71%

Language: Spanish (91%), Nahuatl (2%), Mayan (Yucatec, Tzotzil) (2%), other Native American languages (5%)

Business Language: Spanish, English

Work Force: 31% services, 26% agriculture, 14% commerce, 13% manufacturing, 9% construction, 5% transportation and communication, 2% other

For further information, contact:

> Embassy of Mexico
> 1911 Pennsylvania Avenue, N.W.
> Washington, DC 20036
> Tel.: (202) 728-1600

> Regina Vargo
> U.S. Department of Commerce
> 14th Street and Constitution Avenue, N.W.
> Washington, DC 20230
> Tel.: (202) 482-4303

PERU

Background

Peru is a prodigal son of South America. Peru gained its independence from Spain on July 28, 1821. It was ruled by an oligarchy that included many military officers. Democracy in this century, however, has guaranteed neither stability nor prosperity. Witness the election of Alan Garcia as president. In a few short years, the Garcia administration pushed a struggling nation to the edge of complete collapse. Peru collapsed into a spiral of despair and disaster, and the nation became an international pariah, on the verge of chaos unimaginable to most Americans. In the past decade, happily, Peru has made strides toward getting its economic house in order, as well as restoring its credibility with the international community. As a consequence, it is no longer shut off from the International Monetary Fund and the World Bank. In July 1990, Alberto Fujimori became president and quickly implemented a market-oriented reform program. The hemorrhaging of the nation's finances, its crushing foreign debt, accelerating hyperinflation, and the collapsing economy created much instability. An armed insurrection—the Shining Path and the Tupac Amaru Revolutionary Movement, both terrorist groups—and a thriving drug trade made Peru rather problematic, both at home and within the international community. Alan Garcia, who preceded Alberto Fujimori, was a grand-standing imbecile, similar to Nicaragua's Daniel Ortega. The Garcia administration ruined Peru's fragile economy and his ludicrous policies—the most disturbing centered on his government's decision to change unilaterally its payment schedule to international lending institutions—more than raised eyebrows; they isolated Peru from the international financial community and contributed to a rapid and appalling deterioration in the standard of living of the Peruvian people.

Peru was on the verge of collapse; price levels under Alan Garcia grew by about 2 million percent, which made most calculators useless. The success of the Fujimori administration, therefore, is no small feat. In the 1990s, the austerity and stabilization program has arrested Peru's descent into madness; reasonable exchange rates have eliminated price distortion; labor reforms have rendered sensible the Peruvian labor market; the liberalization of trade is improving export earnings; market-driven reforms have opened up the Peruvian economy to the world; inflation is well under control; Occidental Petroleum, Shell and Mobil are now active in Peru; and calculators are useful once again.

Economic Model

Peru is open for business, with a no-nonsense government and an electorate beginning to see benefits from the austerity program of the first half of this decade. Although dependent on imports of foodstuffs—mostly rice and wheat—from the United States, the country is well on its way to economic stability. This is imperative if the alarming food shortages, from which Peru still suffers, are to be addressed. During the last years of the Garcia administration and well into the first of the Fujimori government, calorie consumption fell dramatically and childhood malnutrition grew. A cholera epidemic swept the country. Terrorist organizations engaged in continuing violence. The deterioration of the economy created enormous hardship on the Peruvian people. The crisis on a human level has been devastating: a country on the mainland of the Americas confronting starvation among its children. The country faced no alternative but to embark on a vigorous market-oriented reform program, get back in good standing with the international community, and implement a shock program.

Political and Market Conditions

Despite the sacrifices the austerity program in place has required of the Peruvian people, the stability it has engendered has been welcome. Alberto Fujimori won reelection in April 1995, this time with the broader grass-roots support of the population. This is a testament to the progress Peru has made; two years ago no one thought the Fujimori administration would serve its full term. The reason for this pessimism lay as much in the economic crisis confronting the nation as in Fujimori's so-called "auto-coup," in which he, backed by the military, seized control of the state, dissolving the Congress. The emergency measures announced then rendered Peru a virtual dictatorship—remarkable only in that this was, in some ways, a democratically elected dictatorship of sorts.

This action was justified by the crisis confronting the nation and by the twin threats to Peruvian sovereignty: terrorist insurrection in the mountains and the drug trade. The United States, while weary of the course of action Fujimori might take, was relieved that the bickering between the executive and legislative branches of government, which made it impossible for any progress to be made, had ended. It was only under the self-proclaimed emergency rule that the reform policies were able to be passed. While the economy continued to stabilize, the arrest of key members of the Shining Path, and greater cooperation with the United States on drug interdiction efforts, has inspired renewed confidence in the Peruvian economy. The continuation of Fujimori's reforms, however severe, is restoring confidence among international investors. Hostilities with Ecuador over a border dispute in 1995 raised the specter of a regional military conflict, but tensions have been eased.

The United States continues to be Peru's largest trading partner. American exports to this Andean nation consists of wheat, rice, machinery parts and equipment, electrical machinery, and refined oil. The more promising prospects continue to be in agricultural, oil, and gas equipment, as well as in food processing and packaging and mining machinery. Demand for electronic equipment, particularly televisions, stereos, and security-related products continues to grow at a healthy pace. The Peruvian currency, the New Sol, is presently overvalued and Peruvian consumers are eagerly buying after years of being unable to purchase durables and consumer goods.

The liberalization of prices, exchange rates, and import/export regulations are integral to the government's effort to transform the Peruvian economy into a market-based one. The systematic dismantling of the statist structure and the wholesale abandoning of the import-substitution model is breathing new life to an otherwise stagnant economy. After years of lackluster growth, Peru is now beginning to witness the blossoming of sustainable growth. The Fujimori administration has successfully cleared the arrears it inherited from the previous regime; Peru is in good standing with the International Monetary Fund, the World Bank, the Inter-American Development Bank, and the United States. The stabilization program now in place has the blessings of the IMF, and the government is steadfast in its commitment to complying with the stringent requirements of its program. This includes a trade surplus and balancing the budgets of the government's federal projects. There is currently a trade surplus, and eliminating the government's debt, to a great extent, depends on the acceleration of the privatization program. Many observers have been disappointed at the slow pace of the privatization efforts during

Fujimori's first term and are anxious to see a more ambitious effort get underway in the second half of the 1990s.

Of equal concern is Peru's foreign debt, which approximates $25 billion US, an enormous amount for a country of this size. The removal of subsidies, the elimination of price controls, and the rationalization of the nation's economic life are expected to allow Peru to emerge from the situation in which it languished during the 1980s. The investment opportunities are only now beginning to emerge. It is expected that in the second half of Fujimori's second term the political risks associated with this nation will be comparable to other risk levels in Latin America. Provided Peru continues on its present course, corporate America can make an important contribution commencing in 1997.

Quick Facts on Peru:

Population: 4,600,000

Ethnic Groups: 45% Native American, 37% mestizo (Native American and European), 15% Asian and African, 3% European

Religions: 85% Roman Catholic, 15% other

Urban: 69%

Language: Spanish (68%), Quechua (27%), Aymara (3%), other (2%)

Business Language: Spanish, English

Work Force: 44% services, 37% agriculture, 19% industry and commerce

For further information, contact:

> Embassy of the United States
> Avenidas Inca Garcilaso de la Vega y España
> Lima, Peru
> Tel.: (51-14) 33-8000
> Fax: (51-14) 31-6682
> Telex: 25212 PE

> Embassy of Peru
> 1700 Massachusetts Avenue, N.W.
> Washington, DC 20036
> Tel.: (202) 833-9860

> Laura Zeiger-Hatfield
> U.S. Department of Commerce
> 14th Street and Constitution Avenue, N.W.
> Washington, DC 20230
> Tel.: (202) 482-4303

NOTES

1. Alice Adams, *Mexico* (Englewood Cliffs, N.J.: Prentice Hall, 1990), pp. 137–38.

2. Macduff Everton, *The Modern Maya* (Albuquerque: University of New Mexico Press, 1991), p. 39.

3. Richard Rodriguez, *Days of Obligation: An Argument with My Mexican Father* (New York: Viking Penguin, 1992), p. 15.

4. Ibid., p. 2.

5. Ibid., p. 19.

6. Octavio Paz, *The Labyrinth of Solitude: Life and Thought in Mexico* (New York: Grove Press, 1961), p. 346.

7. Paul Tillich, *A History of Christian Thought: From its Judaic and Hellenistic Origins to Existentialism* (New York: Simon & Schuster, 1967), p. 210.

8. D. H. Lawrence, *Mornings in Mexico* (New York: Knopf, 1927), p. 34.

9. Jeffrey Meyers, *Edmund Wilson: A Biography* (Boston: Houghton Mifflin, 1995), p. 118.

7

THE CARIBBEAN BASIN NATIONS: BELIZE, CARIBBEAN BASIN ISLANDS, COSTA RICA, CUBA, EL SALVADOR, FRENCH GUIANA, GUYANA, HONDURAS, JAMAICA, NICARAGUA, PANAMA, SURINAME, VENEZUELA

The U.S. government defines the "Caribbean Basin" as the Caribbean islands and the nations of Central America. For the purposes of this discussion, the nations on the northern shoulder of South America, French Guiana, Guyana, Suriname, and Venezuela are included as well. Guatemala is classified as a core country, although it enjoys the same benefits as other nations of the Caribbean Basin. With the exception of Central America, Venezuela, Cuba, the Dominican Republic, and Puerto Rico, English is used as the primary business language throughout the Caribbean Basin, except for the French islands. The Caribbean Basin Initiative (CBI), designed to help the island nations and Central America, offers the most appealing tax incentives anywhere in the Western Hemisphere. There are abundant marketing resources from U.S. government agencies whose mission it is to assist American firms in these markets.

While the Caribbean Basin remains small compared to the other nations of Latin America, there are significant opportunities. The islands that are sprinkled across the Caribbean were once the remaining outposts of colonialism; some islands remain possessions of European powers. The Cayman Islands, the Turks and Caicos Islands, the British Virgin Islands, Anguilla, and Montserrat are territories of the United Kingdom. Guadalupe, Martinique, and St. Martin are departments of France, as is French Guiana in South America. Bonaire, Curacao, Saba, St. Eustatius, and St. Maarten are Dutch parliamentary democracies, as was Aruba until a few years ago, but all remain part of the Netherlands Antilles. The U.S. Virgin Islands are territories of the United States. Puerto Rico is a commonwealth of the United States, as well. And even some independent nations in the Caribbean Basin, such as the Bahamas, Belize, and Bermuda are part of the British Commonwealth. The other nations in this section, too, are among the poorest of the region. But their diversity, history, and people provide reason for optimism for periods of sustained economic growth. Billions of dollars in investment have flowed into the region as part of the Caribbean Basin Initiative, and the area has been swept by market reforms that are only now beginning to make themselves felt. There is every reason to believe that the future of these nations is as bright as the Caribbean sun that shines over the entire region.

BELIZE

Background

Formerly called British Honduras, Belize is the least populous nation in Central America. With a mere quarter-million people, Belize is a small market. A Commonwealth nation, it is a stable democracy that gained independence in September 1981. Neighboring Guatemala still has territorial claims, and on many Guatemalan maps, Belize is occupied by Guatemala. The capital is Belmopan, although the largest city is Belize City.

Economic Model

Belize, under Prime Minister Manuel Esquivel, has been trying to develop an eco-tourist economy, and it is a leader in conservation efforts. The nation is covered mostly by tropical rain forests, dotted with ruins of the ancient Maya civilization. A haven for scuba divers and fishermen, there is little in the way of a developed economy. Not unlike other CBI members, Belize remains a very poor country, with little other than light industry and in-bond facilities. Tourism provides a meager living for its people and, in the age of freer trade, its once-privileged position as a Commonwealth nation offers little benefit.

Political and Market Conditions

The country, along with Costa Rica, is the most stable nation in Central America. In 1990 the National Economic Mobilization Council was set up to design and implement a development plan. Apart from the Coca-Cola Company, the only other recent American firm to make a sizeable investment in the country has been MCI Telecommunications, which purchased 24 percent of Belize Telecommunication Limited from the British in February 1995.

Quick Facts on Belize:

Population: 225,000

Ethnic Groups: 40% mestizo (Native American and European), 29% Creole, 15% Maya (Native American), 13% Spanish, 3% Garifuna

Religions: 55% Roman Catholic, 35% Protestant or Baptist, 10% other

Urban: 27%

Language: English, Spanish, Creole, Maya

Business Language: English

Work Force: 36% commerce, 30% services, 30% agriculture, 4% other

For further information, contact:

> Embassy of Belize
> 3400 International Drive, N.W.
> Washington, DC 20008
> Tel.: (202) 332-9636

> International Trade Administration
> U.S. Department of Commerce
> 14th Street and Constitution Avenue, N.W.
> Washington, DC 20230
> Tel.: (202) 377-0703

CARIBBEAN BASIN ISLANDS

Background

In 1983 the U.S. Congress passed the Caribbean Basin Economic Recovery Act, which was designed to promote political stability through economic growth in the area. The Caribbean Basin Initiative, first included in the Economic Recovery Act, became a permanent part of American foreign policy in 1990. The CBI provides for almost unlimited access to U.S. markets on a duty-free basis for the nations included in this program. Preferential treatment was given to these nations, and the Overseas Private Investment Corporation (OPIC), the Export-Import Bank, and the Inter-American Development Bank were authorized to provide special financing for American companies doing business in the region. In addition, the Internal Revenue Service allowed Section 936 to be applied to the entire region, further reducing the cost of borrowing money for business in the region.

The CBI consists of six major provisions. These are:

1. Duty-free entry into the United States of products manufactured in the Caribbean Basin, with the exception of some items, including most textiles and

apparel, petroleum and petrochemical products, footwear, most leather goods, and canned tuna. In addition, there are restrictions on sugar, beef, and ethanol.

2. Assistance to private-sector initiatives through the creation of development banks, free trade zones, chambers of commerce, and related organizations.

3. In-nation programs to facilitate the development of a stable business environment and business community, the operations of which are consistent with international standards and norms.

4. Assistance from the U.S. development offices and technical assistance programs to American companies exporting or setting up businesses in the CBI nations.

5. Special tax deductions for American firms holding conventions in the CBI nations.

6. Cooperation by the U.S. government with other trading partners assisting in the economic development of the economies of CBI nations.

The participants in the CBI are Antigua and Barbuda, Aruba, the Bahamas, Barbados, Belize, the British Virgin Islands, Costa Rica, Dominica, the Dominican Republic, El Salvador, Grenada, Guatemala, Guyana, Haiti, Honduras, Jamaica, Montserrat, the Netherlands Antilles, Nicaragua, Panama, St. Kitts–Nevis, St. Lucia, St. Vincent/the Grenadines, and Trinidad and Tobago. Those not included are Anguilla, the Cayman Islands, Suriname, and Turks and Caicos Islands.

Information on the opportunities in the CBI is available by calling the Caribbean Basin Information Center Office of the International Trade Administration, U.S. Department of Commerce, at (202) 377-2527.

Puerto Rico and the U.S. Virgin Islands are not included in this survey because they are part of the United States.

COSTA RICA

Background

Costa Rica, wedged between core countries, is out of place. Costa Ricans are an American people of European origins, similar to Argentina and Chile. Descendants of Spaniards, there is a black population centered on the Caribbean port town of Limon. These are descendants of Jamaican immigrants who arrived here in the nineteenth century. The indigenous population stands at fewer than 25,000. A democracy without a military, Costa Rica is referred to as the "Switzerland of Latin America." Under the moral leadership of Oscar Arias, who won the Nobel Peace Prize, this nation has led efforts to mediate the civil wars in other Central American nations.

It is not without its irony that these peace efforts, which at the time were in conflict with U.S. foreign policy, resulted in punitive actions and acts of aggression by the United States. Costa Rica was systematically undermined by the United States in its efforts to seek loans at international lending organizations. A campaign to destabilize the country was also implemented by American intelligence agencies. Costa Rica is nestled between Nicaragua to the north and Panama to the south. This geographic location has made the country of strategic importance—it is situated between the Panama Canal and a war-ravaged neighbor. Indeed, in what proved to be one of the most ludicrous escapades in Central America, American officials in the Reagan administration, for instance, plotted to have the American embassy in San Jose blown up in order to blame neighboring Nicaragua and justify a U.S. invasion of that country (as reported in the U.S. media, including *Vanity Fair*). Costa Ricans, not surprisingly, are restrained in their view of Americans.

The election of Jose Maria Figueres in February 1994, however, is consistent with Costa Rica's democratic traditions. Declaring its independence from Spain in 1821, along with other Central American provinces, it formally became independent in 1838 when the Central American Federation ceased to exist. Democracy became institutionalized in 1889 after the country was able to hold its first free and clean elections. Democracy was interrupted only twice this century. In 1917 Federico Tinoco governed as a virtual dictator for one year. Then, in 1948, after disputed presidential results, Jose Figueres led a popular revolt, and the government that emerged called for new elections and abolished the military. Since then Costa Ricans have enjoyed uninterrupted democratic elections, which is a singular achievement in Latin America. The Nobel Peace Prize in 1987 further strengthened Costa Rican moral authority in the international community. Efforts by the United States to undermine and isolate Costa Rica under the Reagan and Bush administrations have been abandoned.

The government of Oscar Arias was hampered by economic difficulties precipitated by his peace efforts. Isolation created a fiscal crisis for Costa Rica as interest rates rose and pressures on the currency mounted. Rafael Calderon, who succeeded Oscar Arias as president in September 1992, struggled to appease American officials and reverse U.S. efforts to punish this nation for working for peace in Central America. A small nation with a fragile economy, Costa Rica is easily affected by developments in the international scene. The economy remained stagnant until the end of 1993, when it began to show slow improvement. The Calderon administration continued its program of tariff reduction and greater open market reforms. The strengthening of world prices for coffee and bananas has helped Costa Rica, as has the Clinton administration policy of reconciliation.

Costa Rica has successfully rescheduled its debt and bilateral agreements have made greater investments in infrastructure and social spending programs possible. Under the Brady Plan, Costa Rica repurchased 60 percent of its foreign commercial debt in May 1990. It also joined GATT later that year. The election of Jose Maria Figueres in 1994 further spurred economic reform. Costa Rica is in negotiations to enter into free trade agreements with Mexico and has expressed an interest in joining NAFTA. The free trade zone being implemented by Mexico, Colombia, and Venezuela is of interest, as is greater cooperation with the Andean Pact nations. The move to market reforms is accelerating. In the 1980s Costa Ricans grew alarmed at how easily their country could be the object of destabilization, and it was seen as a threat to their national sovereignty. Efforts to diversify the economy began, complemented by a program of structural adjustments and a greater emphasis on an export-led development program.

Economic Model

The economic difficulties encountered by Costa Rica, however, have their foundations in the impressive welfare state in place. The public sector deficit, mostly used for health care and education, contributed to a sharp decline in foreign reserves. An austerity program was put in place while structural adjustments were made on the macroeconomic level. The international support for Costa Rican peace initiatives, moreover, made it easier for the nation to accept the reduced spending; national pride was at stake. While tensions with the United States continued for most of the 1980s—Costa Rica has barred entry to some U.S. officials and a certain chill stemming from the American plot to engage in terrorist activities on Costa Rican soil remains in evidence—since 1990 there have been marked improvements. Costa Rica enthusiastically endorsed the Bush administration's Enterprise for the Americas Initiative. Relations with the United States began to improve considerably when Costa Rica supported the U.S. position and called for a withdrawal of Iraqi forces from Kuwait. Costa Rica was among the most vocal Latin American supporters of Kuwait during the Persian Gulf crisis. In 1991 Costa Rica spearheaded efforts for further liberalization of its economy and trade policies while reducing its fiscal budget deficit and increasing its international reserves. American assistance, through the U.S. Agency for International Development, the Department of Agriculture, the Peace Corps, and the U.S. Information Service, have been invigorated. While inflation remains troublesome, the economic fundamentals are sound and a continuing improvement is expected for the remainder of the decade.

Costa Rica has been successful in operating free trade zone parks. Over 140 foreign companies have operations in these parks. Further information can be obtained by writing:

Corporacion de la Zona Franca de Exportacion, S.A.
Box 96, Montes de Oca
San Jose, Costa Rica
Tel.: (506) 22-5855
Fax: (506) 33-5090

Political and Market Conditions

Costa Rica continues to implement policies consistent with free trade. Reductions in tariffs, standardization of investment norms consistent with the Enterprise for the Americas Initiative, and progress on regional free trade agreements are the centerpieces for economic reform. The growth in nontraditional exports continues to be a bright spot in the economy. The return of democratic rule in Panama and Nicaragua has not only opened these two countries as export markets, but has also eased the social burdens associated with refugee populations. The Commercial Code requires foreign companies to contract with a representative or distributor in Costa Rica. This representative or distributor must have been in business for a minimum of three years. Foreigners who wish to engage in business must prove Costa Rican residency of ten years. These requirements have not proved to be obstacles. The U.S. Department of Commerce can assist American firms in locating an adequate distributor or representative in San Jose. There are few restrictions on foreign ownership or holding equity positions in Costa Rican companies. Foreign investors are afforded the same legal protection as Costa Rican citizens.

There are extensive and complicated procedures for securing foreign exchange. There are no restrictions on capital flows into and out of the country, but official approval is necessary. These requirements entail delays, which may require financing. Investments in Costa Rica, however, can be facilitated through the Private Investment Corporation, known as PIC. PIC may be contacted at:

Private Investment Corporation
A.P. 8609-1000
San Jose, Costa Rica
Tel.: (506) 336-422
Fax: (506) 336-541

The American Embassy in San Jose also houses an office for the U.S. Agency for International Development. Their phone number in Costa Rica is (506) 204-545. Their address is at the end of this survey.

The prospects for Costa Rica continue to improve. The implementation of macroeconomic reform has paid off, as have strategies for export diversification and the liberalization of trade. A strong democracy, Costa Rica defies all the stereotypes of Central America and offers the kind of stability on which sound business plans can be based. While a small economy in and of itself, its privileged position and state of development make Costa Rica an ideal regional base from which to service other markets in Central America, the Caribbean, and the northern shore of mainland South America. The only caveat stems from fallout of the Mexican Meltdown. The Figueres administration confronted a domestic crisis in 1994 and 1995 when the banking system was shaken by a series of bank failures. The problems were exacerbated by the deep recession in Mexico which dashed hopes for increasing trade between both nations, particularly when a free trade agreement between Mexico and Costa Rica took effect on January 1, 1995. These reversals contributed to the 8 percent rise in the fiscal deficit in 1995 and a series of social spending measures, which included a sharp tax increase. The Costa Rican economy stands to decline into a recession if these statist policies continue. The Figueres administration must reduce its fiscal deficit and keep tax increases to a minimum in order to eliminate the nefarious consequences of increased public spending. A recovery in Mexico is crucial for Costa Rica's continued growth.

Quick Facts on Costa Rica:

Population: 3,310,000

Ethnic Groups: 80% European, 15% mestizo (European and Native American), 2% African, 1% Native American, 1% Asian (mostly Chinese), 1% other

Religions: 95% Roman Catholic, 1% Protestant, 4% other

Urban: 45%

Language: Spanish

Business Language: Spanish, English

Work Force: 35% industry and commerce, 33% services, 27% agriculture, 5% other

For further information, contact:

> Embassy of Costa Rica
> 1825 Connecticut Avenue, N.W.
> Washington, DC 20009
> Tel.: (202) 234-2945

> Jay Dowling
> U.S. Department of Commerce
> 14th Street and Constitution Avenue, N.W.
> Washington, DC 20230
> Tel.: (202) 482-1658

CUBA

Background

The United States maintains an economic embargo against Cuba. American firms and their subsidiaries in other countries are prohibited from conducting business with Cuba. To do so constitutes trading with the enemy, which is punishable by law. The inclusion of Cuba in this survey of Latin America does not represent an endorsement of violating the U.S. trade embargo laws. The rationale for the American embargo is based on sound principles. In the aftermath of the Cuban revolution in 1959, the Castro government seized U.S. property without compensating owners. There is a difference between nationalization or expropriation and confiscation. Eminent domain establishes the rights of government to nationalize or expropriate private property, but they are required to compensate those affected. To confiscate property, on the other hand, is theft. The amount of compensation can be negotiated, but the act of confiscating without remuneration is unacceptable. It is because of the failure of the Cuban government to compensate the former owners that the embargo was declared in 1961.

In theory, the embargo will end the moment Fidel Castro agrees to provide compensation for what his government seized. Even if he offers, for example, one dollar, then in principle he has acknowledged the Americans' right to reimbursement and opened the door for negotiation. The U.S. could come back and request *an extra $10 billion,* and the moment that happens, negotiations have commenced and the embargo can be lifted. The Cuban Asset Control Regulations established by the U.S. Treasury Department describe the parameters within which U.S. firms, and their foreign subsidiaries, can operate where trade with Cuba is concerned. That American firms—and Americans—are routinely violating the embargo is another matter. The presentation of a discussion on Cuba is in no way an endorsement that U.S. law should be broken. It is, however, to describe how business in Cuba in the 1990s is conducted.

Economic Model

The economic model of Cuba has been to sell sugar and rum to the Soviet Union at inflated prices, and offer beautiful Caribbean beaches to Soviets and East Europeans who have been rewarded for their efforts with a trip to the tropics. The political development has mirrored this dependence. Cuba, by providing surrogate forces in far-flung places, from Angola to Venezuela, has fomented insurrection and rebellion, which was rewarded by Soviet military protection and subsidies. This, of course, all ended when the Soviet Union dissolved.

It is difficult to understand why Cuba willingly became a colony of the Soviet Union. It is, however, not difficult to see why this island nation is such a mess. On a trip, as in prior ones, there were businessmen at the Hotel Nacional, businessmen from the world over, businessmen who are not pleased with the way the Cubans do business. The excuse that the U.S. trade embargo is the reason why the Cuban economy is in such de-

cline is a fallacious one. The United States does have an economic embargo, but the world isn't the United States, however much Americans act
otherwise. And Cuba is free to do business with any other nation—Canada, France, Germany, Spain, Mexico, Brazil, Japan and the 180-plus other
nations on the face of the earth.

But no one really wants to do business with the Cubans. It is how the
Cubans do business that undermines their economy. They don't pay. The
foreign nationals who live in Havana and front for the Cuban government
have trouble making deposits into their foreign bank accounts to pay their
bills. A Spaniard who travels around Latin America buying for the Cuban
government is unable to make deposits, in a dependable manner, into his
bank account at the ING Bank in Curacao. His checks do not bounce,
but they are not paid. A Venezuelan national also living in Havana is
forced to fly, in a military jet with a diplomatic pouch, to Mexico to pay,
in cash, for merchandise purchased and delivered, after invoices are over-
due by more than 180 days. A Mexican businessman is asked to fly to
Havana to receive payment for items shipped almost a year ago, and then
he is paid in cash, only to find that $3,000 US of the $250,000 US he
received is counterfeit.

Havana, these days, everyone complains, is awash in counterfeit American dollars. There are dozens of businessmen—the German who is trying
to get paid for the Korean steel shipped to Havana, the Mexican who is
threatening to suspend delivery of plastic products to the island, the Brazilian who has sent a container-load of Coke vending machines, the Canadian supplier of souvenirs for the island's hotel chains—who cross
through the lobby of the Hotel Nacional, but they are frustrated businessmen, angry at the capricious and amateurish manner in which the
Cubans handle their economy. On this trip, the familiar grievances and
complaints, the same frustrations and resentments abound. What is
astounding, these businessmen agree, is the contrast among the Cubans:
Miami Cubans are no-nonsense professional businessmen, whereas Havana Cubans are such losers. This is why Havana is not a Casablanca on
the Caribbean, however much it would aspire to be. In Casablanca, deals
were sealed, money changed hands, and buyers and sellers of whatever
commodity walked away satisfied.

There are three ways to do business in Cuba. The first is to sell directly
to the Cuban government, supplying the state. The second is to conduct
business with agents who front for the Cuban government, who typically
are foreigners from other Spanish-speaking countries who reside in Havana. The third is to be granted an exclusive permission to operate an
enterprise as an enclave minieconomy. None are recommended, nor sat-
isfactory. The capricious nature of Cuban officials and the simple fact they
are not very good businessmen makes all three options risky. But returns
reflect the level of risk a venture involves. There are profits to be made,

no doubt, but there is always the possibility that an arrangement may end for any reason, without warning, or for no reason. In the nineteenth century, the Marquis de Custine, an intrepid Frenchman who journeyed through Czarist Russia, made the observation that "[i]n Russia toleration has no guarantee, either in public opinion, or in the constitution of the state: like everything else it is a favour conceded by one man; and that man may withdraw to-morrow what he has granted to-day."[1] This is an accurate appraisal of Cuba at the end of the twentieth century. The whims of a despot govern an entire nation, without any certainty other than the capriciousness. There is a seductive appeal to all of this. For those who long for the adventures of an imagined Wild West, where rules were made to be broken, then Havana in the nineties offers such a business climate. The most perverse manifestations of capitalism, other than that found in illicit activities such as the drug trade, prevail in Cuba.

The sense in Havana is one of frustration. Sitting on the verandah of the Hotel Nacional can be a surreal experience. According to the music, precious and few are the moments we both can share. Then, when conversations are struck with businessmen, things become strange. The stories they tell are out of the Wild West—and to some, there lies the excitement. But the truth is undeniable: frustration suffuses all business transactions. The reason for this is found in the simple fact that Havana Cubans have yet to grasp the fundamental essence of capitalism: When one buys something, one has to pay for it. After decades of Soviet subsidies, the Cubans have forgotten that things cost money, real money and not arbitrary prices set by political committees.

Political and Market Conditions

It is difficult to assess the Cuban situation at present. A few years ago, Spain was the largest foreign investor in Cuba. Today, it is Mexico. This speaks volumes, for the Mexicans, as their eternal emergencies attest, do not have the best judgment in the world. But there are certain things about the Cuban situation that can be said with certainty. To be sure, Cuba remains a potential market for corporate America in the medium and long terms. But even if Castro fell before the reader finishes this sentence, there are significant obstacles impeding the development of lucrative markets on a sustainable basis. Miami Cubans have been masterful in propagating the idea that Cuba is a rich market of over 10 million consumers on America's doorstep, but the reality of the situation is more somber. There are immediate opportunities for consumer goods, but there is a lack of purchasing power, and the initial needs do not constitute a long-term sustainable market. In addition, there are tremendous obstacles to the creation of instant markets on a sustainable basis that are worth considering. Among the areas of concern are:

Political Instability. The idea that exile leaders will assume government positions, even the presidency, is uncertain at best. Other Communist countries have exile communities, yet in none of the former Soviet satellites have exiles returned to take over the government. These countries, particularly Poland and the Czech Republic, have been able to count on financial support from foreign communities of compatriots, but nothing approximates the ambitious plans of exiled Cuban leaders living comfortable lives in Florida. It seems very likely that a series of interim governments will oversee a transition from a Communist to a democratic government, as has been the experience in similar countries. This will entail a period of political instability as the dust settles and a consensus among the Cubans, regardless of where they reside, emerges. Self-styled Cuban exile leader Jorge Mas Canosa indulges in rants similar to those of Fidel Castro, and listening to their rhetoric, it is difficult to tell them apart. The specter of one authoritarian replacing another is not a comforting one. Neither is the prospect of a period of turbulence as a consensus emerges within Cuba and an accommodation is reached with the exile communities abroad. For some reason, Cubans have historically been extreme in their political views. When Castro came to power, for instance, from the beachfront homes of the well-to-do in the Miramar district of Havana, the sunsets were pierced by the sound of firing squads. Men who were not given the benefit of a trial were summarily executed on the beach, which was an effective, if alarming, method for consensus building. The exile community makes heroes of men convicted of blowing up commercial airliners and in Miami, Cuban exiles were involved in a brisk trade with Iran-Contra characters selling weapons to groups planning to overthrow a foreign government. A happy reconciliation among the Cuban people is not too guaranteed.

Impoverished Consumers. Of equal concern is the purchasing power of the Cuban consumer. The collapse of the Cuban economy subsequent to the termination of Soviet subsidies has greatly reduced the incomes of the Cuban people. An individual who lives on $50 a month is not going to purchase many Big Macs or Whoppers—and can only dream about buying a car. The moribund Cuban economy, coupled with a work ethic that is nonexistent, makes it difficult to think that the productivity of the Cuban worker can be raised to adequate levels. It is only natural that Miami Cubans wistfully envision different circumstances, but the Cuban population is woefully unprepared to participate as productive members of a market economy. It is difficult for American executives to envision a nation where everyone loiters around all day because there is nothing to do, and it makes little difference if anything is accomplished, but this is Havana in the 1990s. On a stroll through Havana interviewing residents at random, this becomes evident. When asked what this person studied, ''Russian language'' is the answer. Another person volunteers he studied to work in a nuclear power plant. A third proudly states he worked for the secret police. Fluency in Russian, running nuclear power plants, and state terrorism are not in great demand in capitalist societies, as Russian physicists driving cabs in Moscow have learned. It seems improbable that a nation where people have been, say, memorizing the sayings of Chairman Mao in Russian, has much to offer, other than unskilled manual labor. The Cubans, however, remain oblivious to the humiliating nature of manual labor when forced by unexpected circumstance. Russian cab drivers with Ph.D.s, for instance, are not pleased with their career track under a capitalist system. The same disappointment awaits the Cubans.

Unskilled Labor. Impoverished consumers is what unskilled workers become. There is very little the Cuban worker can do for which a capitalist is prepared to pay. This is most evident in the manner in which the Cuban people have been trained to think for almost forty years. There is a lethargy that is astounding. It is the thinking engendered by the kind of paternalism where the government inculcates the idea that an individual is owed a living by society, whether or not he is prepared to work for it. The lack of ambition among the Cubans is quite remarkable. The Havana Cubans speak in terms of what they are owed—by the Cuban exile communities, by the United States, by the world. It is discomforting to hear people speak in terms of demands. Miami Cubans owe them money. The United States owes them welfare and Social Security and food stamps, not any different from Puerto Ricans. The international community owes them generous grants and aid. But the creation of a welfare state requires revenues. When the question of taxes is mentioned, Havana Cubans stand aghast. The Cuban revolution eliminated taxes, and for almost four decades, no one has paid taxes here. That in a democracy taxes would be necessary is a horrific notion for Cubans who recoil at the prospect of actually paying for something. The mentality of an entire nation that has spent the past forty years living off the largesse of a now-bankrupt philosophy requires time to change. If there is no ambition, there is no foundation for economic growth. It remains unclear how motivation is to be introduced into the Cuban equation, which promises to be challenging given the frustration the Cuban people are bound to feel when they realize they have very few skills that are valued in a market-oriented economy. What is amusing, however, is to hear these demands framed in the archaic vocabulary of Marxism. "Workers" will no longer have their "surplus value" taken for granted and "exploited" by "the bourgeoisie." It is as amusing as listening to an Englishman, who should be cognizant that the U.K. is a member of the G-7 nations for sentimental reasons and not economic ones, speak in terms of empire, or a Mexican, who should be grateful Mexico's creditors have not invaded, speak in terms of revolution. What is not amusing, however, is to witness an entire population, that has nothing to offer a modern economy, demand entitlements of the world with such conviction.

Racism. The question of race is seldom discussed among Cubans. There are, however, racial issues among Cubans. Miami Cubans are white; Havana Cubans are not. A backlash against the 1980 Mariel boatlift that brought over tens of thousands of Cuban refugees to the United States had its origins in racism. For the first time there was a massive wave of nonwhite Cuban exiles arriving in the United States. The educated, professional white Cubans who had steadily arrived since the early 1960s and had successfully settled in south Florida was taken aback by the onslaught of dark-skinned, unskilled Cubans. The frictions within the Cuban exile community was exacerbated by the impact of these refugees on Miami as a whole, and between Cuban Americans and Anglo Americans. Race became an issue and for the first time Miami Cubans, who longingly remembered an "I Love Lucy"–Desi Arnaz image of Cuba, confronted the fact that their homeland was now a nonwhite society. Within Cuba, the irony remained that the Communist Cuban leadership, overwhelmingly was composed of white Cubans ruling over a nation of nonwhites. Fidel Castro, by expelling the professional classes, had inadvertently created an Apartheid government, himself a white man ruling over a nonwhite nation. American silence on this issue is intriguing. If white minority rule in South Africa was immoral, then why is white minority rule in Cuba acceptable? Where are America's senior statesmen such as, say, Jane Fonda, demanding the immediate resignation of Fidel Castro and free elections? It seems very improbable that in free elections Cuba's nonwhite majority would vote for a wealthy white Cuban who has been living a pampered life in the United States. The installation of a white-minority, post-Castro government, therefore, is likely if the same means are used as the ones employed by Castro: force. But for the United States to install a puppet regime in Cuba has domestic political implications among the American people that may or may not be a consideration for Washington politicians. Regardless of who is unfortunate enough to rule, there is no doubt that the question of race will plague Cuba for decades to come. The expected arrival of Miami Cubans as tourists or returning residents will create conflicts, not only because of race, but because they will arrive with money to invest and flaunt, and, needless to say, represent bourgeois decadence.

Absence of Infrastructure. Of equal importance, apart from the human resources of Cuba, there is the question of infrastructure. At a series of meetings with Communist officials, the state of disrepair becomes evident. The investments by the Mexicans in the national telephone company notwithstanding, all other infrastructure—roads, sewers, airports, electrical power generation, water treatment plants—have been languishing for decades. With the exception of unimpressive—by First World standards—structures built for the Pan American Games, Havana is a city collapsing on itself. The declaration of Old Havana as a World Heritage Site by the United Nations' UNESCO has funneled money for the restoration of the colonial part of town. But this is restoring centuries-old structures, not building contemporary buildings or modern infrastructure. The new resorts that dot Varadero, east of Havana, and the restored hotels of Havana itself, are adequate but unimpressive, particularly when compared with the comparable facilities in the Mexican resort of Cancun, just over thirty minutes away by air. Throughout the entire country there is nothing that will provide the basis for sustainable growth for this country into the next century. To make matters more problematic, the kind of infrastructure that is needed will entail years of work, which is to say that it will be a few years into the next century, at the earliest, before Cuba can be ready to participate in a market economy. The funding sources for the billions of dollars in investment remain unclear, particularly when so many capital-starved nations are competing for the same loans. Once funding is secured there will be significant delays until basic infrastructure, such as sufficient electricity and drinking water, comes on-line.

Legal Property Rights. To complicate matters further, there is the question of ownership. A simple stroll through Havana underscores this point. The once-opulent mansions that were seized from or abandoned by their owners have been turned into multiple-family dwellings by the Cuban government. A two-story mansion a block from the Japanese embassy, for instance, is now an apartment building, meaning each room—bedrooms, living rooms, dining hall, salons, and so on—is an efficiency with a family living in it. That these homes have been used by others for so many decades confers legal rights to these occupants, whether or not they are characterized as squatters. At the same time, in most of these cases these homes were not nationalized or expropriated, but confiscated. Competing claims on the same property stand to cause delays as competing rights are contested in legal proceedings. What is the point of opening a McDonald's across from the Hotel Nacional if the property title is in legal limbo for years? If Nicaragua is paralyzed by legal claims after only one decade of Sandinista rule, and the German government has spent fortunes settling competing claims in the former East Germany, then what can be expected of Cuba? The competing claims, both personal and business, are widespread and effusive in Cuban society. There will be tremendous disagreements regardless of how property rights issues are handled. Unless a fund is created to settle these claims, the legal quagmire stands to delay the eventual integration of Cuba into the world economy.

Lack of Exports. The world has changed during the time Cuba has stood still. The Cuban economy of yesteryear, fueled by sugar exports and tourism, will be difficult to revive. There is at present a glut of sugar on world markets. The United States imposes quotas as a way of subsidizing domestic sugar producers whose political lobbyists are influential on Capitol

Hill. That American consumers pay for the inefficiency of American sugar growers is not likely to change. In any event, there are other Caribbean nations that, as part of the Caribbean Basin Initiative, would also increase their sugar exports to the United States if and when America eliminates distortions in this market. The primary Cuban sugar export market, the former Soviet Union, no longer exists, and the component states are not in a position to continue to overpay the Cubans for their sugar. There are few other agricultural products that the island produces in sufficient quantities for the creation of an important export market. Tobacco is a significant industry, but it is as developed as it is likely to get. The U.S. trade embargo has not made it impossible to secure Cuban cigars. While tobacco exports will benefit from the normalization of trade relations with the United States, it cannot be expected to provide the economic basis for sustaining a population of 10 million people. As for tourism, the short-term and medium-term prospects are not promising. The travel ban on Cuba was the impetus for the development of alternative Caribbean resorts, most notably Cancun. The Caribbean is now sufficiently developed to offer an array of choices, and while Varadero is stunning, it is no more beautiful than other resorts. To be sure, there will be an influx of exile Cubans and the curious, but the absence of state-of-the-art facilities will undermine the creation of an instant market. That the Cuban population is so pathetically ill-prepared to participate in a market economy further frustrates efforts to create an in-bond industry in the short term. The development of export markets proves problematic given the relative poverty of what the Cuban economy can offer the world. Cuba may have a shining future, but in the aftermath of the Castro regime, it will be a nation wracked by political instability, filled with poor people who have no marketable skills, obsessed with racial issues, consumed by legal battles over ruined structures, with nothing to sell to the outside world. Through the hype presented by the right-wing elements of the exile community, a more accurate description of Cuba is that of a market of over 10 million impoverished, unemployable, nonwhite consumers, with a bad attitude and worse work ethic. It is quite a somber prospect.

Note: No U.S. law was violated in compiling the information on Cuba.

Quick Facts on Cuba:

Population: 10,450,000

Ethnic Groups: 40% mulatto (European and African), 25% African, 20% European, 15% other

Religions: Atheist state, but 82% Roman Catholic, 15% Santeria, 3% other

Urban: 82%

Language: Spanish

Business Language: Spanish, English

Work Force: Not available

For further information, contact:

Mark Seigelman
U.S. Department of Commerce
14th Street and Constitution Avenue, N.W.
Washington, DC 20230
Tel.: (202) 482-5680

EL SALVADOR

Background

El Salvador has emerged from an eleven-year civil war that cost over $2 billion and resulted in the deaths of over 75,000 civilians. This astounds, considering this nation consists of fewer than six million people, whose average income is below $1,000 US per year. El Salvador is not a large market. Rural and impoverished, the single largest source of income for this nation is U.S. foreign aid and money sent by Salvadorans living in the United States to their relatives. Since the peaceful transition to a multiparty system, the United States has provided over $5 billion in assistance, making El Salvador, along with Israel and Egypt, one of the largest beneficiaries of American largesse in the world.

The economy has experienced modest growth, which stands to become more sustainable as democratic reforms continue. The opening of the economy first began under President Alfredo Cristiani in 1989. A program to transform this economy into a market-driven one began with tremendous enthusiasm. While administrative impediments were removed, and a free-market exchange rate implemented, for an impoverished nation whose population remains uneducated, the benefits of economic reform have only benefited a small elite. Indeed, a familiar problem now threatens to undermine Salvadoran peace: inequitable distribution of wealth. That the former rebels are now members of parliament has done little for the masses of Salvadorans. In this trickle-down economy, nothing has trickled down.

That is, of course, except the benefits parliamentarians with rebel credentials now enjoy. The sad truth remains that by being coopted, former rebel leaders have accumulated wealth and privilege, and have apparently abandoned the work of making Salvadoran society a just one in which all members enjoy the benefits of a market economy. The orthodox fiscal and monetary policies of the 1990s have worked remarkably well, helping El Salvador achieve some semblance of an open economy, and trade has increased. The implementation of IMF-approved development programs, however, have done little to educate the workers, stimulate middle-class growth, or ameliorate the unspeakable poverty in which El Salvador's rural population lives. For American executives these are compelling impediments, for they undermine the development of sustainable economic growth.

This is not to diminish the achievements the Salvadorans have made. El Salvador's foreign debt has been rescheduled, and the country is now in good standing with the World Bank and the Inter-American Development Bank. In 1991 El Salvador became a member of GATT. In the early 1990s, annual growth rates averaged around 3 percent per annum, and thousands of Salvadorans who had fled to Mexico and the United States have returned home, with better educations, more skills, and greater expectations of their leaders. The opening of the economy has continued, and civil unrest is diminished. Once a battlefield, San Salvador is once again a civil place.

Economic Model

El Salvador has been successful in keeping inflation down to single digits. In 1991, for instance, revised figures show a growth rate of 3.5 percent and an inflation rate of 9.8 percent, and the exchange rate between the Salvadoran colon and the U.S. dollar stabilized at about 8 to 1. The market-driven reforms are transforming the economy, and achieving a level of greater integration with the other nations of Central America. The United States remains El Salvador's chief trading partner. The number of Salvadorans now living in the United States—in southern California and southern Florida—has contributed to growth in air travel between these two nations. An open market economy, however, does make it more difficult for people at the bottom, in this case the majority of the population, to have access to the benefits available in a free marketplace.

One of the centerpieces of reforms is the privatization program. The banking system, once a bastion of inefficiency and corruption, is now almost completely privatized. At the same time, monopolies are being ended. Coffee, El Salvador's chief export, and sugar, long the bases of wealth for Salvadoran oligarchies, are entering the age of competition. The stability of world prices and the increased attractiveness of Salvadoran currency have unleashed a wave of new planting. The boost in real prices, the introduction of competition, and remarkably good weather for the past several years is shown in the robust harvests throughout most of the 1990s. Previous declines in the cotton business have been reversed, and it is hoped this sector will register growth for the rest of the decade. The agricultural sector continues to improve all around, but remains indicative of how dependent the nation's economy is on the export of primary goods.

The prospects for industry, however, are not as promising. Long benefiting from protectionism, the inefficiency of Salvadoran manufacturing is legendary. Since the lowering of tariffs and the dismantling of protectionism, industry has not been successful in coping with international competition. Apart from in-bond facilities, mostly in the textile area, most foreign investors are in El Salvador to take advantage of the lower labor costs a weaker colon represents, and to benefit from the Caribbean Basin Initiative. The free trade zones in which these plants operate, however, are all filled to capacity and are not a major source of employment. While Salvadoran workers are able and disciplined, there are not facilities in place to mass assemble American components. For the nation, too, it is not clear if this kind of dependence on rote manual work is a sound economic development policy. For now, however, El Salvador is clearly on the road to an open market economy, and the resolution of the nation's civil war is welcome, for it is evidence that a stable business environment is possible once hostilities end.

Political and Market Conditions

The Foreign Investment Promotion and Guarantee Law of 1988 and the Export Promotion Law of 1990 have done much to restore El Salvador's credibility to the international community. El Salvador is a very small market, without a doubt. There is not much money to be made there, nor are the opportunities compelling. What is significant about El Salvador, however, is that it shows how an entire society can be transformed by democratic reform and a market economy. It is almost impossible to believe that the peace accord signed in 1992 has worked so well. Walking around San Salvador, the changes are remarkable. A few years ago, right-wing death squads roamed the streets and left-wing guerrillas placed car bombs in front of shopping centers. Across the political spectrum, death and terror reigned upon a hapless civilian population. In contrast, and without irony, the Farabundo Martí National Liberation Front (FMLN) and the Nationalist Republican Alliance (ARENA) now share offices in the National Congress Building, one floor away from each other. They dominate the Legislative Assembly and have embarked on reform programs. But in the twelve-year civil war, there was much damage done not only to the political structure and economy of the nation, but also to the Salvadoran people.

There are critics, and their concerns are valid. The progress in El Salvador, however, merits the benefit of the doubt. It is impossible to do everything at once. And while not enough has been done to alleviate the disturbing poverty of the urban poor and rural populations, then again, significant progress has been made in ensuring that terror will not befall this nation in the future. The dismantling of the National Guard and the Treasury Police, for instance, does much to allay fears that police security forces could be engaged in terrorism. These organizations, replaced by a new National Civilian Police, violated human rights as a matter of course, as did the army, which has been cut by 60 percent. Under the auspices of the United Nations, much progress has been made in institutionalizing democratic processes. Human rights abuses have become rare, and not a single "disappearance" has been reported in almost four years. The business climate has improved dramatically, which is often the case when stability is thrown into the equation. American aid has fostered the return of economic growth. Foreign investment, once unthinkable, is coming back after a generation, as are Salvadorans who fled the violence of their homeland.

On the social front, however, much remains to be done. The poor remain poor. One central aspect of the peace plan calls for a redistribution of land to over 40,000 former combatants from both sides. This has not been completed, and the slow pace further undermines the ability of rural farmers to take advantage of the planting season. Soldiers and peasant rebels alike wish to return to their homes, their lands, and their livelihoods. The implementation of land reform and supporting agricultural development programs will be the centerpiece of lasting peace. The costs of reconstruction, too, have been higher than anticipated; one car bomb can ruin more than a whole block. Of equal concern, too, is the failure to agree upon a coherent, market-oriented development plan. To depend on foreign aid is not a long-term development model that should be entertained for long. A program to educate the people, increase agricultural exports, and establish a manufacturing industry—whether in-bond or light industrial—is a prudent course of action. The geographic location of the country is ideally suited for making the most of the free trade agreement among the nations of Central America. The progress, overall, has been tremendous and El Salvador now offers hope.

Quick Facts on El Salvador:

Population: 5,625,000

Ethnic Groups: 75% mestizo (European and Native American), 15% European, 10% other

Religions: 93% Roman Catholic, 7% other

Urban: 43%

Language: Spanish (95%), other (5%)

Business Language: Spanish, English

Work Force: 55% agriculture, 25% services, 18% industry and commerce, 2% other

For further information, contact:

> Embassy of El Salvador
> 2308 California Street, N.W.
> Washington, DC 20008
> Tel.: (202) 265-9671

> Helen Lee
> U.S. Department of Commerce
> 14th Street and Constitution Avenue, N.W.
> Washington, DC 20230
> Tel.: (202) 482-2528

FRENCH GUIANA

Background

French Guiana is a colonial possession of France. The French established Cayenne as a settlement in 1604. Not much has happened since. By this it is understood that, like Suriname and Guyana, French Guiana seems to have been forgotten by its European colonizer. With just over 100,000 people, mostly descendants of renegade black slaves and indigenous tribespeople, French Guiana remains mostly unpopulated.

Economic Model

The economy survives on small commerce, gold mining, the exploitation of roundwood production, a small fishing fleet comprised of seventy-two shrimping vessels, and light agriculture. French Guiana's budget expenditures are authorized by the French government. The colony remains a colony.

Political and Market Conditions

Apart from periodic satellite launches by Arianespace, the commercial arm of the European Space Agency, little is heard from French Guiana. There is little interest in developing French Guiana at present. Its limited market can be served from Suriname.

Quick Facts on French Guiana:

Population: 115,000

Ethnic Groups: 66% Creole, 28% Native American, 6% European

Religions: Not available

Urban: 27%

Language: French (Official)

Business Language: French

Work Force: Not available

For further information, contact:

> Embassy of France
> 4101 Reservoir Road, N.W.
> Washington, DC 20007
> Tel.: (202) 944-6000

> International Trade Administration
> U.S. Department of Commerce
> 14th Street and Constitution Avenue, N.W.
> Washington, DC 20230
> Tel.: (202) 377-0703

GUYANA

Background

Guyana gained its independence from the United Kingdom in 1966, but it was only in 1992 that the Guyanese people have been freed. Prior to independence, Cheddi Jagan was elected president of Guyana in free elections. The United Kingdom and the United States, however, feared that the Jagan administration would be too sympathetic to leftist causes, most notably the Cuban revolution, which had only then consolidated power. After a series of meetings in Washington at which Cheddi Jagan attempted to reassure the Kennedy White House that Guyana would re-main in the Western camp of the cold war, John F. Kennedy instructed the Central Intelligence Agency to overthrow the government of Guyana.

The ensuing chaos prompted the United Kingdom to delay independ-ence until 1966. Guyana was subsequently ruled by Forbes Burnham, who was characterized even by the British as an opportunist. The only achieve-ment during this period was the amassing of a vast fortune by the Burn-ham family and their friends. Guyana descended into a backward spiral of economic stagnation and repressive political rule. In 1985 Hugh Des-mond Hoyte was elected president. He implemented an Economic Re-covery Program (ERP) designed to arrest the nation's dramatic decline. It proved a successful program in that the free market reforms and the liberalization of both trade and the currency markets produced results. By 1990 Guyana's GNP approximated that of 1976, which is, incredibly, an achievement. Since then, currency stability and the gradual opening of the economy have offered stability to this ravaged country, so much so that in 1992's presidential elections, Cheddi Jagan won again.

That a Jagan administration is now in power after having been deposed by the U.S. government creates certain delicate problems for both countries. The situation is further aggravated by American law: Secret documents detailing the Kennedy administration's directives to overthrow the government of Guyana are scheduled to be declassified, which is being fought by the CIA. The possibility of embarrassment remains great, but the Jagan administration has not sought to exploit the situation thus far. The prospects for American companies are ambivalent. While there are limited opportunities in this impoverished country, there is also the embarrassment of new reminders of a shameful chapter in U.S.–Guyana relations making headlines in the 1990s.

Economic Model

The economic policies now underway attempt to rationalize the economy. The privatization of the telephone company and the selling of stakes in the timber, fishing, rice, bauxite, and sugar industries have not only revitalized the private sector, but increased state revenues. Guyana is currently working with international lending bodies on reducing its foreign debt while diversifying its economy. An export-led strategy, however, is tempered by the nature of Guyana exports. It depends on sugar and rice, for instance, which are volatile commodities. The privatization of the Guyana Sugar Corporation has been slow in coming, and the protective measures implemented by the United States limits Guyana's access to American consumers. The market for rice, however, enjoys the advantage of a quota established by European countries to assist this nation, as well as neighboring Suriname, to increase its exports. The area of greatest growth potential remains forest and forestry products. An Amazon nation, Guyana has the potential of supplying forest products through renewal efforts. Timber exports are expected to generate about $75 million US in 1995, which compares favorably with the growth prospects of the mining industry.

The Jagan administration is committed to market reform and greater regional integration. The diversification of the economy depends on increased tourism; this remains difficult as Americans remember Guyana as the site of the mass suicide of Jim Jones and his followers. Other nontraditional industries require significant development time, particularly given the low urbanization of the country and the almost nonexistent infrastructure. The World Bank and International Monetary Fund are active in seeking solutions to the pressing development needs of the nation. The World Bank, for instance, is seeking greater investments in Guymine, the nation's mining company, for the more efficient production of export products such as bauxite and gold. There are several programs in place to increase the export of seafood and seafood products, as well.

Political and Market Conditions

The political turmoil in Guyana can best be summed up with one sta-
tistic: Guyana's major export is people. The socioeconomic conditions in
the country have resulted in emigration on a continuing basis. Only in
the past three years has this trend been arrested. Guyana remains poor
and underdeveloped from the poverty of its human resources. As such,
the relative size of the Guyanan economy, and regional integration efforts,
make it more viable to service this market from Venezuela. Unless the
economic conditions in Venezuela deteriorate, Guyana will continue to
receive about a third of its total imports from this neighbor. The market
for consumer products remains small, but can be serviced from Caracas.
The export of capital goods and equipment, however, will continue to
come from the United States directly. The markets for telecommunications and electric power generation continue to grow. Atlantic Tele-
Network, of the U.S. Virgin Islands, acquired 80 percent of Guyana's
telephone company in 1991. Investment has opened up new opportunities. Mobil Oil is involved in oil exploration off the coast of Guyana.
United Parcel Service now has a subsidiary in Georgetown. Corporate
America is slowly entering this nation. The continuing infrastructure problems, however, pose serious impediments to the development of the country. International aid programs center on securing the investment capital
required to establish investor confidence and provide the foundation for
sustainable economic growth. American firms are encouraged to contact
the U.S. Department of Commerce for information on current development projects.

Quick Facts on Guyana:

Population: 755,000

Ethnic Groups: 50% East Indian, 44% African, 4% Native American, 2% European,
2% Chinese

Religions: 57% Christian, 33% Hindu, 9% Muslim, 1% other

Urban: 35%

Language: Creole English (78%), English (15%), other (7%)

Business Language: English

Work Force: 45% industry and commerce, 32% agriculture, 23% services

For further information, contact:

> Embassy of Guyana
> 2490 Trace Place, N.W.
> Washington, DC 20008
> Tel.: (202) 265-6900

William Dowling
U.S. Department of Commerce
14th Street and Constitution Avenue, N.W.
Washington, DC 20230
Tel.: (202) 482-1648

HONDURAS

Background

Honduras has enjoyed greater stability than its neighbors. A small, impoverished country, opportunities in Honduras are relatively insignificant. An undeveloped economy, its chief exports are agricultural products and its impoverished consumers do not represent a significant market for consumer products. Nevertheless, Honduras is on the road to sustainable growth. Honduras is well positioned to take advantage of the Central American Common Market. In the 1980s and early 1990s, however, the situation in the country was strained due to the influx of refugees from both El Salvador and Nicaragua. That Honduras was a staging area for U.S.–backed guerrillas plotting to overthrow the Nicaraguan government in the 1980s made the nation something of an international pariah. The new government, however, has been forceful in claiming Honduran sovereignty and asserting itself on the world stage. Honduras, for instance, agreed to receive 5,000 Cuban rafters rescued by the U.S. Coast Guard in the fall of 1994, which was a significant contribution to American foreign policy objectives in the area.

Economic Model

Economic policies now underway attempt to rationalize the economy, although there are certain caveats. Honduran president Carlos Roberto Meina assumed office in September 1993 and has continued the reforms of his predecessor, Rafael Leonardo Callejas. The fiscal deficit was reduced, the Honduran lempira was sharply devalued, foreign exchange was liberalized, and most restrictions on commercial lending were lifted. As a consequence, the economy began to grow, a modest 2.2 in 1991 and approximately the same in both 1992 and 1993. The agricultural sector enjoyed the greatest benefits, although banana exports declined, caused by both bad weather and trade disagreements with the Europeans. That coffee prices were depressed in the first half of the 1990s undermined the growth of exports.

As a result of these obstacles, greater emphasis has been placed on encouraging light industrial assembly plants. Apparel exports, for example, more than doubled, from $80 million to over $195 million, from 1990 to 1991. The creation of industrial parks further encourages growth in this area. Other efforts have not been as successful, but Honduras remains committed to developing within the framework of a market-driven economy. It has to be noted that the Meina administration was alarmed by the Mexican Meltdown. Fearful that this is the inevitable consequence of economic liberalization, Honduras in 1995 moved with greater prudence and reservation.

Political and Market Conditions

The political stability of Honduras is unquestioned; its commitment to economic reform is not. A return of statist ideas has marked the Meina administration, more as a reaction to the economic upheaval in Mexico than out of political conviction. The consequences are the same, nevertheless. Honduras is threatened by an economic slowdown precipitated by fiscal policies designed to moderate the opening of the economy. The nefarious effects of statist policies, unfortunately, stand to undermine the progress made thus far. While these have been small steps, which have not produced the benefits to meet the needs of its people, they have to be given time, particularly since Hondurans are so poor and uneducated. It is impossible to bring instant prosperity when there are so many pressing needs. The economic consequences of political decisions could set the nation back. The temptations to increase social spending, raise barriers, and increase taxes are very much in evidence. The Meina administration, however, must resist the hasty conclusion that the Mexican Meltdown is an inevitable aspect of economic integration.

Quick Facts on Honduras:

Population: 5,250,000

Ethnic Groups: 80% mestizo (European and Native American), 15% European, 15% Native American, 5% black

Religions: 93% Catholic, 7% other

Urban: 43%

Language: Spanish (97%), black Caribbean (2%), other (1%)

Business Language: Spanish, English

Work Force: 30% industry and commerce, 30% agriculture, 25% services, 10% other

For further information, contact:

> Foundation for Investment and Export Development (FIDE)
> A. P. 2029
> Tegucigalpa, D.C.
> Honduras

Tel.: (504) 320-937
Fax: (504) 321-808

Helen Lee
U.S. Department of Commerce
14th Street and Constitution Avenue, N.W.
Washington, DC 20230
Tel.: (202) 482-2528

Consulate General of Honduras
80 Wall Street, Suite 915
New York, NY 10005
Tel.: (212) 269-3611

JAMAICA

Background

Encountered by Christopher Columbus in 1494, the Spanish settled Jamaica for most of the sixteenth century. In 1670 Britain took possession of the island, following the signing of the Treaty of Madrid. In 1958 Jamaica joined nine other British colonies to form the West Indies Federation. It withdrew three years later and in 1962 gained independence from the United Kingdom. Jamaica, like Belize, is a member of the Commonwealth. The island nation is a multiracial society, with immigrant populations from various parts of the world. While class and race are an issue, Jamaica remains a socially harmonious society. Impressive gains have been made in education, and the emergence of a middle class is a significant reason for the greater social and economic mobility that are erasing the vestiges of colonialism.

Economic Model

Historically, Jamaica's economy has been based on plantations. The export of sugar, citrus fruit, coffee, bananas, coconuts, and allspice are integral to the economy. Indeed, in efforts to increase coffee exports, massive deforestation is taking place on this, the third largest island in the Caribbean. Industry is relegated to the export of minerals, including alumina and bauxite, and light industry such as garments, processed food, rum, molasses, and cement. Tourism plays a crucial role; since the imposition of the U.S. trade embargo against Cuba, Jamaica has benefited and world-class resorts have been developed in the intervening decades.

Jamaican economic growth has been restrained by the damage suffered during Hurricane Gilbert in 1988 and by its foreign debt, which, at $4 billion, exacts a heavy burden on the nation's finances. The limits imposed by debt have created tensions in the political economy of the country. Jamaica has struggled to engineer sustainable growth, and it has not always been successful. Unemployment has been high, as has the inflation rate. Severe foreign exchange shortages undermined economic growth. Jamaica, desperate to alleviate its problems, became a champion for leftist causes; Jamaican Prime Minister Michael Manley, for instance, made it a practice to drop in on Fidel Castro in Havana and took a leadership role in calling for a repudiation of the Third World's debt. This George McGovern of the Caribbean, as he was mocked in some circles, found himself helpless as shantytowns spread and Kingston became more violent. Edward Seaga replaced Manley, but he was unable to improve upon the situation. Apart from breaking diplomatic ties with Cuba, Jamaica's problems lingered.

In 1989 Michael Manley became prime minister again, but by this time, his views had changed. His first state visit was to Washington, where he met with President George Bush. A wide-sweeping program to revitalize the Jamaican economy was then embarked upon. Jamaican cooperation on narcotics control efforts, and a more efficient Caribbean Basin Initiative, have helped. Nontraditional exports have increased substantially following the liberalization of trade. Tariffs were reduced, reforms implemented, and the size of government reduced. The result has been a market-driven economy that has resulted in renewed growth rates for most of this decade. The sale of state-owned companies has bolstered state revenue, alleviating both the chronic shortages of foreign exchange and the debt servicing needs required.

Michael Manley resigned in March 1992 because of health reasons. He was replaced by Persival Patterson, who has continued the economic reforms initiated by his predecessor. Indeed, two years after assuming office, the most crucial reform was enacted: Foreign exchange controls were abolished and the Jamaican dollar was allowed to float freely in the markets. This resulted in a devaluation, which has assisted in eliminating the distortions that have plagued the Jamaican economy for years, while proving a drain on the government's foreign reserves. There remain lingering effects in the medium term—only tourism and bauxite exports have benefited structurally from a weaker Jamaican dollar—but the economy now shows signs of growing, without distortions. One reason Jamaica has been able to avoid the trap of heightened inflation after a devaluation is found in how the country has been able to benefit from the Caribbean Basin Initiative. Over half of the nation's exports to the United States entered duty free, within the provisions set forth in the agreements in place. This has helped to diversify the economy at a time of short-term problems associated with economic liberalization and has encouraged Jamaican leaders to stay the course.

Political and Market Conditions

Jamaica has made great strides in dismantling the statist policies that undermined growth. It is committed to market reforms and to participating fully under the terms set forth in the Caribbean Basin Initiative. Its robust tourism industry is one of the fastest-growing sectors of the economy; there are more flights from Miami to Jamaican resorts than to any other Caribbean nation. Prime Minister Patterson is still operating under austerity measures designed to reign in public spending, freeing more capital to the private sector. The reform initiatives have been helpful, but more needs to be done. Inflation and unemployment remain high, and job creation still lags. With a per capita income of $1,600 US, internal demand is small, although Jamaica falls within the average range for most developing countries. This figure underestimates the significant parallel economy that operates informally. Jamaica's "higglers," which is to say, sidewalk and street vendors, are the engines of an informal economy that operates parallel to the official one. The economic contribution of these informal businesses is enormous, by some estimates exceeding $120 million US.

Jamaica's membership in the Caribbean Common Market (Caricom) and governmental success at making significant gains in the economic realm assure political stability. Jamaicans, by nature, are merchants, and the level of economic activity on the streets of Kingston is astounding. That this island nation is now embarked on a program of greater economic integration with its Caribbean neighbors and the whole of Latin America is a welcome development. The misguided socialist policies of the 1960s and 1970s brought much hardship to the Jamaican people. Only in the past decade have the fundamental reforms been made that are laying the groundwork for sustainable growth. The economic liberalization program has met with important success; American Airlines, IBM and W. R. Grace are some of the members of corporate America now doing business on the island nation, and total foreign investment has grown by over $1 billion since the market reforms have been introduced, which is vital to sustainable growth in the years ahead.

Quick Facts on Jamaica:

Population: 2,575,000

Ethnic Groups: 77% African, 15% Afro-European, 3% East Indian, 3% European, 1% Chinese, 1% other

Religions: 60% Anglican, 15% Baptist, 15% Roman Catholic, 10% other

Urban: 51%

Language: Creole English (70%), English (27%), other (3%)

Business Language: English

Work Force: 42% industry, 30% agriculture, 27% services, 2% other

For further information, contact:

> Embassy of Jamaica
> 1850 K Street, N.W.
> Washington, DC 20008
> Tel.: (202) 452-0660

> Mark Seigelman
> U.S. Department of Commerce
> 14th Street and Constitution Avenue, N.W.
> Washington, DC 20230
> Tel.: (202) 482-5680

NICARAGUA

Background

In 1979, Anastasio Somoza, a dictator and U.S. puppet, was overthrown by the Sandinistas. Nicaragua at the time was the quintessential banana republic, run by authoritarian rulers as a private fiefdom. The oligarchical elite remained in power through the National Guard, whose human rights violations were legendary. When the Sandinistas came to power it was difficult to believe that things could become worse. Under the leadership of Daniel Ortega, however, they did. The eleven years of Sandinista rule proved, once again, that despots, whether of the right or the left, are nothing but despots. The country was systematically sacked, and the foreign aid other Latin American nations and the Europeans gave was plundered. That the Reagan administration made overthrowing the Sandinistas the centerpiece of its foreign policy in Central America only made things more ludicrous.

The unbearable nature of the situation was more than evident when in 1990, in free elections, the Sandinistas were soundly defeated. Violeta Barrios Vd. de Chamorro was elected president and, upon assuming office, she discovered that the outgoing Sandinistas had taken everything they were able to, including the toilets. This is as outlandish as when, in 1976, Mexican president Luis Echeverría had the door handles removed when he vacated Los Pinos, the official residence. If the toilets were missing, then what could the incoming administration expect to find in its bank accounts? In fact, they found nothing. Nicaragua, then, has been forced to live through an emergency period, relying on foreign aid, desperately trying to recover from a period of systematic looting.

Economic Model

The economy in 1990 suffered from hyperinflation, bankrupt financial institutions, historic unemployment, a bloated bureaucracy, and a massive brain drain in which 15 percent of the nation's population had fled under Sandinista rule. It has not been easy reviving the moribund economy, or winning back investor confidence. Indeed, 1994 was the first year of growth in more than a decade. Foreign investment was an almost insignificant $50 million and the country has been facing the problems associated with a returning population. Almost 150,000 Nicaraguans fled to Miami and another 75,000 were scattered throughout Latin America. Since 1990 almost 200,000 have returned to their homeland to rebuild their country and their lives. It has not been an easy matter, particularly when economic growth remains tenuous at best. That President Barrios Vd. de Chamorro is committed to market reform is unquestionable. That she will be able to dismantle the statist apparatus the Sandinista left in place is a difficult task.

Her record has been a mixed one. Critics point out that she does too little, too late. In October 1990, for example, the Superior Council of Private Enterprise refused to sign the "Concertación" agreement, in which the government agreed to retain most state employees. The Sandinistas agreed to grant her government civil peace, by which they would refrain from agitating during a six-month grace period. Of greater concern was her inability to remove the Sandinistas from command of the army. It was not until February 21, 1995, that General Humberto Ortega transfered power to General Joaquin Cuadra, which was the first peaceful transfer of the top military post in Nicaraguan history. To her defense, it must be noted that she, in essence, had to work as if in a coalition government. The Sandinistas, while themselves splintering and falling into factions now, commanded tremendous power—and wealth accumulated after a decade of plunder—and could very easily undermine market reforms.

Political and Market Conditions

Since the lifting of the U.S. trade embargo in 1990, Nicaragua has made progress in returning to the community of civilized nations. An embarrassment for neighboring Costa Rica, things have improved tremendously. The nation is only now recovering from the contractions experienced under Sandinista rule. Manufacturing, for instance, dropped by 42 percent during the last three years of Sandinista rule, and agricultural exports declined by a third during the same period. The Barrios Vd. de Chamorro government has made significant progress in dismantling the Nicaraguan Corporation of Public Companies, CORNAP, which was an umbrella agency for the almost 400 state-owned firms nationalized by the Sandinistas. When she took office, her administration found itself in control of over 40 percent of the nation's industrial assets, few of which were being utilized. The ambitious privatization program initiated in 1991 has provided the foundation for economic recovery. What has made progress difficult is the state of disrepair of industrial plant capacity in Nicaragua. The privatization program, for example, only managed to raise $25 million, and foreign investment is about twice that amount.

For further information on Nicaragua's privatization program, contact:

> Corporation for Privatization
> Km. 7-1/2, Carretera Norte
> Apartado 1909
> Managua, Nicaragua
> Tel.: (505) 2-31-100
> Fax: (505) 2-31-193

Nicaragua is a nation whose development plans are on a shoestring. To overcome these obstacles the new government has entered into an impressive liberalization program. These reforms, however, have not taken off as quickly as they would have otherwise, because of the continuing foreign exchange shortage in the country; Nicaraguan exports are insufficient to provide the foreign reserves required for economic growth. While progress has been slow, the political stability of Nicaragua during these austerity years of the new government demonstrate the resilience of the Nicaraguan people. The economy is growing once again, and demand is picking up. The reforms in place will require a few years to take hold, and it is expected that Nicaragua will become an increasingly attractive market as the decade ends. The opportunities in Nicaragua are only now beginning to reveal themselves.

Quick Facts on Nicaragua:

Population: 3,975,000

Ethnic Groups: 72% mestizo (European and Native American), 25% European, 10% Native American, 3% black

Religions: 96% Catholic, 4% other

Urban: 59%

Language: Spanish (95%), Miskito (4%), Creole English (1%)

Business Language: Spanish, English

Work Force: 35% agriculture, 30% industry and commerce, 25% services, 10% other

For further information, contact:

> Embassy of Nicaragua
> 1627 New Hampshire Avenue, N.W.
> Washington, DC 20009
> Tel.: (202) 939-6570

> Jay Dowling
> U.S. Department of Commerce

14th Street and Constitution Avenue, N.W.
Washington, DC 20230
Tel.: (202) 482-1658

PANAMA

Background

Panama is more a convenience than a nation. A former province of Colombia that declared its independence on November 3, 1903, after Colombia rejected a U.S. proposal to build a canal, Panama came into existence for the exclusive purpose of building the Panama Canal. After Mexico and Brazil, Panama is the largest beneficiary of American investment in Latin America. Panama uses the U.S. dollar as its own currency, which not only guarantees a stable exchange rate and complete freedom in capital flows in and out of the country, but has made this country the center for the laundering of drug money. The commercial activities in this nation are enormous; the Panama Canal united the Pacific Ocean with the Caribbean and Atlantic Ocean, creating one of the most important strategic transportation routes in the world.

Panama was a democracy from its creation until 1968 when General Omar Torrijos overthrew the government. A charismatic leader of great intelligence, General Torrijos pursued a nationalist policy that culminated with the signing of an agreement to return the Panama Canal to Panamanian control. Populism was the power base of General Torrijos, whose rule ended when he died in a plane crash in 1981. The general's death notwithstanding, the Panama Defense Forces dominated Panamanian politics. More important, General Manuel Noriega dominated the Panama Defense Forces and ruled with complete control. That General Noriega was involved in drug smuggling and trading with Cuba, and embarked on a radical nationalist policy, did little to improve relations between the United States and Panama. In 1987, after the United States suspended economic and military assistance to Panama, President Eric Devalle attempted to remove General Noriega from heading the Panama Defense Forces. General Noriega removed President Devalle instead.

President Ronald Reagan invoked the International Economic Powers Act and froze all Panamanian government assets in the United States in April 1988. When elections in May the following year indicated a repudiation of General Noriega by the Panamanian electorate, tensions between the United States and Panama mounted. General Noriega refused to accept the election results and prevented the elected officials from taking office, unleashing a wave of violence and terror. A crisis gripped Panama, which culminated with a U.S. invasion in December 1989. That the United States would arrest General Noriega, a sitting head of state of a nation with whom the United States had full diplomatic relations, proved problematic for American courts. Nevertheless, the general was brought to the United States and tried on various charges. The winner of the 1989 election, Guillermo Endara, assumed office. In 1994 Ernesto Perez Ballardes became president, vowing to "close the Noriega chapter."

Economic Model

Panama has experienced strong, stable growth following the return to democracy. In 1991, for instance, the economy grew at an annual rate of 9.3 percent, one of the highest in the developing world. Throughout the 1990s the economy has continued to expand at an impressive rate. The return of civilian rule has also meant the return of Panama's traditional role as a client state for U.S. interests. This is true in the economic realm, where the highly developed services sector accounts for almost 75 percent of the nation's economic activity, and in the political realm as well. The sophisticated banking, financing, and insurance sector continues to register impressive gains, and Panama was one of the few Latin American countries to respond favorably to American requests for assistance in relocating Cuban refugees rescued from sea. The Colon Free Trade Zone is once again contributing to the nation's economic life, which is particularly useful in this period of transition as authority over the Panama Canal Zone is being transfered in phases. Established in 1948, the Colon Free Trade Zone is the largest free trade zone in Latin America and generates almost $8 billion in economic activity, rivaling only Hong Kong. Indeed, Japanese and Korean firms have been aggressive in using the Colon Free Trade Zone as a springboard for supplying markets in Central and South America. The result has been the transformation of Panama into one of the most export-driven in-bond economies in the world, contributing greatly to a diversified economy.

Agricultural exports, which include coffee, bananas, cacao, dairy products, livestock, fisheries, and sugar, contribute 12 percent of the GDP, making Panama one of the least dependent nations on this kind of export. The sustainable economic model has successfully allowed significant income to be derived from the export of agricultural products, while not being dependent on agriculture. The relatively sophisticated state of Panamanian agriculture makes it the most modern agribusiness sector of any Central American nation. Light industry and construction have also experienced impressive rebounds in the 1990s. Demand for construction materials grew, for instance, after there was significant damage from bombing during the capture of General Noriega. In addition to the economic activity generated by rebuilding, domestic industry has done well, particularly in the areas of consumer products, beverages, food processing, and the manufacture of clothing. Unlike its neighbors where this kind of light industry is carried out in in-bond plants for subsequent export, this activity is geared toward domestic consumption. The Bilateral Investment Treaty between the United States and Panama was signed in May 1991, which has done much to increase trade and investment in the country. That Panama also joined GATT that same year has done much to accelerate its integration into the world economy.

Political and Market Conditions

As it stands now, with a few reforms and precautions in place to prevent drug money laundering, the Endara administration has done an admirable job of restoring Panama as an offshore haven and banking center. With over 100 banks in its international banking center, Panamanian banks have over $25 billion US in deposits. Mexico, which has a population almost thirty times that of Panama, barely had $8 billion when it devalued the peso in December 1994. Only two banks, the National Bank of Panama and the National Savings Bank, are state owned, and major U.S. banks, including Bank of America, Citibank, and Chase Manhattan, have offices in Panama City.

If banking and finance are the engines that drive the Panamanian economy, revenues from the Panama Canal traffic tolls are an important aspect of the economy. Rebounding from the marked decline experienced in the late 1980s, revenues are up. For Panamanians, the orderly operation of the Panama Canal, and confidence expressed in traffic, are integral to fostering nationalist identities. The rise in the early 1990s, however, was the result of changes in trade traffic patterns arising from the Persian Gulf War, and growth is expected to be slower for the remainder of the 1990s. What is remarkable is how effortlessly Panama has returned to civility. While there are occasional conflicts from the presence of U.S. armed forces, these are minor compared to the tensions when General Noriega ruled. The nation enjoys political stability, and the only areas of continuing concern are money laundering and drug trafficking activities. Since the return of civilian rule, the transition to sustainable economic growth within a democratic framework has been impressive despite the rehabilitation of some of the discredited characters from the Noriega regime. While the Endara administration includes some men associated with disreputable elements, including drugs and money laundering, the new administration is creating more distance between previous governments and the present one.

Quick Facts on Panama:

Population: 2,575,000

Ethnic Groups: 70% mestizo (European and Native American), 14% West Indian, 10% European, 6% Native American

Religions: 93% Roman Catholic, 6% Protestant, 1% other

Urban: 52%

Language: Spanish (81%), Creole English (14%), Guaymi (2%), Kuna (2%), other (1%)

Business Language: Spanish, English

Work Force: 27% government and services, 25% agriculture, 15% tourism and related services, 10% manufacturing, 6% transportation, 4% construction, 2% canal zone, 11% other

For further information, contact:

> Embassy of Panama
> 2862 McGill Terrace, N.W.
> Washington, DC 20008
> Tel.: (202) 483-1407

> Jay Dowling
> U.S. Department of Commerce
> 14th Street and Constitution Avenue, N.W.
> Washington, DC 20230
> Tel.: (202) 482-1658

SURINAME

Background

In 1975 Suriname gained independence from the Netherlands. With a population of only 400,000 people, this is one of the smallest markets in South America. Impoverished and tormented by turmoil, there are few ready markets in this country. In 1980 and in 1990 coups overthrew the democratically elected governments. Internal strife is only one of the nation's problems. In 1982, for instance, the CIA recommended to the Reagan Administration that the United States should overthrow the government. Secretary of State George Shultz rejected the notion outright, but this suggests how fertile this land is for the absurd.

Economic Model

Prime Minister Jule Ajodhia has embarked on a program of economic reform. Independent from the Netherlands for twenty years, Suriname remains very much impoverished. Bauxite production is still the most commercial mineral, and basic agriculture is the driving force of the economy. Although Gencor Limited, the South African mining concern, has operations in Suriname from when it invested $15 million in bauxite and alumina mines, it is one of the few foreign companies to have a presence in the country. Agricultural production is undermined because it is restricted to the coastal alluvial zone. There are small fisheries and wood processing operations in the country.

Political and Market Conditions

Impoverished and unstable, the political stability of the country cannot be assumed.

Quick Facts on Suriname:

Population: 400,000

Ethnic Groups: 35% Creole, 33% Indian, 16% Javanese, 10% blacks, 3% Native American

Religions: Not available

Urban: 35%

Language: Dutch

Business Language: Dutch

Work Force: Not available

For further information, contact:

Embassy of Suriname
4301 Connecticut Avenue, N.W.
Washington, DC 20008
Tel.: (202) 244-7488

International Trade Administration
U.S. Department of Commerce
14th Street and Constitution Avenue, N.W.
Washington, DC 20230
Tel.: (202) 377-0703

VENEZUELA

Background

It is difficult to believe that a country with the oil wealth that Venezuela is blessed with can be in such a state of chaos. Venezuela has not been able to escape the boom-bust cycle so prevalent throughout Latin America. In some ways, it can be argued that oil has been a curse for this country; other Latin American nations with far fewer resources have managed to achieve more sustainable economic and political developments. An attempted military coup on February 4, 1992, began a chain of events in this country that culminated with a sharp devaluation of the currency, a banking crisis of unprecedented proportions, and economic chaos that has torn asunder the fabric of Venezuelan life. Despite the desperate efforts of President Rafael Caldera, who took office in December 1993, the country languishes in a severe recession that includes a Draconian austerity program, and Venezuela has the dubious distinction of having been the worst performing economy on the mainland of South America in 1994.

The political situation in Venezuela is deteriorating at an alarming rate. The suspension of some constitutional rights remains in effect, with hundreds of people being arrested and detained without charge. The Caldera administration has placed so many controls on the economy that only Communist Cuba has greater government intervention in the economy. The severe recession and high inflation registered in the first three-quarters of 1995 stand to make Venezuela the worst performing economy in South America for the second consecutive year. The banking crisis remains unresolved and the government remains unable to provide the necessary liquidity for a turnaround. In the span of a few short years the positive growth rates registered—Venezuela enjoyed a remarkable 10.4 percent growth rate in 1991—have vanished. In the 1990s, no other country demonstrates more vividly the argument that in Latin America there are no miracles, only mirages.

Economic Model

Venezuela is confronting a crisis of unprecedented proportions. The Caldera administration has reversed the free market reforms implemented in the 1980s by then-president Carlos Andres Perez. There are now so many controls in place that in no other country on the mainland of the Americas does the government exercise as much discretionary power to intervene in the economy as in this nation. The collapse of Venezuela has been a great disappointment to corporate America. "American businessmen are very disillusioned, particularly American businessmen who were planning to use Venezuela as a regional base," an American diplomat was quoted in the *New York Times* in the spring of 1995.

The abandonment of free market reforms, the currency controls in place, and the desperate attempt to control the economy have all met with disappointing failure. The economic consequences of these political decisions are everywhere in evidence; American Airlines, which is expanding in every South American country, reduced by half its air service to Venezuela because of a drop in demand and the new foreign exchange controls in effect. The severing of air links is a shocking reminder of the extent of the crisis to the people of Venezuela. Air service to Miami, for instance, had become so routine that Caracas was jokingly referred to as "Miami Beach South."

The chain of events in the bust of this once-booming nation is monumental in the lessons it holds. Not unlike Mexico, which suffered a devastating reversal, the official Venezuelan government position is that the crisis is a short-term phenomenon and that the restrictions now in place are temporary. Nevertheless, after the failed coup attempt, the country quickly entered a period of continuing crisis. Former President Carlos Andres Perez was charged with corruption and embezzlement and was arrested in May 1995. Three months later the Caldera administration issued decrees suspending basic constitutional rights, permitting the government to seize private property, make arrests without making charges, restrict the travel of its citizens, implement wide-ranging price controls, and extend foreign exchange controls indefinitely. These drastic measures, coming in the midst of a severe banking crisis in which a total of eighteen banks were seized by the government with a total loss of over $7.5 billion US, led to a state of panic among Venezuelans. Many financiers and bankers have fled to exile in Miami, and there is little hope of restoring the liquidity in the banking sector in the short term.

The Caldera administration has gone through two finance ministers, two Central Bank presidents, four planning ministers, and eight economic plans in the first fourteen months of office. As 1995 ended, inflation continued to increase as the recession deepened. Social tensions continued to mount as public discontent became more widespread. The government retaliated by arrests and forcing critics into exile. Venezuela had no coherent economic development plan in force that could address the problems confronting the nation.

Political and Market Conditions

Not since gaining independence from Spain on July 5, 1811, has Venezuela confronted as profound a dilemma as it does at present. The cyclical nature of these crises in Venezuela resides in how dependent the government is on the oil sector. Living in a make-believe economy, oil revenues provide over 80 percent of the government's revenues. Corporate and personal taxes provide less than 7 percent, which creates distortions in a country that has a sizable population and tremendous development needs. The administration of the oil industry, too, continues to prove problematic; Venezuela's oil wealth is too often plundered by politicians and their cronies and surrogates. The stunning charges of embezzlement against former president Carlos Andres Perez reveal how corruption in Venezuela reaches the highest levels of government. This pattern is consistent with other oil-rich Latin American countries, including Mexico and Ecuador.

The susceptibility of the currency to speculation—and devaluation—also reveals the limits of some economies to manage a currency. An economy as dollarized as Venezuela's—oil in the international markets is priced in American dollars—has no reason to have its own currency. If, as is the analytical case in Argentina, vanities are to be indulged, then the local currency should act as a voucher for the U.S. dollar on a fixed ratio. Only then will the value of the currency be sustainable against the U.S. dollar over the long term. Venezuela, however, has not been able to break free of the inflation/devaluation/liquidity crisis cycle.

This is not to say the end is near. As is often the case, this kind of crisis provides opportunities for the next cycle. Venezuela, in all probability, will continue its boom-bust cycles, which means that within thirty-six months, strong growth rates will be registered. It is not likely that these will be sustainable, but for a few years there will be lucrative opportunities. The telecommunications sector, for instance, is one bright spot. The privatization of the national telephone company demonstrated the enormous potential in Venezuela when market reforms are carried out. Pharmaceuticals and processed food, in the early 1990s, also suggested the underlying fundamentals of the Venezuelan economy when permitted to flourish.

In these time of crisis, however, the only priority is the oil sector. The irony is evident: Economic reforms are being reversed that will render Venezuela very much a state-dominated economy dependent on the export of oil. By concentrating on expanding the export of a primary material, Venezuela is falling farther and farther behind its neighbors not only in developing a market-based, open economy, but in diversifying that economy to withstand a future drop in oil prices. However desperate an economic crisis, the suspension of constitutional rights is alarming, for it demonstrates the whimsical and arbitrary nature of the Venezuelan government. If by presidential decree citizens can be arrested without charges being made, then what guarantees do foreign investors have that favorable investments laws will not at some point be changed retroactively?

Despite its expressed commitment to joining Mexico and Colombia in a free trade zone, there is little to ease the mind that this will be permitted to take place. More to the point, it is unclear how tariff and nontariff barriers can be eliminated when there are so many price controls and such government intervention in the domestic economy. If there is no free movement of capital and foreign exchange, it is dubious that free trade can take place in the first place. That Venezuela fails to meet acceptable international protection for intellectual property further complicates the present situation. "Business has come to a complete halt," an American businessman stated to the *New York Times* in the summer of 1995. "Without foreign exchange controls being lifted, no one can pay for anything."

American firms are advised to contact the U.S. embassy in Caracas to ascertain the latest information on developments in the Venezuelan crisis.

Embassy of the United States of America
Avenidas Francisco de Miranda y Principal de la Floresta
Caracas, 1060-A, Venezuela
Tel.: (58-2) 285-2222
Fax: (58-2) 285-0336
Telex: 25501 AMEMB VE

It remains unclear if the Caldera administration plans to return to the market-driven reforms initiated in 1989. A systematic lowering of tariffs and restrictions on the equity participation of foreigners had made the country more attractive. The privatization program in place had created an atmosphere for positive growth. The average tariff on imported goods had dropped to 9 percent and the sweeping economic reforms had laid the foundation for sound, sustainable economic development and regional integration. The reversal, then, is that much more devastating; many American companies had only begun to tap the promising Venezuelan market when the present crisis exploded.

For the short and medium term, however, it is the lack of direction of the Caldera administration, the absence of a sound recovery program, and the deteriorating social, economic and political conditions in the country that cause alarm. Rescue packages are slow in coming when the government is resorting to reprisals and mass arrests. The threat of civil strife looms ominously over Caracas, especially as inflation rages on and there is no order in the foreign exchange markets. The disarray in Venezuela has caused concern among the member nations of OPEC. Venezuela, a founding member of that organization, is seen as a weak link in the cartel's efforts to maintain stability in world oil markets. American companies, including AT&T and GTE, which, as members of a consortium, acquired 40 percent of Venezuela's state-owned telephone monopoly, known as CANTV, are watching developments closely. Foreign debt obligations continue to drain state resources, despite the debt reduction plan reached in December 1990. The outlook through the beginning of 1998 is not encouraging. Over a dozen major banks had to be rescued throughout 1995, adding significantly to the sense of panic and chaos throughout the country as it moved toward a statist economic development model. Venezuela has many matters to attend to before it can convince the foreign investment community that a sustainable economic program is in place.

Quick Facts on Venezuela:

Population: 21,200,000

Ethnic Groups: 67% mestizo (European and Native American), 21% European, 10% African, 2% Native American

Religions: 96% Roman Catholic, 2% Protestant, 2% other

Urban: 83%

Language: Spanish

Business Language: Spanish, English

Work Force: 56% services, 28% industry and commerce, 16% agriculture

For further information, contact:

>   Embassy of Venezuela
>   1099 30th Street, N.W.
>   Washington, D.C. 20007
>   Tel.: (202) 342-2214

>   Laura Zeiger-Hatfield
>   U.S. Department of Commerce
>   14th Street and Constitution Avenue, N.W.
>   Washington, DC 20230
>   (202) 482-4303

NOTE

1. Marquis de Custine, *Empire of the Czar: A Journey through Eternal Russia* (New York: Doubleday, 1989), p. 112.

EPILOGUE

We are having lunch at Fonda del Refugio in Mexico City's Zona Rosa. It is the summer of 1995 and Mexicans are reeling from the austerity program in place. The restaurant is all but empty, and after strolling about for an hour or so, the tension is palpable as Mexicans quietly go about the business of maintaining some dignity during this crisis. Mexico continues to struggle from economic turmoil and political unrest. The political assassinations continue, as does electoral fraud. The country continues to be polarized—the northern states, industrialized and ambitious, their eyes firmly set on the United States, are challenging the authority of the federal government and asserting states rights, while the southern states, rural and poor, reminiscent of banana republics further south, descend into despair and ungovernability. The mounting problems, coupled with the manner in which Ernesto Zedillo has capitulated to foreign interests, inspire little confidence.

Mexico's recovery is underway, to be sure, but it is an irresponsible recovery. The frantic manner in which Zedillo has surrendered Mexico's long-term interests to short-term IMF dictates and the excessive demands of the United States undermine future sustainable growth. What the Mexicans are doing is laying the foundation for future disappointment. By desperately rewriting their laws to allow American banks to come in and take over the financial system, by sabotaging the national symbol of oil, by enacting an austerity program that destroys the middle class, the Zedillo administration is repeating Mexico's mistakes made last century. At that time the whole of the country was controlled by foreigners, and Mex-

icans were reduced to being the mere servants of foreigners. In time this
created a resentment, not unlike how Americans felt in the 1970s when
public perceptions were that Arabs were buying up the country, or how
some Americans now feel about the Japanese.

Corporate America cannot afford to ignore history. There are enormous new opportunities unfolding in Mexico now. But there is a difference between seizing opportunity and becoming an opportunist. The
irresponsible manner of current Mexican leaders should not be an invi-
tation to undermine long-term business in the country. According to Gene
Smith, this is how nineteenth-century Mexico foolishly surrendered its sovereignty and brought ruin upon itself:

In the country which had been New Spain chaos reigned supreme. . . . In a country
larger in size than France, Austria, England, Ireland, Scotland, Italy, Holland, Portugal and Belgium put together, there was not a road that was safe from bandits,
hardly a business that was not in the hands of a foreigner . . . the Acapulco–Mexico
City road was impassable for any wheeled vehicle, and it took a good horse or
mule to travel it; and the road to Vera Cruz was so dangerous that it was not
uncommon for a diligence to arrive at its destination bearing passengers who had
been robbed by one band after another. . . . [1]

Mexico threw itself into the arms of crass European scoundrels in the
nineteenth century, and now ends the twentieth century by throwing itself
recklessly into the arms of corporate America. There will be a backlash of
resentment if corporate America proceeds in an arrogant manner, and
rightfully so.

In the first year of Ernesto Zedillo's six-year presidency it has been
alarming to witness how Mexico's integrity has been compromised. The
regional polarization of the country is disquieting. The threat of disintegration lingers fast precisely because the Mexican revolution is such a
miserable failure. It is seen in the stunned faces of the Mexican people
as they struggle to endure hardship in a dignified manner. Over lunch at
that excellent restaurant, not far from where Emperor Maximilian once
ruled, his lament flashed across my mind. Thinking back at how Finance
Minister Guillermo Ortiz had conducted himself during the emergency
negotiations in Washington and New York in order to save the country in
1995, the enduring problem with Mexico—ruled by men who had never
had responsibility and did not understand it—the prescience of the
doomed Emperor had never before rung so true.

The gentlemen with me—three Americans, one Canadian and a
Frenchman—were all engaged in different business ventures. Quantifying
losses, restructuring present operations, analyzing present opportunities,
a consensus emerged: Mexico had a brilliant future in the medium and
long terms, but it was the short term that was complicated. Looming over

our conversation was concern—fear in fact—at the reckless manner in which the present rulers of Mexico were accumulating debt. In the short span of a few frantic months, Mexico's foreign debt exploded to over $160 billion, the largest foreign debt of any nation in the developing world. Then we discussed the importance of diversifying; four of my companions would fly off to Chile and Argentina, which were booming. And it was clear that Mexico, which was bust, needed time to pick up the pieces of former president Carlos Salinas's ambitions and dreams. Mexico would begin to grow once more in the last quarter of 1996 according to the Mexican government and the IMF.

But as is often the case in Latin America's boom-and-bust cycles, it is important to remember that the opportunities are tremendous, because so are the risks. Profits have to be handsome because the down cycles are devastating. Prudence, however, is always in order. It also bears remembering that even submerging markets offer emerging opportunities. But it is not without irony that Latin Americans turn to religion to bolster their faith.

NOTE

1. Gene Smith, *Maximilian and Carlota: A Tale of Romance and Tragedy* (New York: William Morrow, 1973), p. 100.

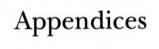

Appendices

APPENDIX I
Newsletters/Journals

Caribbean Update
52 Maple Avenue
Maplewood, NJ 07040
Tel.: (201) 762-1565
Fax: (201) 762-9585

Latin America Index
Welt Publishing
1413 K Street, N.W.
Washington, DC 20005
Tel.: (202) 371-0555

Latin America Monitor
56–60 St. John Street
London, England
Tel.: (44-71) 608-3646
Fax: (44-71) 608-3620

Mexico Business Monthly
52 Maple Avenue
Maplewood, NJ 07040
Tel.: (201) 762-1565
Fax: (201) 762-9585

Mexico Finance
3033 Chimney Rock
Suite 300
Houston, TX 77056
Tel.: (713) 266-0861

Trade Winds
Desert Scribe Publications
P.O. Box 487069
Phoenix, AZ 85068
Tel.: (602) 244-2864

U.S./Latin Trade
Freedom Communications, Inc.
One Biscayne Tower
2 South Biscayne Blvd.
Suite 2950
Miami, FL 33131
Tel.: (305) 358-8373

U.S.–Mexico Free Trade Reporter
1725 K Street, N.W.
Suite 200
Washington, DC 20006
Tel.: (202) 785-8851

U.S./Mexico Trade Pages
The Global Source
1511 K Street, N.W.
Suite 927
Washington, DC 20005
Tel.: (202) 429-5582

Washington Letter on Latin America
1117 North 19th Street
Arlington, VA 22209
Tel.: (703) 783-1717

APPENDIX II
U.S. Trade Promotion Organizations and Resource Foundations

American Association of Exporters and Importers (AAEI)
11 West 42nd Street
New York, NY 10036
Tel.: (212) 944-2230

Caribbean/Latin America Action
1211 Connecticut Avenue, N.W.
Suite 510
Washington, DC 20036
Tel.: (202) 466-7464

Council of the Americas
1625 K Street, N.W.
Suite 1200
Washington, DC 20006
Tel.: (202) 659-1547

Enterprise Development International Foundation
5619 Bradley Boulevard
Bethesda, MD 20814
Tel.: (301) 652-0141

Export/Small Business Development Center
110 E. Ninth Street, Suite A761
Los Angeles, CA 90079
Tel.: (213) 892-1111

Federation of International Trade Associations (FITA)
1851 Alexander Bell Drive
Reston, VA 22091
Tel.: (703) 391-6108

Institute of the Americas
10111 North Torrey Pines Road
La Jolla, CA 92037
Tel.: (619) 453-5560

Latin American Development Corporation
4903 Edgemoor Lane, Suite L-03
Bethesda, MD 20814
Tel.: (301) 652-0179

Latin American Manufacturing Association
419 New Jersey Avenue, S.E.
Washington, DC 20003
Tel.: (202) 546-3803

National Council on International Trade and Documentation (NCITD)
350 Broadway
New York, NY 10013
Tel.: (212) 925-1400

North American Free Trade Association
1130 Connecticut Avenue, N.W.
Suite 500
Washington, DC 20036
Tel.: (202) 296-3019

U.S. Chamber of Commerce
1615 H Street, N.W.
Washington, DC 20062
Tel.: (202) 463-5488

U.S. Council for International Business
1212 Avenue of the Americas
New York, NY 10036
Tel.: (212) 354-4480

World Trade Center Association
One World Trade Center
55th Floor
New York, NY 10048
Tel.: (212) 313-4600

APPENDIX III
U.S. Government Resources

U.S. Department of Commerce
14th Street and Connecticut Avenue,
  N.W.
Washington, DC 20230
Tel.: (202) 482-2000

U.S. Department of State
Office of Commercial, Legislative and
  Public Affairs

Bureau of Economic and Business
  Affairs
Washington, DC 20520
Tel.: (202) 647-1942

APPENDIX IV
Regional Trading Blocs

In December 1994, at the conclusion of the Summit of the Americas, all the nations of the New World, with the exception of Cuba, agreed in principle to form a hemispherewide free trade zone by the year 2005. The Mexican Meltdown occurred two weeks after this historic announcement, but negotiations are on schedule. At present, however, there are regional trading blocs. Following is a list of these trade agreements and the member nations comprising them.

Andean Free Trade Zone

Member nations: Bolivia, Colombia, Ecuador, Peru, and Venezuela

Caribbean Basin Initiative (CBI)

Member nations: Antigua, Aruba, Bahamas, Barbados, Belize, British Virgin Islands, Costa Rica, Dominica, Dominican Republic, El Salvador, Grenada, Guatemala, Guyana, Haiti, Honduras, Jamaica, Montserrat, Netherlands Antilles, St. Kitts and Nevis, St. Lucia, St. Vincent and the Grenadines, Trinidad and Tobago

Caricom (Caribbean Community)

Member nations: Antigua and Barbuda, Bahamas, Barbados, Belize, Dominican Republic, Grenada, Guyana, Jamaica, Montserrat, St. Kitts and Nevis, St. Lucia, St. Vincent and the Grenadines, Trinidad and Tobago

Central American Common Market

Member nations: Costa Rica, El Salvador, Guatemala, Honduras, Nicaragua

Group of Three

Member nations: Colombia, Mexico, Venezuela

Mercosur–Southern Cone Market

Member nations: Argentina, Brazil, Paraguay, Uruguay

North American Free Trade Agreement (NAFTA)

Member nations: Canada, Mexico, United States

APPENDIX V
Development Banks

Andean Development Corporation
P.O. Box 5086, Carmelitas
Altamira, Caracas
Venezuela
Tel.: (582) 285-5555

Banque Francaise de Commerce
  Exterior
21, Boulevard Haussmann
75427, Paris, France
Tel.: (331) 4800-4800

Caisse Centrale de Cooperation
  Economique
Cite du Reito
Rue Boissy d'Anglas, 35-37
75379, Paris, France
Tel.: (331) 4006-3131

Canadian International Development
  Agency (CIDA)
Place du Centre
200 Promenade du Portage
Hull, Quebec
K1A 0G4, Canada
Tel.: (819) 997-7901

Caribbean Development Bank
Wildey, P.O. Box 408
St. Michael, Barbados
Tel.: (809) 426-1152

Central American Bank for Economic
  Integration
Apartado Postal 722
Tegucigalpa, Honduras
Tel.: (504) 372-253

Centre for the Development of
  Industry
Rue de l'Industrie 28
1040, Brussels, Belgium
Tel.: (322) 513-4100

Commonwealth Development
  Corporation
1 Bessborough Gardens
London, England
Tel.: (4471) 828-4488

Commonwealth Development
  Corporation of Australia
Prudential Building, 1st Floor
39 Martin Place
G.P.O. Box 2719
Sydney, NSW, 2001
Australia
Tel.: (612) 227-711

De Nederlandse Investeringsbank voor
  Ontwikkelingslanden NV
P.O. Box 380
Camegieplein 4
The Hague, Netherlands
Tel.: (3170) 342-5455

European Bank for Reconstruction
  and Development
6 Broad Gate
London, England
Tel.: (4471) 496-0060

European Investment Bank (EIB)
100, Boulevard Konrad Adenauer
Luxembourg, Luxembourg
Tel.: (352) 437-91

German Agency for Technical
  Cooperation
Dag Hammarskjold Weg 1
P.O. Box 5180
6236 Eschborn 1, Germany
Tel.: (49) 6196-790

Industrial Fund for Developing
  Countries
P.O. Box 2155

Bremerholm 4
DK-1016, Copenhagen, Denmark
Tel.: (4533) 142-575

Inter-American Development Bank
  (IDB)
1300 New York Avenue, N.W.
Washington, D.C. 20577
Tel.: (202) 623-3900

Japan Development Bank
9-1, Otemachi 1-Chome
Chiyoda-ku, 100
Tokyo, Japan
Tel.: (813) 270-3211

Nordic Investment Bank
Unioninkatu 30
P.O. Box 249
SF-00171, Helsinki, Finland
Tel.: (3580) 1800-1

OPEC Fund for International
  Development
Parkring 8
A-1010 Vienna, Austria
Tel.: (421) 515-640

Overseas Economic Cooperation Fund
Takebashi Godo Building
4-1, Otemachi 1-Chome
Chiyoda-ku, 100
Tokyo, Japan
Tel.: (813) 215-1311

Swedish International Enterprise
  Development Corporation
  (SWEDECORP)
P.O. Box 3144
S-10362, Stockholm, Sweden
Tel.: (468) 667-6600

APPENDIX VI
American Chamber of Commerce Offices in Latin America

Argentina
Union Carbide Argentina
Virrey Loreto No. 2477/81
1426 Buenos Aires, Argentina
Tel.: (54) 782-6016

Bolivia
The Anschutz Corporation
A.P. 160
La Paz, Bolivia
Tel.: (591) 35-5574

Brazil
R. J. Reynolds do Brasil
Raia de Botafogo No. 440/25
P.O. Box 3588
22.250, Rio de Janeiro, Brazil
Tel.: (55) 286-6162

Chile
Fundacion Chile
Casilla 773
Santiago, Chile
Tel.: (56) 28-1646

Colombia
Fiberglass Colombia, S.A.
A.P. 9192
Bogota, Colombia
Tel.: (57) 255-7900

Costa Rica
Peat, Marwick, Mitchell & Co.
A.P. 10208
1000, San Jose, Costa Rica
Tel.: (506) 21-5222

Ecuador
Xerox de Ecuador, S.A.
A.P. 174-A
Quito, Ecuador
Tel.: (593) 245-229

El Salvador
Moore Comercial, S.A. de C.V.
29 avenida Sur No. 817
A.P. 480
San Salvador, El Salvador
Tel.: (503) 71-1200

Guatemala
Foodpro International, Inc.
12 calle 1-25, No. 1114
A.P. 89-A, Zona 10
Guatemala City, Guatemala
Tel.: (502) 320-490

Honduras
Camara de Comercio
21 Avenida S.O. 9 y 10
A.P. 500
San Pedro Sula, Honduras
Tel.: (504) 54-2743

Mexico
Embotelladora Tarahumara, S.A.
  de C.V.
Rio Amazonas, No. 43
06500, Mexico, D.F.
Tel.: (52) 591-0066

Nicaragua
Vigil y Caligaris
A.P. 202
Managua, Nicaragua
Tel.: (505) 262-491

Panama
Citibank, N.A.
A.P. 555
9A, Panama City, Panama
Tel.: (507) 64-4044

Peru
M. J. Godoy & Company, S.A.
A.P. 5661
100, Lima, Peru
Tel.: (51) 28-7006

Uruguay
General Motors Uruguay, S.A.
Sayago No. 1385
Casilla 234
Montevideo, Uruguay
Tel.: (598) 38-1621

Venezuela
Carton de Venezuela, S.A.
A.P. 609
1010, Caracas, Venezuela

Regional Headquarters
Association of American Chambers of
   Commerce in Latin America
National Distillers do Brasil
Avenida Brig. Faria Lima, 4 e 5 Andar
01451, Sao Paolo, Brazil
Tel.: (55) 813-4133

APPENDIX VII
Latin American Banks with New York Offices

Argentina
Banco de Galicia y Buenos Aires
300 Park Avenue, 20th Floor
New York, NY 10022
Tel.: (212) 906-3700
Fax: (212) 906-3777

Banco de la Nacion
299 Park Avenue, 2nd Floor
New York, NY 10071
Tel.: (212) 303-0600
Fax: (212) 303-0805

Banco de la Provincia de Buenos Aires
650 Fifth Avenue, 30th Floor
New York, NY 10019
Tel.: (212) 397-7650
Fax: (212) 397-7676

Banco Quilmes
366 Madison Avenue, Suite 1052
New York, NY 10017
Tel.: (212) 867-3460
Fax: (212) 867-4193

Banco Rio de la Plata
650 Fifth Avenue, 29th Floor
New York, NY 10019
Tel.: (212) 974-6800
Fax: (212) 974-6828

Brazil
Banco Bamerindus do Brasil
10 East 50th Street, 28th Floor
New York, NY 10022
Tel.: (212) 478-5700
Fax: (212) 888-5878

Banco Bandeirantes
280 Park Avenue, 38th Floor
New York, NY 10017
Tel.: (212) 972-7455
Fax: (212) 949-9158

Banco Bradesco
450 Park Avenue, 32nd Floor
New York, NY 10022
Tel.: (212) 688-9855
Fax: (212) 754-4032

Banco do Brasil
550 Fifth Avenue
New York, NY 10036
Tel.: (212) 626-7000
Fax: (212) 626-7045

Banco do Credito Nacional
499 Park Avenue
New York, NY 10022
Tel.: (212) 980-8383
Fax: (212) 755-0626

Banco Economico
499 Park Avenue
New York, NY 10022
Tel.: (212) 758-3700
Fax: (212) 758-3881

Banco do Estado do Parana
125 West 55th Street, 9th Floor
New York, NY 10019
Tel.: (212) 956-0011
Fax: (212) 956-0506

Banco do Estado do Rio Grande do
  Sul
500 Fifth Avenue, 12th Floor
New York, NY 10110
Tel.: (212) 827-0390
Fax: (212) 869-0844

Banco do Estado do Rio de Janeiro
55 East 59th Street, 18th Floor
New York, NY 10022
Tel.: (212) 759-7878
Fax: (212) 759-7288

Banco do Estado do Sao Paolo
153 East 53rd Street
New York, NY 10022
Tel.: (212) 888-9550
Fax: (212) 371-1034

Banco Itau
540 Madison Avenue
New York, NY 10022
Tel.: (212) 486-1280
Fax: (212) 888-9342

Banco Mercantil do Sao Paolo
450 Park Avenue, 14th Floor
New York, NY 10022
Tel.: (212) 888-0030
Fax: (212) 888-4631

Banco Nacional
645 Fifth Avenue
New York, NY 10022
Tel.: (212) 935-6920
Fax: (212) 593-2611

Banco Real
680 Fifth Avenue, 3rd Floor
New York, NY 10019
Tel.: (212) 489-0100
Fax: (212) 307-5627

Banco Safra
1114 Avenue of the Americas
New York, NY 10036
Tel.: (212) 382-9200
Fax: (212) 768-8972

Unibanco
555 Madison Avenue
New York, NY 10022
Tel.: (212) 832-1700
Fax: (212) 754-4872

Chile
Banco Central de Chile
200 Liberty Street, Suite 5127
New York, NY 10048
Tel.: (212) 432-0680
Fax: (212) 423-0747

Banco de Chile
124 East 55th Street
New York, NY 10022

Tel.: (212) 758-0909
Fax: (212) 593-9770

Banco Santiago
375 Park Avenue, 26th Floor
New York, NY 10152
Tel.: (212) 826-0550
Fax: (212) 826-1218

Banco Sudamericano
200 Liberty Street, Suite 8947
New York, NY 10048
Tel.: (212) 938-5896
Fax: (212) 938-5985

Colombia
Banco de Bogota Trust
375 Park Avenue
New York, NY 10152
Tel.: (212) 826-0250
Fax: (212) 715-4313

Banco Popular Dominicano
  BPD International
4186 Broadway
New York, NY 10033
Tel.: (212) 581-4430
Fax: (212) 581-4520

Mexico
Mexico liberated its financial laws in 1995 to allow foreign banks, mostly American, greater options in entering the Mexican market. The Mexican banking system is in a free fall and, with the exception of Banamex and Bancomer, major consolidation within the industry may result in the disappearance of many Mexican banks.

Banca Serfin
88 Pine Street, 26th Floor
New York, NY 10005
Tel.: (212) 574-9500
Fax: (212) 344-0727

Banco de Comercio (Bancomer)
115 East 54th Street
New York, NY 10022

Tel.: (212) 759-7600
Fax: (212) 635-2086

Banco Internacional
45 Broadway, 16th Floor
New York, NY 10006
Tel.: (212) 480-0111
Fax: (212) 635-2086

Banco Mexicano Somex
235 Fifth Avenue
New York, NY 10016
Tel.: (212) 679-8000
Fax: (212) 951-2085

Banco Nacional de Mexico (Banamex)
767 Fifth Avenue
New York, NY 10153
Tel.: (212) 751-5090
Fax: (212) 303-1489

Multibanco Comermex
1 Exchange Plaza, 16th Floor
New York, NY 10006
Tel.: (212) 701-0100
Fax: (212) 422-3559

Nacional Financiera
450 Park Avenue, Suite 401
New York, NY 10022
Tel.: (212) 753-8030
Fax: (212) 753-8033

Panama
Banco Latinoamericano de
  Exportaciones
750 Lexington Avenue, 26th Floor
New York, NY 10022
Tel.: (212) 754-2600
Fax: (212) 754-2606

Uruguay
Banco de la Republica Oriental de
  Uruguay
1270 Avenue of the Americas
New York, NY 10036
Tel.: (212) 307-9600
Fax: (212) 307-6786

Venezuela
Venezuela is experiencing severe financial difficulties. There are exchange
controls in place and a bailout involving
government takeovers of major banks is
underway, putting at risk the liquidity of
the Venezuelan economy.

Banco Consolidado
220 East 51st Street
New York, NY 10022
Tel.: (212) 980-1770
Fax: (212) 644-9809

Banco de la Guaira
55 East 59th Street
New York, NY 10022
Tel.: (212) 888-9400
Fax: (212) 838-9629

Banco Industrial de Venezuela
400 Park Avenue
New York, NY 10022
Tel.: (212) 688-2200
Fax: (212) 832-1588

Banco Interamericano
630 Fifth Avenue, 31st Floor
New York, NY 10111
Tel.: (212) 459-0310
Fax: (212) 459-0315

Banco Mercantil
410 Park Avenue, 16th Floor
New York, NY 10022
Tel.: (212) 838-4455
Fax: (212) 374-1711

Banco Union
609 Fifth Avenue, 2nd Floor
New York, NY 10017
Tel.: (212) 735-1500
Fax: (212) 735-1551

Banco de Venezuela
500 Park Avenue
New York, NY 10022
Tel.: (212) 980-0350
Fax: (212) 593-3948

APPENDIX VIII
Trade Organizations in the United States

Argentine Trade Office
900 Third Avenue, 4th Floor
New York, NY 10022
Tel.: (212) 759-6477

Argentine Trade Office
3580 Wilshire Blvd., Suite 1412
Los Angeles, CA 90010
Tel.: (213) 623-3230

Brazilian Government Trade Office
551 Fifth Avenue, Suite 201
New York, NY 10176
Tel.: (212) 916-3200

British Trade and Investment Office
845 Third Avenue
New York, NY 10022
Tel.: (212) 745-0495

Canadian Commercial Corporation
501 Pennsylvania Avenue, N.W.
Washington, DC 20001
Tel.: (202) 682-1740

Colombian Export Promotion Agency
259 Park Avenue
New York, NY 10177
Tel.: (212) 972-7474

Colombian Export Promotion Agency
One Biscayne Tower, Suite 2570
2 South Biscayne Blvd.
Miami, FL 33131
Tel.: (305) 374-3144

Invest-in-France
610 Fifth Avenue, Suite 301
New York, NY 10020
Tel.: (212) 757-9340

APPENDIX IX
U.S. Trade Promotion Organizations

American Association of Exporters and
  Importers
11 West 42nd Street
New York, NY 10036
Tel.: (212) 944-2230

Federation of International Trade
  Associations
1851 Alexander Bell Drive
Reston, VA 22091
Tel.: (703) 391-6108

National Council on International
  Trade and Documentation

350 Broadway
New York, NY 10013
Tel.: (212) 925-1400

U.S. Council for International Business
1212 Avenue of the Americas
New York, NY 10036
Tel.: (212) 354-4480

World Trade Centers Association
One World Trade Center, 55th Floor
New York, NY 10048
Tel.: (212) 313-4600

APPENDIX X
Inter-American Development Bank Offices in Latin America

Argentina
Calle Esmeralda No. 130, Pisos 19 y 20
Casilla de Correo No. 181, Sucursal 1
Buenos Aires, Argentina

Bahamas
IBM Building, Fourth Floor
Box N-3743
Nassau, Bahamas

Barbados
Maple Manor, Hastings
Box 402
Christ Church, Barbados

Bolivia
Edificio "BISA," 5o Piso
Avenida 16 de julio, No. 1628
La Paz, Bolivia

Brazil
Praia do Flamengo, No. 200
Caixa Postal 16209, Z0-01
Rio de Janeiro, Brazil

Chile
Avenida Pedro de Valdivia No. 193,
  11o Piso
Casilla No. 16611, Correo 9,
  Providencia
Santiago de Chile, Chile

Colombia
Avenida 40-A, No. 13-09, 8o Piso
Apartado Aereo No. 12037
Bogota, Colombia

Costa Rica
Edificio Centro Colon, 12o Piso
Paseo de Colon, por calles 38 y 40
San Jose, Costa Rica

Dominican Republic
Avenida Winston Churchill
Esquina Calle Luis F. Thomen, Torre
  BHD
Apartado Postal No. 1386
Santo Domingo, Dominican Republic

Ecuador
Avenidas Amazonas No. 477 y Roca
Edificio Banco de los Andes, 9o Piso
Apartado Postal 9041, Sucursal 7
Quito, Ecuador

El Salvador
Condominio Torres del Bosque
Colonia La Moascota, 10o Piso
Apartado Postal No. 01-199
San Salvador, El Salvador

Guatemala
Edificio Geminis No. 10
12 Calle 1-25, Zona 10, Nivel 19
Apartado Postal 935
Ciudad Guatemala, Guatemala

Guyana
47 High Street, Kingston
Box 10867
Georgetown, Guyana

Haiti
Batiment de la Banque Nationale de
  Paris
Angle de la Rue Lemarre et Calve
Boite Postale 1321
Port-au-Prince, Haiti

Honduras
Edificio Los Castanos, 5o y 6o Pisos
Colonia Los Castanos
Apartado Postal C-73
Tegucigalpa, Honduras

Jamaica
40-46 Knutsford Boulevard, 6th Floor
Box 429
10, Kingston, Jamaica

Mexico
Paseo de la Reforma No. 379, 7o Piso
Colonia Cuauhtemoc
06500, Mexico, D.F.

Nicaragua
Edificio BID
Kilometro 4-½, Carretera a Masaya
Apartdo Postal 2512
Managua, Nicaragua

Panama
Avenida Samuel Lewis
Edificio Banco Union, 14o Piso
Apartado Postal 7297
5, Panama City, Panama

Paraguay
Edificio Aurora I
Calle Caballero
Esquina Eligio Ayala, 2o y 3o Pisos
Casilla 1209
Asuncion, Paraguay

Peru
Paseo de la Republica No. 3245, 14o
  Piso
Apartado Postal No. 3778
San Isidro
27, Lima, Peru

Suriname
Zwartenhovewn Brugstraat
32 Boven
Paramaribo, Suriname

Trinidad and Tobago
Tatil Building, 11 Maravel Road
Box 86
Port of Spain, Trinidad

Uruguay
Andes No. 1365, 13o Piso
Casilla de Correo 5029, Sucursal 1
Montevideo, Uruguay

Venezuela
Nucleo A, 16o Piso
Conjunto Miranda
Multicentro Empresarial del Este
Avenida Liberador, Chaco
1060, Caracas, Venezuela

APPENDIX XI
Foreign Chambers of Commerce in the United States

Argentine–American Chamber of
  Commerce
10 Rockefeller Plaza, Suite 1001
New York, NY 10020
Tel.: (212) 698-2238

Argentine Trade Office
Two Illinois Center, Suite 1408
233 North Michigan Avenue
Chicago, IL 60601
Tel.: (312) 565-2466

Brazilian–American Chamber of
  Commerce
80 South 8th Street, 18th Floor
Miami, FL 33130
Tel.: (305) 579-9030

Colombian–American Chamber of
  Commerce
150 Nassau Street, Suite 2015
New York, NY 10038
Tel.: (212) 233-7776

Latin American Manufacturing
  Association
419 New Jersey Avenue, S.E.
Washington, DC 20003
Tel.: (202) 546-3803

Mexican Chamber of Commerce of
  the County of Los Angeles
125 Paseo de la Plaza, Suite 404
Los Angeles, CA 90012
Tel.: (213) 688-7330

Mexican Chamber of Commerce of
  the United States
730 Fifth Avenue, 9th Floor
New York, NY 10019
Tel.: (212) 333-8728

North American–Chilean Chamber of
  Commerce
220 East 81st Street
New York, NY 10028
Tel.: (212) 288-5691

Puerto Rican Chamber of Commerce
  of the United States
212 West 79th Street
New York, NY 10024
Tel.: (212) 724-4731

Trinidad and Tobago Chamber of
  Commerce of the United States
Trintoc Services, Ltd.
400 Madison Avenue, Suite 803
New York, NY 10017
Tel.: (212) 759-3388

U.S.–Mexican Chamber of Commerce
1900 L Street, N.W., Suite 612
Washington, DC 20036
Tel.: (202) 296-5198

Venezuelan–American Association of
  the United States
115 Broadway, Suite 1110
New York, NY 10006
Tel.: (212) 233-7776

APPENDIX XII
Central American Trade Organizations

Costa Rica

Costa Rican Coalition of Development
Initiatives (CINDE)
Box 7170-1000
San Jose, Costa Rica
Tel.: (506) 20-0036
Fax: (506) 20-4754

Federation of Private Businesses of
Central America and Panama
Apartado Postal 539-1002
Barrio Francisco Peralta
Avenida 8, entre calles 33 y 35
San Jose, Costa Rica
Tel.: (506) 53-9815
Fax: (506) 25-2025

El Salvador

National Association of Private
Enterprise
Apartado Postal 1207
Alameda Roosevelt y 55 Avenida Sur,
No. 2827
San Salvador, El Salvador
Tel.: (503) 24-1236
Fax: (503) 23-8932

Salvadoran Foundation for Economic
and Social Development
(FUSADES)
Edificio La Centroamericana,
Apartado Postal 01-278
San Salvador, El Salvador
Tel.: (505) 23-2738
Fax: (505) 23-4723

Guatemala

Entrepreneurial Chamber of
Commerce
Edificio de Industria
9 Nivel, Ruta 6, 9-21

Zona 4, Guatemala City, Guatemala
Tel./Fax: (502-2) 316-513

Honduras

Foundation for Investments and
Development of Exports
2 Nivel, Centro Comerical Maya
Boulevard Morazan, Apartado Postal
2029
Tegucigalpa, Honduras
Tel.: (504-3) 2-9345
Fax: (504-3) 1-1808

Honduran Council of Private
Enterprise
Edificio la Plazuela, 1o Piso
Barrio la Plazuela, Honduras
Tel.: (504) 3 7-4371
Fax: (504) 3 7-4339

Nicaragua

Superior Council of Private Enterprise
Apartado Postal 5430
Managua, Nicaragua
Tel.: (505-2) 2-7130
Fax: (505-2) 2-7136

Panama

National Association for the Economic
Development of Panama
Apartado Postal 503
Panama, 9A, Panama
Tel.: (507) 63-5878
Fax: (507) 64-9280

National Council of Private Enterprise
Apartado Postal 1276
Zona 1, Calle Aquilino de la Guardia
No. 19
Panama, 1, Panama
Tel.: (507) 63-5197
Fax: (507) 64-2384

Panama Promotion Group
Apartado Postal 55-1297
Estafeta de Paitilla
Panama, 1, Panama
Tel.: (507) 64-3000
Fax: (507) 64-2815

APPENDIX XIII
Mexican Trade Offices in the United States

California
8484 Wilshire Blvd., Suite 808
Beverly Hills, CA 90211
(213) 655-6421

Florida
New World Tower
100 N. Biscayne Blvd., Suite 1601
Miami, FL 33132
(305) 372-9929

Georgia
229 Peachtree Street, N.E., Suite 917
Atlanta, GA 30343
(404) 522-5373

Illinois
225 N. Michigan Avenue, Suite 708
Chicago, IL 60601
(312) 856-0316

New York
150 East 58th Street, 17th Floor
New York, NY 10155
(212) 826-2916

Texas
2777 Stemmons Freeway, Suite 1622
Dallas, TX 75207
(214) 688-4096

Washington
Plaza 600, 600 Stewart Street, Suite
703
Seattle, WA 98101
(206) 441-2833

Washington, DC
Embassy of Mexico
1911 Pennsylvania Avenue, N.W., 7th
Floor
Washington, DC 20006
(202) 728-1700

APPENDIX XIV
Mexican Trade Organizations

Industry Associations

Asociación de Fabricantes de la
Cerveza
(Beer Manufacturing National
Chamber)
Avenida Horacio No. 1556, Colonia
Chapultepec Morales
11570, Mexico, D.F.

Asociación de Ingenieros de Minas,
Metalurgistas y Geologos de Mexico,
A.C.
(Mining Engineers, Metallurgists
and Geologists Association)
Tacuba No. 5-19 B,
Apartado Postal 1260
06000, Mexico, D.F.

Asociación Mexicana de Agencias de
Publicidad
(Advertising Agency Association)
Plaza Carlos J. Finlay No. 6, 4o Piso
06500, Mexico, D.F.

Asociación Mexicana de Caminos
(Mexican Road Association)
Río Tiber No. 103, 2o Piso
06500, Mexico, D.F.

Asociación Mexicana de Criadores de
Ganado Suizo
(Mexican Association of Swiss Cattle
Breeders)
Andalucia No. 162,
03400, Mexico, D.F.

Asociación Mexicana de Distribuidores
de Gas Licuado y Empresas
Conexas, A.C.
(Mexican Association of Gas
Distributors)
Filadelfia No. 119, 1o Piso, Colonia
Nápoles
Mexico, D.F.

Asociación Mexicana de Fabricantes
de Válvulas
(Valves Manufacturers National
Association)
Copérnico No. 47, Colonia Anzures
11590, Mexico, D.F.

Asociación Mexicana de Hoteles y
Moteles de la República, A.C.
(Mexican Hotel and Motel
Association)
Hamburgo No. 108-104
06600, Mexico, D.F.

Asociación Mexicana de la Industria
Automotriza, A.C.
(Automotive Industry Association)
Ensenada No. 90
06100, Mexico, D.F.

Asociación Mexicana de Restaurantes
(Mexican Restaurant Association)
Torcuato Tasso No. 325-103
11560, Mexico, D.F.

Asociación Nacional de Fabricantes de
Aparatos Domésticos
(Household Appliance National
Association)
Zacatecas No. 155, Colonia Roma
06067, Mexico, D.F.

Asociación Nacional de Fabricantes de
Tableros de Madera, A.C.
(Lumber Manufacturers National
Association)
Acapulco No. 35-501
06700, Mexico, D.F.

Asociación Nacional de la Industria
del Café
(Coffee Industry National Association)
Avenida Insurgentes Sur No. 682
03100, Mexico, D.F.

Asociación Nacional de la Industria
  Química
(Chemical Industry National
  Association)
Avenida Providencia No. 1118
03100, Mexico, D.F.

Asociación Nacional de Fabricantes de
  Medicamentos
(Pharmaceutical Manufacturers
  National Association)
Eugenia No. 13-601
03810, Mexico, D.F.

Asociación Nacional de Fabricantes de
  Pinturas y Tintas
(Paint and Ink Manufacturers National
  Association)
Gabriel Mancera No. 309,
03100, Mexico, D.F.

Asociación Nacional de Industrias de
  Plástico, A.C.
(Plastic Industry National Association)
Doctor Vertiz No. 546
03500, Mexico, D.F.

Asociación National Hotelera
(National Hotel Association)
Edison No. 84, 2o Piso, Colonia
  Tabacalera
Mexico, D.F.

Asociación Nacional de Productores
  de Aguas Envasadas
(Bottled Water Producers National
  Association)
Paseo de la Reforma No. 195-301
06500, Mexico, D.F.

Asociación Nacional de
  Vitivinicultores, A.C.
(National Association of Grape
  Growers and Wine Producers)
Calzada de Tlalpan No. 3515
04650, Mexico, D.F.

Industry Chambers of Commerce
Camara Minera de Mexico
(Mining Chamber of Mexico)

Sierra Vertientes No. 369, Colonia
  Lomas de Chapultepec
11000, Mexico, D.F.

Camara Nacional del Aerotransporte
(Air Transport National Chamber)
Paseo de la Reforma No. 76, 17o Piso
06600, Mexico, D.F.

Camara Nacional de Cemento
  (Canacem)
(Cement National Chamber)
Leibnitz No. 77
11590, Mexico, D.F.

Camara Nacional de Hospitales
(Hospital National Chamber)
Vito Alessio Robles No. 23, 6o Piso
01030, Mexico, D.F.

Camara Nacional de la Industria de
  Aceites, Grasa y Jabones
(Oil, Grease and Soap Industry
  National Chamber)
Melchor Ocampo No. 193, Torre A,
  Colonia Veronica Anzures
11300, Mexico, D.F.

Camara Nacional de Industria de Artes
  Gráficas
(Graphic Arts Industry National
  Chamber)
Avenida Río Churubusco No. 428, 2o
  Piso, Colonia Del Carmen Coyoacan
04100, Mexico, D.F.

Camara Nacional de la Industria
  Azucarera y Alcoholera
(Sugar and Alcohol Industry National
  Chamber)
Río Niagara No. 11, Colonia
  Cuauhtemoc
06500, Mexico, D.F.

Camara Nacional de la Industria del
  Calzado
(Shoe Industry National Chamber)
Durango No. 24S, 12o Piso
06700, Mexico, D.F.

Camara Nacional de la Industria
  Cinematográfica
(Cinematography Industry National
  Chamber)
Gen. Anaya No. 198
04210, Mexico, D.F.

Camara Nacional de la Industria de la
  Construcción
(Construction Industry National
  Chamber)
Periférico Sur No. 4839
14010, Mexico, D.F.

Camara Nacional de la Industria de la
  Curtiduría
(Tannery Industry National Chamber)
Tehuantepec No. 255, 1o Piso
06760, Mexico, D.F.

Camara Nacional de la Industria
  Electrónica y de Comunicaciones
  Eléctricas
(Electronic and Electronic
  Communications National
  Chamber)
Guanajuato No. 65
06700, Mexico, D.F.

Camara Nacional de la Industria del
  Embellecimiento Físico
(Physical Fitness Industry National
  Chamber)
Salamanca No. 5
06700, Mexico, D.F.

Camara Nacional de la Industria
  Farmaceutica
(Pharmaceutical Industry National
  Chamber)
Avenida Cuauhtemoc No. 1481,
  Colonia Santa Cruz Atoyac
03380, Mexico, D.F.

Camara Nacional de la Industria del
  Hierro y del Acero
(Iron and Steel Industry National
  Chamber)

Amores No. 338, Colonia Del Valle
03199, Mexico, D.F.

Camara Nacional de la Industria
  Hulera
(Rubber Industry National Chamber)
Manuel María Contreras No. 133-115
06500, Mexico, D.F.

Camara Nacional de la Industria
  Maderera y Similares
(Lumber and Related Products
  Industry National Chamber)
Santander No. 15-301
03920, Mexico, D.F.

Camara Nacional de la Industria
  Panificadora
(Bakery Industry National Chamber)
Doctor Liceaga No. 96
06620, Mexico, D.F.

Camara Nacional de la Industria de la
  Pesca
(Fishing Industry National Chamber)
Manuel María Contreras No. 133,
  Colonia Cuauhtemoc
06500, Mexico, D.F.

Camara Nacional de la Industria de la
  Platería y la Joyería
(Silver and Jewelry Industry National
  Chamber)
Reynosa No. 13
06100, Mexico, D.F.

Camara Nacional de la Industria de
  Radio y T.V.
(Radio and T.V. Industry National
  Chamber)
Horacio No. 1013
11550, Mexico, D.F.

Camara Nacional de la Industria
  Textile
(Textile Industry National Chamber)
Plionio No. 20, Esquina Horacio
11560, Mexico, D.F.

Camara Nacional de la Industria del
  Vestido

(Garment Industry National Chamber)
Tolsa No. 54
06040, Mexico, D.F.

Camara Nacional de las Industrias de
la Celulosa y el Papel
(Cellulose and Paper Industries
National Chamber)
Priv. de San Isidro No. 30, Colonia
Reforma Social
11650, Mexico, D.F.

Camara Nacional de Industrias de la
Leche
(Milk Products Industry National
Chamber)
Benjamin Franklin No. 134
11800, Mexico, D.F.

Camara Nacional de las Industrias de
la Silvicultura
(Forest Products and Derivatives
Industries National Chamber)
Baja California No. 225, Edificio A,
12o Piso
06170, Mexico, D.F.

Camara Nacional de las Manufacturas
Eléctricas (Caname)
(Electric Manufacturers National
Chamber)
Ibsen No. 13
11560, Mexico, D.F.

Camara Nacional de Transportes y
Comunicaciones
(Communication and Transportation
National Chamber)
Pachuca No. 158
06140, Mexico, D.F.

National Associations
Asociación Mexicana de Bancos
(Mexican Bank Association)
Lázaro Cárdenas No. 2, 9o Piso
06079, Mexico, D.F.

Asociación Nacional de Importadores
y Exportadores de la República
Mexicana
(National Association of Importers and
Exporters of the Mexican Republic)
Monterrey No. 130, Colonia Roma
06700, Mexico, D.F.

Camara Nacional de Comercio de la
Ciudad de México
(Mexico City National Chamber of
Commerce)
Paseo de la Reforma No. 43, 3er Piso
06048, Mexico, D.F.

Camara Nacional de la Industria de la
Transformación (Canacintra)
(Manufacturing Industry National
Chamber)
Avenida San Antonio No. 256,
03849, Mexico, D.F.

Confederación de Camaras
Industriales de los Estados Unidos
Mexicanos (Concamin)
(Confederation of the National
Chambers of Industry)
Manuel María Contreras No. 133, 8o
Piso
06500, Mexico, D.F.

Confederación de Camaras Nacionales
de Comercio (Concanaco)
(Confederation of National Chambers
of Commerce)
Balderas No. 144, 3er Piso
06079, Mexico, D.F.

Consejo Coordinador Empresarial
(CCE)
(Businessmen's Coordinating
Council)
Homero 527–6o Piso
11570, Mexico, D.F.

BIBLIOGRAPHY

Adams, Alice. *Mexico*. Englewood Cliffs, N.J.: Prentice Hall, 1990.

Custine, Marquis de. *Empire of the Czar: A Journey through Eternal Russia*. New York: Doubleday, 1989.

Didion, Joan. *Miami*. New York: Simon & Schuster, 1987.

Everton, Macduff. *The Modern Maya*. Albuquerque: University of New Mexico Press, 1991.

Hamilton-Peterson, James. *The Great Deep: The Sea and its Thresholds*. New York: Random House, 1992.

Lawrence, D. H. *Mornings in Mexico*. New York: Knopf, 1927.

Meyers, Jeffrey. *Edmund Wilson: A Biography*. Boston: Houghton Mifflin, 1995.

Paz, Octavio. *The Labyrinth of Solitude: Life and Thought in Mexico*. New York: Grove Press, 1961.

Rieff, David. *The Exile*. New York: Simon & Schuster, 1993.

Rodriguez, Richard. *Days of Obligation: An Argument with My Mexican Father*. New York: Viking Penguin, 1992.

Smith, Gene. *Maximilian and Carlota: A Tale of Romance and Tragedy*. New York: William Morrow, 1973.

Tillich, Paul. *A History of Christian Thought: From its Judaic and Hellenistic Origins to Existentialism*. New York: Simon & Schuster, 1967.

INDEX

About the Author

LOUIS E.V. NEVAER is Director of Political Analysis at International Credit Monitor, a consulting firm specializing in political risk assessment, located in Coral Gables, Florida. He has consulted worldwide to governments, corporations, and nonprofit organizations. Among his various journal publications and five previous Quorum books is *Strategies for Business in Mexico* (1995), a timely and authoritative account of the recent "Mexican Meltdown."